The LGBTQ BOOK OF DAYS – 2019 Revised Edition

BY OWEN KEEHNEN

The LGBTQ Book Of Days – 2019 Revised Edition

© 2019 Owen Keehnen/OutTales Publishing

The LGBTQ Book Of Days - 2019 Revised Edition
© 2019 Owen Keehnen

Previously Published in the US and Australia
as The LGBT Book of Days by Wilde City Press 2013
Published by Wilde City Press

THE LGBTQ BOOK OF DAYS –
2019 Revised Edition

A Fun and Comprehensive Guide to Important Dates in LGBT History

Owen Keehnen

Foreword by Victor Salvo
Creator and Executive Director of The Legacy Project

For Carl,

Thank you for making May 11, 2017
one of the happiest days of my life

Foreword

To any casual observer – regardless of their political agenda, personal values, or where they fit on the Kinsey Scale – it is obvious that the rate of acceptance of LGBTQ people in contemporary society seems to be accelerating at a pace deemed unimaginable even a decade ago. Court cases, legislation and electoral victories have helped point the way to a brighter future for LGBTQ people. But political winds change and there are established, well-financed interests vocally committed to reversing progress – to the point of erasing not only those hard-fought gains, but LGBTQ people themselves. Such efforts could very well succeed if the history of LGBTQ achievements is not firmly and aggressively reintegrated into humanity's story.

Other minority groups have the benefit of generational memory passed from old to young upon which to build long-term cultural cohesion and an historic frame of reference. However, LGBTQ people, because of the negative social forces arrayed against them for millennia, have been denied a fluid understanding of themselves and their collective role in shared human history. This has condemned generation after generation to the social isolation and cultural marginalization that challenges LGBTQ self-esteem and fuels bullying.

The summary redaction of the lives of influential LGBTQ individuals such as social justice advocate Jane Addams, famed Russian composer Pyotr Tchaikovsky, acclaimed Mexican artist Frida Kahlo, British mathematician Alan Turing, human rights activist Eleanor Roosevelt, acclaimed Maestro Leonard Bernstein, legendary artist Michelangelo – and hundreds of others – has robbed LGBTQ youth – ALL youth – of historically significant LGBTQ role models.

When one considers that, for the average person, their only awareness of history comes from what they can recall of their high school education, it is a small wonder LGBTQ people are so easily denigrated as modern social aberrations – willful "deviants" who consciously eschew heterosexuality – instead of being accepted as fully integrated, whole people who, though somewhat different, have been around for a very, very long time.

To counter the effects of an education bereft of LGBTQ contributions, the Legacy Project explores that history which has been hidden from LGBTQ people. We seek out stories of struggle and change and triumph to highlight the obscure, the famous – and those who would have been famous if their being LGBTQ had not kept them out of America's textbooks. Through the Legacy Walk outdoor museum in Chicago, the traveling Legacy Wall interactive exhibit, and the Legacy Project Education Initiative's lesson plans, study guides, resource links and multimedia tools, we offer a variety of tools to help both LGBTQ youth and the people who care about them bridge the gap left by education systems which fail to include LGBTQ historic contributions.

Another such tool is Owen Keehnen's splendid compendium *The LGBTQ Book of Days*, which has been updated with new eye-opening, life-affirming revelations. Mr. Keehnen has done an impressive job of culling through vast reams of obscure data to capture nuggets of information which remind all of us that every single day is also the anniversary of a pivotal achievement, or the launch of an influential publication, a celebration of an historic milestone, or the birth or passing of a person whose contributions altered the trajectory of LGBTQ advancement. Keehnen's daily journal of timely tidbits captures our contributions to history in a concise fashion which is both easily accessible and a pleasure to read. Whether this information inspires you to explore our history further, makes you feel better about being LGBTQ, or just gives you fun facts to toss out at a cocktail party, *The LGBT Book of Days: 2019 Revised Edition* will be an important addition to your library. Keep it handy – I certainly do.

Victor Salvo | Creator and Executive Director
of the Legacy Project

Introduction

Since the initial publication of *The LGBT Book of Days* by Wilde City Press in 2013, much has changed. In that period of time the LGBTQ community has experienced momentous political, social, and cultural advances, but that progress has been tempered by malevolent measures from our enemies who are more determined than ever to curtail our victories. By fanning the flames of fear and demonizing change, these homophobic political forces seek to silence and erase LGBTQ people as well as our history and accomplishments. We will not go back or return to the closet. We refuse to be erased. The time was right for an updated version of *The LGBTQ Book of Days – 2019 Revised Edition.*

We owe it to many of the brave pioneers, the activists, and the martyrs named in these pages to keep moving forward, for the sake of ourselves as well as LGBTQ folk in the future. For that reason, the importance of celebrating, honoring, and exploring our LGBTQ history has never been more important.

The LGBTQ Book of Days – 2019 Revised Edition is a reference book, an illuminative and fun trivia compilation, and a tool for further investigation into our rich, colorful - and profoundly challenging - past. All events and individuals included in this book merit greater reading and supplementary research.

The specific labels LGBTQ are only recent additions to history. Many of the people named in this book did not identify themselves as such in their place and time. As an alternative to our modern labels of LGBT or Q - and to understand sexual behavior in different eras and parts of the globe - a preferable term might be *non-hetero normative* to denote behaviors outside that of exclusively male/female relations. The inclusions in this book have been made with this in consideration.

The LGBTQ Book of Days – 2019 Revised Edition is an exploration of the LGBTQ/non-hetero normative contributions and milestones that have shaped us - the people and events included are, for the most part, historical figures. All individuals persons mentioned are deceased unless they were part of a watershed moment. For example, Ellen DeGeneres's birth date is not included, but the publication date of the *TIME Magazine* with Ellen on the cover declaring, 'Yep, I'm Gay' is listed.

The LGBTQ Book of Day – 2019 Revised Edition is by no means a completed work. The book in its current state is merely the basis, the foundation, for additional entries and dates of interest. This reference book is an organic body of material that is meant to evolve and grow as the accomplishments and notable dates in our LGBTQ story continue to unfold.

If you have an event or person you wish to suggest for future inclusion, or a correction or clarification of existing data, please forward the information. All commentary and suggestions are welcomed.

Owen Keehnen
OwenKeehnen@yahoo.com

"We are powerful because we have survived."

Audre Lorde

JANUARY

January 1, 1632

Poet Katherine Philips (*Poems by the Incomparable Mrs. K.P.*, *Poems*, *Pompey: A Tragedy*) - the first British woman to find wide public acclaim as a poet during her lifetime - is born in London, England.

January 1, 1879

Novelist and author E.M. Forster (*Howards Erd*, *Maurice*, *A Passage to India*, *Where Angels Fear to Tread*, *A Room with a View*) is born in Marylebone, London, England.

January 1, 1928

Modern dance and theatrical lighting techniques pioneer Loie Fuller best known for *The Serpentine Dance* and who opened at the Folies Bergere in her *Fire Dance* - dies at age 65 of pneumonia in Paris, France.

January 1, 1933

Playwright and author Joe Orton (*Entertaining Mr. Sloane*, *Loot*, *What the Butler Saw*) is born in Leicester, England.

January 1, 1962

Illinois becomes the first state in the U.S. to decriminalize homosexuality by repealing its sodomy laws.

January 1, 1967

LAPD New Year's Eve raids on two Los Angeles gay bars, the Black Cat Tavern and New Faces, results in injuries to patrons. Several hundred participate in a spontaneous demonstration outside the Black Cat.

January 1, 1982

Actor Victor Buono - who was nominated for an Oscar and a Golden Globe Award for his work in *Whatever Happened to Baby Jane?* and who found enduring fame in recurring villain roles on the 1960s TV series *Batman* and *The Wild Wild West* - dies of a heart attack at age 43 in Apple Valley, CA.

January 1, 1994

Prolific actor Cesar Romero (*Week-End in Havana, The Thin Man, Ocean's 11*) - perhaps best known for his role as The Joker on the television series *Batman* - dies at age 86 from bronchitis and pneumonia in Santa Monica, CA.

January 1, 2018

Openly transgender individuals are allowed to join the United States military.

January 2, 1557

Painter Jacopo Pontormo aka Pontormo (*The Deposition from the Cross, The Visitation, Madonna with Child and Saints*) - an early Mannerist painter from the Florentine School who focused primarily on religious subjects with some portraiture work - dies at age 62 in Florence, Italy.

January 2, 1857

M. Carey Thomas, educator, suffragist, and second president of Bryn Mawr College - where she demanded the highest standards from both faculty and students - is born in Baltimore, MD.

January 2, 1900

Popular silent film and early talkies actor Billy Haines (*Show People*, *Alias Jimmy Valentine*, *Brown of Howard*) – who turned his back on Hollywood when he was given an ultimatum about hiding his homosexuality by entering into a lavender marriage – is born in Staunton, VA.

January 2, 1991

Singer and stage actor Gilbert Price - who received Tony nominations for *Lost in the Stars*, *The Night That Made America Famous*, and *Timbuktu!* - dies of accidental asphyxiation at age 48 in Vienna, Austria.

―――――――――○―――――――――

January 3, 1824

Educator Sophia B. Packard, who would eventually cofound a school for African American women that would eventually become Spelman College, is born in New Salem, MA.

January 3, 1897

Filmmaker Dorothy Arzner (*The Wild Party, Craig's Wife, Christopher Strong, The Bride Wore Red*) – who invented the boom microphone, was the first woman to direct a talking film, and the first woman to join the Directors Guild of America – is born in San Francisco, CA.

January 3, 1905

Anna May Wong, the first Asian-American actress to gain international recognition in films like *The Shanghai Express, The Toll of the Sea, The Thief of Bagdad,* and *Piccadilly,* is born in Los Angeles, CA

January 3, 1948

The official publication date of the groundbreaking *Sexual Behavior in the Human Male* aka The Kinsey Report, by Indiana zoologist Dr. Alfred Kinsey, which revolutionized the way Americans viewed sex and sexuality. The companion volume, *Sexual Behavior in the Human Female,* would follow in 1953.

January 3, 1992

Transgender philanthropist Reed Erickson (founder of the Erickson Educational Foundation, who donated millions to the early development of the LGBTQ movement from 1964-1984) dies at age 74 in Mexico.

January 3, 1992

Actress Dame Judith Anderson (*Laura, Cat on a Hot Tin Roof, And Then There Were None, Kings Row, The Strange Love* of *Martha Ivers, Star Trek III: The Search for Spock*) dies at age 94 in Santa Barbara, CA. Anderson is best known for her role as Mrs. Danvers in *Rebecca* and won two Emmys, a Tony Award, and was nominated for an Oscar.

January 3, 2003

Writer and feminist theorist Monique Wittig (*Les Guerilleres, The Straight Mind and Other Essays, The Lesbian Body*) dies of a heart attack at age 67 in Tucson, AZ.

January 4, 1877

Artist and poet Marsden Hartley (*Handsome Drinks, The Ice Hole, Art and the Personal Life, Adelard the Drowned, Master of the Phantom, German Officer, Twenty-five Poems*) - whose work was often influenced by the rural and rugged landscape and people of Maine - is born in Lewistown, ME.

January 4, 1904

Society photographer, set and costume designer, and writer Cecil Beaton (*My Fair Lady, Gigi*) - recipient of several Tony Awards and three Oscars - is born in Hampstead, England.

January 4, 1952

National Urban League founder Frances Kellor - a social reformer and activist who specialized in the rights and care of immigrants, domestic workers, and women, who championed adult education, and who was responsible for having women's suffrage on national party platforms - dies in New York City at age 78.

January 4, 1970

The articles are filed in the office of the California Secretary of State for The Gay Community Services Center (now the Los Angeles Gay and Lesbian Center) a non-profit center which will provide a variety of social services to members of the gay and lesbian community.

January 4, 1986

Writer Christopher Isherwood (*A Single Man*, *The Berlin Diaries*, *Christopher and His Kind*) - whose work inspired *Cabaret* - dies at age 81 in Santa Monica, CA.

―――――――――――○―――――――――――

January 5, 1931

Choreographer and dance pioneer Alvin Ailey - founder of the Alvin Ailey American Dance Theater in 1958, choreographer of such productions as *Revelations*, and recipient of the Kennedy Center Honors - is born in Rogers, TX.

January 5, 1943

Scientist, botanist, agricultural chemist, and inventor George Washington Carver - who was committed to the improvement of farming and is credited with, among other things, the concept of crop rotation - dies at age 78 in Tuskegee, AL.

January 5, 1959

Dr. Margaret "Mom" Chung - the first known American-born Chinese female physician who lobbied for the creation of the U.S. Women's Naval Reserve (the WAVES) - dies at age 59.

January 5, 1996

Lincoln Kirstein – writer (*Flesh is Heir, Mosaic, Quarry*), critic, and co-founder of the New York City Ballet - whose numerous awards include the American Guild of Musical Artists Award, the Distinguished Service Award from the National Institute of Arts and Letters, and who was also nominated for a National Book Award – dies at age 88 at his home in Manhattan, N.Y.

January 5, 2011

Long-time Chicago activist and attorney Renee Hanover - who opened what is often cited as the first law office in the U.S. to focus on women's issues and who was also believed to be the first "out" lesbian attorney in the county - dies at age 84 in Los Angeles, CA.

January 6, 1798

Actress and sensation of the French stage Marie Dorval (*Chatterton, Lucrèce, Marie-Jeanne*) - who was also rumored to be a lover of female writer George Sand - is born in France.

January 6, 1946

Adolph de Meyer - photographer of such celebrities as Mary Pickford, John Barrymore, Lillian Gish, and Billie Burke - dies in Los Angeles, CA at age 77.

January 6, 1974

Inspired by Patricia Nell Warren's novel *The Front Runner*, the initial Front Runners running group holds its first Sunday "fun run" in San Francisco's Golden Gate Park.

January 6, 1990

Actor Ian Charleston (*Gandhi, Opera*) - best known for his role as Eric Liddell in the 1981 film *Chariots of Fire* - dies at age 40 of an AIDS-related illness in London, England.

January 6, 1993

Ballet dancer, choreographer, film star and media personality Rudolf Nureyev *(Romeo and Juliet, Sleeping Beauty, Swan Lake)* - the first dancer to defect from the Soviet Union, and who appeared with over 30 ballet and modern dance companies - dies at age 54 from an AIDS-related illness in Levallois-Perret, France.

January 6, 2004

Fashion photographer Francesco Scavullo (*Scavullo on Beauty, Scavullo*) - known for his many covers of *Cosmopolitan* magazine - dies of heart failure at age 82 in New York City.

January 7, 1891

Author, anthropologist, and folklorist Zora Neale Hurston (*Their Eyes Were Watching God, Mules and Men, Spunk, Every Tongue Got to Confess*) - active during the time of the Harlem Renaissance - is born in Notasulga, AL.

---○---

January 8, 1896

Poet Paul Verlaine (*Sagasse*, *Selected Poems*), associated with the Symbolist movement - which sought to express states of mind rather than objective reality through the power of words and images - dies at age 51 in Paris, France. His torrid affair with poet Arthur Rimbaud ended in disaster.

January 8, 1901

Forman Brown - puppeteer, composer, songwriter (*Mrs. Pettibone*), and novelist (*Better Angel*) and co-founder of the Turnabout Theater in Hollywood - is born in Otsego, MI.

January 8, 1925

Lighting designer Tharon Musser - who was nominated for ten Tony Awards and won three times for her work on the Broadway productions *Follies*, *A Chorus Line*, and *Dreamgirls* - is born in Roanoke, VA.

January 8, 1926

Actor Kerwin Mathews (*The 7th Voyage of Sinbad*, *Maniac*, *The 3 Worlds of Gulliver*, *Jack the Giant Killer*, *The Devil at 4 O'Clock*) - popular in several swashbuckling and action films of the 1950s and 1960s - is born in Seattle, WA.

January 8, 1941

Comedian, writer, and actor Graham Chapman (*Monty Python's Flying Circus*, *Monty Python and the Holy Grail*, *The Life of Brian*, *Yellowbeard*, *A Liar's Autobiography*) is born in Leicester, England.

January 8, 1947

Influential singer (*Changes, Let's Dance, Fame*), songwriter, performer, and actor (*Labyrinth, The Man Who Fell to Earth*) David Bowie is born in London.

January 8, 1948

Violet Gordon-Woodhouse, keyboard player who specialized in the harpsichord (*The Harpsichord Virtuoso*) and clavichord, was the first person to record the harpsichord, and the first to broadcast harpsichord music, dies at age 75 in London.

January 8, 1978

Harvey Milk is sworn in as a member of the San Francisco Board of Supervisors.

January 8, 2013

Jeanne Manford, community ally and activist who, in 1973, became the co-founder of the support organization PFLAG, Parents and Friends of Lesbians and Gays, dies at age 92 in Daly City, CA.

January 9, 1857

Writer Henry Blake Fuller (*With the Procession, Bertram Cope's Year*) - a pioneering author of the gay novel and the realist style of writing - is born in Chicago, IL.

January 9, 1923

Modernist short story writer Katherine Mansfield (*The Garden Party: And Other Stories, Bliss: And Other Stories, Prelude*) - who enchanted and influenced writers from Virginia Woolf to D.H. Lawrence - dies of a pulmonary hemorrhage (as a result of tuberculosis) at age 34 in Fontainebleau, France.

January 9, 1946

Countee Cullen – poet (*Color, Copper Sun*), playwright (*St. Louis Woman*), and leading figure of the Harlem Renaissance – dies in New York City at age 42.

January 9, 1962

Professor, serviceperson and author (*The Narrow Land*) Elizabeth Reynard, who helped to establish the WAVES (Women Accepted for Volunteer Emergency Service) and was the first woman to be appointed lieutenant in the United States Navy Reserve, dies at age 64 in Mount Kisco, NY.

January 9, 1996

Visual artist and sculptor Felix Gonzalez-Torres - known for his minimalist sculptures and installations which were defined by the AIDS epidemic - dies of an AIDS-related illness at age 38 in Miami, FL.

---○---

January 10, 1959

Photographer and performance artist Mark Morrisoe (*Mark Morrisoe: My Life, Mark Morrisoe*) - who often colored and wrote on his Polaroid snapshots, utilized varied photographic mediums, and experimented with Super 8 film stills in his art as well - is born in Malden, MA.

January 10, 1927

Singer Johnny Ray (*Cry, Just Walking in the Rain, The Little White Cloud That Cried*) - who was known as "Mr. Emotion" for his uninhibited vocal delivery and who also appeared in the film *There's No Business Like Show Business* - is born in Hopewell, OR.

January 10, 1939

Actor Sal Mineo (*Rebel Without a Cause, Exodus, The Gene Krupa Story*) - nominated for two Oscars and winner of a Golden Globe Award - is born in The Bronx, N.Y.

January 10, 1948

Female impersonator Craig Russell - whose artistry is captured in the films *Outrageous!* and *Too Outrageous!* and whose list of impersonations included Peggy Lee, Shirley Bassey, Bette Davis, Barbra Streisand, Mae West, Carol Channing, Sophie Tucker, Bette Midler, and many others - is born in Toronto, Ontario, Canada.

January 10, 1957

Poet and diplomat Gabriela Mistral, the first Spanish American author to receive the Nobel Prize in Literature, dies at age 67 in Hempstead, NY.

January 10, 1978

Painter and feminist Hannah Gluckstein aka Gluck (*Medallion, Gluck, Sir James Crichton-Brown, Rage, Rage Against the Dying of the Light*) - who painted primarily portraits, landscapes, and flowers - dies at age 82 following a stroke in Steyning, Sussex, England.

January 10, 1982

Comic actor of stage, screen, and especially television, Paul Lynde (*Hollywood Squares*, Uncle Arthur on *Bewitched, Send Me No Flowers, Donny and Marie, The Paul Lynde Show, Bye Bye Birdie*) - a five time Emmy Award nominee - dies of a heart attack at age 55 in Beverly Hills, CA.

January 10-12, 1994

The mini-series adaption of the first book of Armistead Maupin's beloved *Tales of the City* airs over three nights on PBS in the U.S. (after first being shown in the U.K. on Channel 4) to high ratings and controversy. The cast includes Laura Linney, Olympia Dukakis, Donald Moffat, and Parker Posey. Television adaptations of the other books in the series will follow.

January 10, 1996

Forman Brown - puppeteer, composer, songwriter (*Mrs. Pettibone*), and novelist (*Better Angel*) and co-founder of the Turnabout Theater in Hollywood - dies at age 95 in Los Angeles, CA.

January 10, 2015

Actor Taylor Negron (*The Last Boy Scout, Angels in the Outfield, Vamps, Fast Times at Ridgemont High*) dies of liver cancer at age 57 in Los Angeles, CA.

January 10, 2016

Influential singer (*Changes, Let's Dance, Fame*), songwriter, performer, and actor (*Labyrinth, The Man Who Fell to Earth*) David Bowie dies of liver cancer in Manhattan.

January 11, 1899

Stage actress Eva Le Gallienne- recipient of a special Tony Award in 1964 for her body of work (*The Swan, Resurrection, Alison's House, To Grandmother's House We Go, Peter Pan*) - is born in London, England.

January 11, 1973

An American Family debuts on PBS. The groundbreaking reality series helps redefine the traditional family when Lance Loud, the eldest son, becomes the first openly gay man to appear on television as part of American family life.

January 11, 1984

The Wall Street Journal allows use of the word 'gay' as a synonym for 'homosexual' in articles and headlines for the first time.

January 11, 1985

Entertainer, actor, female impersonator Lynne Carter (star of the Jewel Box Revue and who, in 1971, became the first female impersonator to play Carnegie Hall) dies of AIDS related pneumonia at age 60 in Manhattan.

January 11, 1997

The episode "The Day the Earth Moved" of the short-lived TV series, *Relativity*, shows the first open-mouth kiss between two lesbians on prime time television. The characters, Rhonda and Suzanne, are portrayed by actresses Lisa Edelstein and Kristin Dattilo.

January 11, 2006

Sarah Aldridge (pen name of lawyer Anyda Marchant) - co-founder of Naiad Press (1972) and A&M Books (1995) as well as author of 14 novels including *The Latecomer*, *All True Lovers*, *The Nesting Place* - dies at age 94 in Rehoboth Beach, DE.

January 12, 1896

Bestselling writer Nobuko Yoshiya (*Flower Tales*, *Two Virgins in the Attic*, *To the Ends of the Earth*) - an out lesbian in Japan in the 1920s who also began her own magazine *Black Rose* - is born in the Niigata Prefecture, Japan.

January 12, 1965

Essayist, playwright, activist, and editor Lorraine Hansberry (*A Raisin in the Sun, To Be Young, Gifted and Black*) - winner of the New York Critics' Circle Award, and whose play *A Raisin in the Sun* ran 530 performances and was the first play produced on Broadway written by an African-American woman - dies in New York City from cancer at age 34.

January 12, 1910

Film, stage, and radio actress Patsy Kelly (*Rosemary's Baby, Freaky Friday, Pigskin Parade*) - who won a Tony Award for Best Featured Actress in a Musical for *No, No, Nanette* - is born in Brooklyn, N.Y.

January 13, 1832

Author Horatio Alger Jr., best known for his juvenile rags-to-riches novels (*Ragged Dick, The Young Bank Messenger, Paul the Peddler, The Life of Edwin Forrest*) is born in Chelsea, MA.

January 13, 1931

TV and stage actor Charles Nelson Reilly (*The Ghost & Mrs. Muir, Match Game*) - who also won a Tony Award in 1962 as Best Featured Actor in a Musical for *How to Succeed in Business Without Really Trying* - is born in the Bronx, N.Y.

January 13, 1958

The U.S. Supreme Court (ONE Inc. V. Olesen) upholds

the distribution of homosexual publications under the First Amendment.

January 13, 1973

On *The Mary Tyler Moore Show* episode "My Brother's Keeper" [Season 3, Episode 17] airs. In this episode Rhoda goes on a date with Phyllis' brother, Ben, who turns who turns out to be gay.

January 13, 1974

Poet, playwright, writer, translator Salvador Novo (*Our Land, Short History of Coyoacan, Mexico City in 1867*) - who was also a chronicler of politics, history, culture and social life in Mexico City - dies at age 69 in Mexico.

———————————○———————————

January 14, 1925

Writer Yukio Mishima (*Confessions of a Mask, Way of the Samurai, The Sound of Waves*) – whose conflicted bisexuality belied his hyper-masculine persona – is born in Shinjuku, Tokyo, Japan.

January 14, 1926

Actor and author Tom Tryon - whose roles included his Golden Globe nominated performance in *The Cardinal* and roles in such films as *In Harm's Way* and *The Story of Ruth* is born in Hartford, CT. Tryon's best-selling novels include *The Other, Crowned Heads,* and *Harvest Home.*

January 14, 1961

Stage and film actor Ernest Thesiger (*Frankenstein, The Old Dark House, The Bride of Frankenstein, They Drive By Night*) - an expert embroiderer who also published the book *Adventures in Embroidery* - dies one day before his 82nd birthday in London, England.

January 14, 1977

Author, artist. and popular diarist Anais Nin (*Delta of Venus, Little Birds*) - who enjoyed living on the artistic edge for five decades and also helped establish the publishing house Siana Editions when no one would publish her oftentimes intimate and erotic work - dies of cancer at age 73 in Los Angeles, CA.

January 14, 1987

Sam Wagstaff - curator, photography collector (whose collection was comprised of thousands of masterworks) and benefactor of Robert Mapplethorpe - dies at age 65 of AIDS-related pneumonia in New York City.

January 14, 2009

Transgender composer Angela Morley (*The Little Prince, The Slipper and the Rose, Watership Down, Julie Andrews: The Sound of Christmas, Dallas*) - who was nominated for two Oscars and won three Emmy Awards for her scores - dies from complications after a fall at age 84 in Scottsdale, AZ.

---○---

January 15, 1815

Actress and beauty Mlle Francoise Raucourt (*Gaston et Bayard, Henriette*) - who also led the lesbian society la Secte Androgyne in Paris - dies at age 58 in France.

January 15, 1862

Modern dance and theatrical lighting techniques pioneer Loie Fuller - best known for *The Serpentine Dance* and who opened at the Folies Bergere in her *Fire Dance* - is born in Fullersburg, IL.

January 15, 1879

Stage and film actor Ernest Thesiger (*Frankenstein, The Old Dark House, The Bride of Frankenstein, They Drive By Night*) - an expert embroiderer who also published the book *Adventures in Embroidery* - is born in London, England.

January 15, 1893

Singer, composer, and actor Ivor Novello (*Keep The Home Fires Burning, The Lodger, The White Rose*) - a force in the entertainment field for thirty-five years - is born in Cardiff, Wales. Until the advent of Andrew Lloyd Webber, Novello was the most consistently successful composer of British musicals.

January 15, 1958

Poet and journalist Brian Howard (*God Save the King*) - a key figure among England's "Bright Young Things", a group of wealthy, talented, and often hard partying artists - commits suicide by overdose at age 52 in Nice, France.

January 15, 1971

Stage and film actor John Dall (*Gun Crazy, Another Part of the Forest, Spartacus*) - who was nominated for a Best Supporting Actor Oscar for his role in the 1945 film *The Corn is Green* but is best remembered as one of the two prep school killers in Alfred Hitchcock's *Rope* - dies of a heart attack at age 52 in Hollywood, CA.

January 15, 2016

The film, *Carol,* (based on Patricia Highsmith's lesbian romance novel *The Price of Salt* which Highsmith wrote as Claire Morgan) is released starring Cate Blanchett and Rooney Mara. The Todd Haynes' directed film will eventually be nominated for six Academy Awards.

January 15, 2016

Award-winning poet and educator Francisco Xavier Alarcon (*Iguanas in the Snow and Other Winter Poems, From the Other Side of Night, Snake Poems, Body in Flames*) dies of cancer at age 61 in Davis, CA.

———————————— ○ ————————————

January 16, 1898

Film director Irving Rapper (*Now, Voyager, Deception, Marjorie Morningstar, The Corn is Green, The Glass Menagerie, The Christine Jorgensen Story*) - best remembered for the films he did with Bette Davis - is born in London, England.

January 16, 1921

Fashion photographer Francesco Scavullo (*Scavullo on Beauty*, *Scavullo*) - known for his many covers of *Cosmopolitan* magazine - is born in Staten Island, N.Y.

January 16, 1946

Photographer, filmmaker, activist Honey Lee Cottrell, who was also the co-founder of the San Francisco Lesbian and Gay History Project, is born in Astoria, OR.

January 17, 1886

Author Ronald Firbank (*Five Novels*, *The Flower Beneath the Foot*) - whose novels were greatly inspired by the society aesthetes - is born in London, England.

January 17, 1905

Jazz saxophonist and bandleader Peggy Gilbert (Peggy Gilbert and the Dixie Belles, Peggy Gilbert and Her Metro Goldwyn Orchestra) - subject of the documentary film *Peggy Gilbert and Her All Girl Band* - is born in Sioux City, IA.

January 17, 1927

Dr. Thomas Dooley III - physician, soldier, humanitarian, and recipient of the Congressional Gold Medal - is born in St. Louis, MO.

January 17, 1996

U.S. Congresswoman Barbara Jordan (D-Texas) dies of pneumonia, after a long battle with leukemia. Jordan was the first African American woman to be elected to Congress from a Southern state and the first to deliver the keynote address at a national presidential convention (1976).

January 18, 1904

Definitive Hollywood leading man, Cary Grant (*North By Northwest, The Philadelphia Story, Charade, Arsenic and Old Lace, An Affair to Remember*), is born in Bristol, U.K.

January 18, 1928

Lambda Literary Award winning author and psychotherapist Betty Berzon, (*Permanent Partners, Positively Gay, The Intimacy Dance*) - known for her work with gays and lesbians - is born in St. Louis, MO.

January 18, 1955

Frankie Knuckles, the Grammy Award winning DJ, record producer, and re-mixer known as "The Godfather of House Music," is born in the Bronx.

January 18, 1960

Gladys Bentley (*How Much Can I Stand?, Worried Blues, Red Beans and Rice*) - iconic gender-bending blues singer of the Harlem Renaissance who typically wore her trademark white tuxedo and top hat and was known for her suggestive lyrics and delivery - dies of pneumonia at age 52 in Los Angeles, CA.

January 18, 1961

Dr. Thomas Dooley III - physician, soldier, humanitarian, and recipient of the Congressional Gold Medal - dies of malignant melanoma at age 34.

January 18, 1980

Society photographer, set and costume designer, and writer Cecil Beaton (*My Fair Lady, Gigi*) - recipient of several Tony Awards and three Oscars - dies of a heart attack in Wiltshire, England at age 76.

January 18, 1986

The single *That's What Friends Are For*, a record by Dionne Warwick with friends Elton John, Stevie Wonder, and Gladys Knight - to benefit the AIDS organization amfAR, climbs to #1 on Billboard's Hot 100 where it will remain for four weeks.

January 18, 1989

Novelist, adventurer, and travel writer Bruce Chatwin (*The Songlines, In Patagonia, Utz, The Viceroy of Ouidah*) dies at age 48 of an AIDS-related illness in Nice, France.

January 18, 1996

The *Friends* episode "The One With the Lesbian Wedding," features the TV's first primetime lesbian wedding. The couple is played by Jane Sibbett (Carol) and Jessica Hecht (Susan).

January 18, 2004

The L Word debuts on Showtime. The show will run for six seasons through March 8, 2009, and will become the first successful U.S. television series to focus on lesbians.

January 19, 1897

Set and costume designer, screenwriter, and dancer Natacha Rambova - remembered as one time wife of Rudolph Valentino and for her Art Deco and Art Nouveau sets and lavish costumes of Alla Nazimova's silent films *Camille* and *Salome* - is born in Salt Lake City, UT.

January 19, 1921

Novelist and writer Patricia Highsmith (*Strangers on a Train, The Talented Mr. Ripley, The Two Faces of January, Deep Water*) - who also wrote the lesbian novel *The Price of Salt* under the pseudonym Claire Morgan - is born in Fort Worth, TX.

January 19, 1943

Electrifying singer and songwriter Janis Joplin (*Piece of My Heart, Mercedes Benz, Summertime, Me and Bobby McGee*) - a main attraction at both Woodstock and the Monterey Pop Festival - is born in Port Arthur, TX.

January 19, 1973

The collective Olivia Records is formed to record and market women's music. The first 45 released has a song with Meg Christian on one side and Cris Williamson on the other.

January 19, 1999

Bill Clinton becomes the first president to mention LGBT issues in a State of the Union Address.

January 19, 2003

Morris Kight - activist, founder/co-founder of several early gay organizations including Gay Liberation Front/Los Angeles, Aid for AIDS, and the Stonewall Democratic Club - dies at age 83 in Los Angeles, CA.

———————————○———————————

January 20, 1872

Architect Julia Morgan (Hearst Castle in San Simeon, Riverside Art Museum, Los Angeles Examiner Building) - the first woman to be admitted to the architecture program at the Ecole des Beaux-Arts in Paris and later California's first licensed woman architect - is born in San Francisco, CA.

January 20, 1944

Poet, activist, and founder of the Black Women's Revolutionary Council - Pat Parker (*Jonestown & Other Madness*, *Child of Myself, Pit Stop, Movement in Black*) is born in Houston, TX.

January 21, 1885

Painter and designer Duncan Grant (*Garden Path in Spring, Self-Portrait, Vanessa Bell in Armchair, Paul Roche, Girl at the Piano, George Mallory*) - a member of the Bloomsbury Group and whose lovers included Maynard Keynes and David Garnett - is born in Aviemore, Scotland.

January 21, 1895

Cristobel Balenciaga, fashion designer and founder of the Balenciaga fashion house, is born in Getaria, Spain.

January 21, 1905

Designer and founder of one of the world's top fashion houses - Christian Dior is born in Granville, France.

January 21, 1989

Transgender jazz musician and bandleader Billy Tipton dies at age 74 of a hemorrhaging peptic ulcer in Spokane, WA.

January 21, 2013

President Barack Obama becomes the first president to use the word gay in his inaugural address in reference to sexual orientation.

January 22, 1561

Sir Francis Bacon - statesman and philosopher who served as both Attorney General and Lord Chancellor of England is born in London. He also developed the scientific method in which natural laws or theories are reached though observation.

January 22, 1788

Poet George Gordon Byron - who later became known as Lord Byron (*Don Juan*, *The Corsair*, *Childe Harold's Pilgrimage*) and was a leading figure of the Romantic Movement - is born in London, England.

January 22, 1957

Cabaret singer and entertainer Claire Waldoff (*Fritze Bollmann*, *Hannelore*, *Es Gibt Nur Ein Berlin*) - who reached the height of her fame in Berlin during the decadent period between 1910-1920 - dies at age 72 in Bad Reichenhall, Germany.

January 22, 1986

Carl Wittman - activist, early proponent of the Radical Faeries, author of *Amerika: A Gay Manifesto* (originally published by the Red Butterfly cell of the Gay Liberation Front in January, 1970) and member of the national council of the Students for a Democratic Society (SDS) - commits suicide at age 69 to end his suffering from an AIDS-related illness.

January 22, 2000

Food journalist and author Craig Claiborne (*The New York Times Cookbook*, *Craig Claiborne's Southern Cooking*, *The Chinese Cookbook*, *The Best of Craig Claiborne*) - food editor and restaurant critic for *The New York Times* - dies in New York City at age 79.

---◯---

January 23, 1889

Actor Franklin Pangborn (*Hail the Conquering Hero, Now, Voyager, International House*) - whose fussy mannerisms and delivery enlivened over 200 films and television shows - is born in Newark, N.J.

January 23, 1898

Screen actor and top 10 film box office draw, Randolph Scott (*Ride the High Country, The Tall T, My Favorite Wife*) is born in Orange County, VA.

January 23, 2015

Essayist, chronicler, and novelist Pedro Lemebel (*Poco Hombre, My Tender Matador, La Esquina Es Mi Corazon)* dies of cancer of the larynx at age 62 in Santiago, Chile.

January 23, 2017

Actor and singer Gorden Kaye (*'Allo 'Allo, Brazil, Born and Bred, Coronation Street*) dies at age 75 in Yorkshire, England.

---◯---

January 24, 76 A.D.

Hadrian - the Roman emperor best known for rebuilding the Pantheon as well as constructing Hadrian's Wall to mark to northern limit of Roman Britain - is born.

January 24, 1874

Popular author W. Somerset Maugham (*The Razor's Edge,*

The Moon and Sixpence, Of Human Bondage, Rain) is born in Paris, France.

January 24, 1944

New wave countertenor Klaus Nomi (*Encore*, *Simple Man*, *Eclipsed: The Best of Klaus Nomi*) is born in Immenstadt, Bavaria, Germany.

January 24, 1975

The television sitcom *Hot L Baltimore* debuts on ABC featuring one of the medium's first depictions of an older gay couple, George and Gordon.

January 24, 1983

Film director George Cukor (*The Women*, *The Philadelphia Story*, *My Fair Lady*, *Gaslight*, *A Star is Born*) - who was nominated for five Oscars and won once - dies of a heart attack at age 83 in Los Angeles, CA.

January 24, 1998

Publisher and diarist Donald Vining (*A Gay Diary*, *How Can You Come Out If You've Never Been In?*) - who also founded Pepys Press - dies at age 80 in New York City.

January 24, 2006

Lambda Literary Award winning author and psychotherapist Betty Berzon (*Permanent Partners*, *Positively Gay*, *The Intimacy Dance*) - known for her work with gays and lesbians - dies of breast cancer at age 78 in the San Fernando Valley, CA.

January 25, 1882

Modernist literary legend Virginia Woolf (*Mrs. Dalloway, A Room of One's Own, The Waves, To the Lighthouse, Orlando*) is born in London, England.

January 25, 1996

Composer and playwright Jonathan Larson (*Rent*) - who won a Pulitzer Prize for Drama as well as two Tony Awards, all posthumously - dies of an aortic dissection at age 35 in New York City.

January 25, 2005

Architect Philip Johnson - who in 1930 founded the Department of Architecture and Design at the Museum of Modern Art in New York City and who is celebrated for championing both the International and Post-Modern styles of architecture - dies at age 98 in New Canaan, CT.

January 26, 2011

David Kato, activist and founder of Sexual Minorities Uganda (SMUG) - often described as "Uganda's first openly gay man" after he came out publicly at the nation's first gay rights news conference - is bludgeoned to death in Mukono Town, Uganda. This followed incidents in which the names, photos, and addresses of several gay rights activists were published in the Ugandan tabloid *Rolling Stone* under the headline, "Hang Them!"

January 27, 1911

Sarah Aldridge (pen name of lawyer Anyda Marchant) - co-founder of Naiad Press (1972) and A&M Books (1995) as well as author of 14 novels including *The Latecomer*, *All True Lovers*, *The Nesting Place* - is born in Rio de Janeiro, Brazil.

January 28, 1873

Novelist Colette (*The Vagabond, Cheri, Gigi, Claudine in Paris, The Gentle Libertine*) - whose literary forte was passion and love and who did not shy away from the sensual in her work - is born in Yonne, France. Colette was only the second woman in history to be made a grand officer of the Legion of Honor.

January 28, 1941

Actor Joel Crothers - two time Daytime Emmy nominee for his role as Miles Cavanaugh in *The Edge of Night* and well remembered for his role as Joe Haskell/Nathan Forbes on the daytime soap opera *Dark Shadows* - is born in Cincinnati, OH.

January 28, 1947

Composer, conductor, and director for the Paris Opera - Reynaldo Hahn (*Ciboulette, A Chloris, If My Verse Had Wings*) - rumored lover at one time of writer Marcel Proust - dies at age 72 in Paris, France.

January 28, 1960

Author, anthropologist, and folklorist Zora Neale Hurston (*Their Eyes Were Watching God, Mules and Men, Spunk, Every Tongue Got to Confess*) - active during the time of the Harlem Renaissance - dies of hypertensive heart disease at age 69 in Fort Pierce, FL.

January 28, 1961

The Illinois legislature votes to strike down that state's sodomy statute - effective January 1, 1962 - making Illinois the first state in the U.S. to do so.

January 28, 2002

Author Paul Reed - who wrote one of the first AIDS novels in 1984, *Facing It: A Novel of AIDS*, as well as books such as *Vertical Intercourse* and *Longing* - dies of an AIDS-related illness at age 45 in San Francisco, CA.

January 29, 1960

Supermodel Gia Marie Carangi - popular during the late 1970s and early 1980s and portrayed by Angelina Jolie in the 1998 HBO movie *Gia* - is born in Philadelphia, PA.

January 29, 1990

The term "outing" is introduced to the general public via William A. Henry III's piece "Forcing Gays Like Mike Howes Out of the Closet" in *TIME Magazine*. Henry cited *OutWeek* columnist Michelangelo Signorile as the originator of the practice in which individuals such as David Geffen, Malcolm Forbes, and Liz Smith were "outed" as gay and/or lesbian.

———————————◯———————————

January 30, 1925

Writer and poet Jack Spicer (*My Vocabulary Did This To Me*, *After Lorca*, *The Holy Grail*) - often associated with the San Francisco Renaissance and winner of the National Book Award - is born in Los Angeles, CA.

January 30, 1961

Journalist and radio personality Dorothy Thompson (*On the Record*, *I Saw Hitler*, *Let the Record Speak*) - once the second most influential woman in the U.S. behind First Lady Eleanor Roosevelt - dies at age 67 is Lisbon, Portugal.

January 30, 1978

Singer and actress Marie-Louise Damien aka Damia (*Napoleon*, *Tu Ne Sais Pas Aimer*, *C'est Mon Gigolo*) - part of the Paris circle which included Natalie Clifford Barney, Romaine Brooks, Loie Fuller, etc. - dies at age 88 following a fall in the metro in La Celle-Saint-Cloud, France.

———————————◯———————————

January 31, 1900

Artist and art dealer Betty Parsons - who championed the avant-garde and is known primarily for her work with and promotion of Abstract Expressionism – is born in New York City.

January 31, 1902

Theater and film actress Tallulah Bankhead (*Lifeboat, A Royal Scandal, Devil and the Deep*) - a stage sensation in the 1920s, and later became as famous for her outrageous behavior and larger than life personality as for her acting - is born in Huntsville, AL.

January 31, 1942

Filmmaker, designer, and diarist Derek Jarman (*Edward II, Aria, Wittgenstein, Caravaggio*) - who was awarded a BAFTA Award and directed three videos for the rock band The Smiths - is born in Northwood, England.

January 31, 1948

Singer and songwriter Paul Jabara - who wrote such disco hits as *Last Dance, The Main Event,* and *It's Raining Men* - is born in Brooklyn, NY.

Janaury 31, 2017

The Alan Turing Amnesty Law receives Royal Assent, poshtumously pardoning 50,000 British men.

FEBRUARY

February 1990

The first OutWrite lesbian and gay writer's conference is held in San Francisco, CA, conceived and produced by the editors of *OUTLOOK* magazine.

February 1, 1902

Poet, writer and activist Langston Hughes (*The Ways of White Folks*, *Not Without Laughter*, *The Selected Poems of Langston Hughes*) - known for his work during the Harlem Renaissance - is born in Joplin, MO.

February 1, 1927

Transgender journalist and author Nancy Hunt Bowman (*Mirror Image: The Odyssey of a Male-to-Female Transsexual*) - who won four Associated Press Awards for her reportage during the Vietnam War as Ridgely Hunt and was a featured writer with the *Chicago Tribune* - is born in New York City.

February 2, 1923

Gossip columnist Liz Smith, known as the Grand Dame of Dish, who wrote for *The New York Daily News*, *The Washington Post*, etc., is born in Fort Worth, TX.

February 2, 1940

Science fiction author, critic, and poet Thomas M. Disch (*The Dreams Our Stuff is Made Of, 334, The Genocides, On Wings of Song, The Word of God, Camp Concentration*) - who was also nominated for several Hugo and Nebula Awards for his fantasy/speculative fiction writing and won a Hugo Award for his non-fiction writing - is born in Des Moines, IA. Disch was also the author of the popular children's book *The Brave Little Toaster: A Bedtime Story for Small Appliances.*

February 2, 1956

Author, publisher, and literary expatriate Robert McAlmon (*Village: It Happened Through a Fifteen Year Period, A Hasty Bunch, Not Alone Lost, A Scarlet Pansy, McAlmon and the Lost Generation: A Self-Portrait*) dies at age 60 in Desert Hot Springs, CA.

February 2, 1957

Architect Julia Morgan (Hearst Castle in San Simeon, Riverside Art Museum, Los Angeles Examiner Building) - the first woman to be admitted to the architecture program at the Ecole des Beaux-Arts in Paris and later California's first licensed woman architect - dies at age 85 in San Francisco, CA.

February 2, 1972

Writer Natalie Clifford Barney (*A Perilous Advantage, Adventures of the Mind*) – a U.S. expatriate in Paris known for her artist salon on the West Bank – dies of heart failure at age 95 in Paris, France.

February 2, 1994

Writer and journalist Robert Ford (*Thing Magazine*) dies at age 32 from an AIDS-related illness in Chicago, IL.

February 2, 2003

Prolific composer, conductor, musician and environmentalist Lou Harrison (*Suite for Percussion, Young Caesar, Elegiac Symphony*) - who had over 300 diverse compositions to his credit and was known for his synthesis of styles - dies of a heart attack at age 85 in Lafayette, IN.

February 2, 2009

The reality drag contest television show, *RuPaul's Drag Race*, debuts on Logo.

February 3, 1874

Writer Gertrude Stein (*Tender Buttons, The Autobiography of Alice B. Toklas, Three Lives*) – a U.S. expatriate in Paris known for her salon as well as her literary and artistic influence – and partner of Alice B. Toklas – is born in Allegheny, N.Y.

February 3, 1900

Celebrated cabaret and jazz singer Mabel Mercer, recipient of the Presidential Medal of Freedom and whose notable recordings include *From This Moment On* and *Just One of Those Things*, is born at Burton upon Trent, UK.

February 3, 1938

Prolific actor Victor Buono - who was nominated for an Oscar and a Golden Globe Award for his work in *Whatever Happened to Baby Jane?* and who found enduring fame in recurring villain roles on the 1960s TV series *Batman* and *The Wild Wild West* - is born in San Diego, CA.

February 3, 1957

Filmmaker, activist, and educator Marlon Riggs (*Tongues Untied, Color Adjustment, Ethnic Notions*) - who won an Emmy and a Peabody Award for his documentary work - is born in Fort Worth, TX.

February 3, 1961

Anna May Wong, the first Asian-American actress to gain international recognition in films like *The Shanghai Express, The Toll of the Sea, The Thief of Bagdad,* and *Piccadilly,* dies of a heart attack at age 56 in Santa Monica, CA.

February 3, 1991

Character actress Nancy Kulp - best known for her portrayal of Jane Hathaway on the 1960s sitcom *The Beverly Hillbillies* - dies of cancer at age 69 in Palm Desert, CA.

February 3, 2011

Actress Maria Schneider (*Last Tango in Paris, The Passenger*) dies from cancer at age 58 in Paris, France.

February 3, 2015

Journalist, arts critic, interviewer, broadcaster, and author I.F. Stone *(I.F. Stone: a Portrait; A Portrait in Four Movements: The Chicago Symphony under Barenboim, Boulez, Haitink, and Muti)* dies of a bacterial infection at age 55 in Chicago, IL.

February 4, 1938

Author, editor, historian, and lecturer Martin Greif *(The Gay Book of Days, The World of Tomorrow)* is born in the Bronx, N.Y.

February 4, 1960

Composer and playwright Jonathan Larson *(Rent)* - who won a Pulitzer Prize for Drama as well as two Tony Awards, all posthumously - is born in Mount Vernon, N.Y.

February 4, 1980

Disco, nightclub, and rich and famous playground, Studio 54 closes, with a final party called "The End of Modern-day Gomorrah."

February 4, 1987

Pianist, personality, and flamboyantly dressed showman Liberace *(The Loved One, A Liberace Christmas, Sincerely Yours, The Liberace Show)* - whose many awards include two Emmys and six gold records - dies from an AIDS-related illness at age 67 in Palm Springs, CA.

February 4, 1995

Novelist and writer Patricia Highsmith (*Strangers on a Train, The Talented Mr. Ripley, The Two Faces of January, Deep Water*) - who also wrote the lesbian novel *The Price of Salt* under the pseudonym Claire Morgan - dies of aplastic anemia and cancer at age 74 in Locarno, Switzerland.

February 4, 2002

Golden Globe Award winning actor George Nader (*Robot Monster, Carnival Story, Away All Boats*) - who also wrote the 1978 gay science-fiction novel *Chrome* - dies at age 80 in Woodland Hills, CA.

February 4, 2018

Award winning stage, TV, and screen actor John Mahoney (*Frasier, Barton Fink, Say Anything*) dies of brain disease and lung cancer at age 77 in Chicago, IL.

February 5, 1912

Author William S. Burroughs (*Naked Lunch, The Wild Boys, The Soft Machine, Cities of the Red Night, Junkie, Queer*) - one of the key writers of the Beat Generation - is born in St. Louis, MO.

February 5, 1982

The Robert Towne lesbian themed film, *Personal Best*, about the American women's track and field team is released in theaters. The Warner Brothers film stars Mariel Hemingway, Scott Glenn, and Patrice Donnelly.

February 5, 1992

Danny Sotomayor – the first nationally syndicated, openly gay political cartoonist, and co-founder of ACT-UP/Chicago – dies at age 33 of an AIDS-related illness in Chicago, IL.

February 5, 2013

Gay rights advocacy groups and members of Congress applaud reports that the Pentagon plans to propose extending benefits to some same sex spouses of U.S. military members.

―――――――――――⊖――――――――――――

February 6, 1899

Silent film actor and MGM box office star Ramon Novarro (*Ben-Hur, Mata Hari, The Student Prince at Old Heidelberg*) – one of the greatest stars of the era – is born in Durango, Mexico.

February 6, 1995

Poet and writer James Merrill (*The Changing Light at Sandover, Divine Comedies, Nights and Days, Mirabell: Books of Numbers, A Scattering of Salts*) - whose many honors and awards include two National Book Awards, the National Book Critics Circle Award, and the Pulitzer Prize - dies of an AIDS-related heart attack at age 68 in Tucson, AZ.

February 6, 1995

The made-for-TV movie, *Serving in Silence: The Margarethe Cammermeyer Story* first airs on NBC. Featuring Glenn Close and Judy Davis, the film chronicles a decorated soldier's dishonorable discharge from the army and challenges the U.S. military's position on gays and lesbians. Close and Davis will both go on to win Emmys for their roles.

February 6, 2014

The award winning comedy-drama television series, *Transparent*, debuts.

February 6, 2017

Out film and stage actor Sir Alec McCowen (*Henry V, Frenzy, Travels With my Aunt, Never Say Never Again, Waiting for Godot, Caesar and Cleopatra),* dies at age 91 in London.

———————————◦———————————

February 7, 1977

The U.S. State Department announces it will no longer automatically prevent the hiring of gays and lesbians for employment.

February 7, 1991

The first kiss lesbian airs on network TV during the "He's a Crowd" episode of the NBC drama *L.A. Law* [Season 5, Episode 12]. In the episode Abby Perkins (Michele Greek) and C.J. Lamb (Amanda Donohoe) exchange a kiss after Abby receives a raise. Advertisers threaten to pull their ads over the scene.

February 7, 2012

The three judge panel of the Ninth Circuit Court of Appeals in California rules 2–1 that Proposition 8, the referendum that banned same-sex marriage in the state, is in violation of the Equal Protection Clause of the 14th Amendment and therefore unconstitutional.

February 8, 1875

Operatic soprano, actress and author Georgette Leblanc (*The Choice of Life*, *Carmen*, *Mary Magdalene*, *La Navarraise*, *Sapho*) is born in Rouen, France.

February 8, 1911

Poet Elizabeth Bishop (*Geography III*, *A Cold Spring*, *The Complete Poems*, *North and South*) - whose awards include the Pulitzer Prize and the National Book Award for Poetry - is born in Worcester, MA.

February 8, 1931

Iconic film actor James Dean (*East of Eden*, *Giant*, *Rebel Without a Cause*) - who was nominated for two Oscars and one Hollywood's brightest stars during his brief, meteoric career – is born in Marion, IN.

─────────────────────○─────────────────────

February 9, 1874

Poet Amy Lowell (*Pictures of the Floating World, The Complete Poetical Works of Amy Lowell*) - who was posthumously awarded the Pulitzer Prize for Poetry in 1926 for *What's O'clock* - is born in Boston, MA.

February 9, 1971

TV series *All in the Family* airs the "Judging Books By Covers" episode [Season 1, Episode 5] - written by Burt Styler and Norman Lear – one of the first times a gay character is brought into America's living rooms.

February 9, 1977

The first gay film festival takes place in San Francisco, CA. At the time it is called The Gay Film Festival of Super-8 Films but will eventually become the Frameline Film Festival.

February 9, 1999

The Reverend Jerry Falwell, former spokesman for the Moral Majority, claims that Tinky Winky (the purple-colored Teletubby from the PBS toddler series *Teletubbies*) is gay because he carries a purse, is purple - the gay pride color, and his hat is in the shape of a triangle.

February 9, 2019

Award winning author Patricia Nell Warren (Harlan's Race, Billy's Boy) whose novel The Front Runner was one of the first works of contemporary gay fiction to make the New York Times best seller list, dies at age 82.

February 10, 1893

Tennis great Bill Tilden - the world's number one player for seven years during the 1920s, and the winner of seven United States championships - is born in Philadelphia, PA.

February 10, 1897

Actress Dame Judith Anderson (*Laura, Cat on a Hot Tin Roof, And Then There Were None, Kings Row, The Strange Love of Martha Ivers, Star Trek III: The Search for Spock*) is born in Adelaide, Australia. Anderson is best known for her role as Mrs. Danvers in *Rebecca* and won two Emmys, a Tony Award, and was nominated for an Oscar.

February 10, 1944

Oscar, Grammy, and Golden Globe winning songwriter and entertainer Peter Allen (*I Go To Rio, Arthur's Theme, I Honestly Love You*) is born in Tenterfield, New South Wales, Australia.

February 10, 1975

Activist and journalist Lige Clarke - who wrote *The Homosexual Citizen* column in *Screw Magazine* in 1968, as well as the books *Men's Liberation, I Have More Fun With You Than Anybody* and *Roommates Can't Always Be Lovers*, with his partner Jack Nichols - is shot and killed at age 32 near Vera Cruz, Mexico.

February 10, 1995

Author Paul Monette (*Borrowed Time*, *Last Watch of the Night*) - who won the National Book Award in 1992 for his gay memoir *Becoming a Man: Half a Life Story* and was the winner of two Lambda Literary Awards as well as a Stonewall Book Award - dies of an AIDS-related illness at age 49 in West Hollywood, CA.

February 11, 1967

Over three dozen picketers from various counterculture groups descend upon the Black Cat Tavern in Los Angeles to protest continued police mistreatment following the arrests at the nightspot on New Year's Eve.

February 11, 2010

Innovative fashion designer Alexander McQueen - four time winner of the British Designer of the Year award as well being named International Designer of the Year at the Council of Fashion Designers Awards - commits suicide by hanging himself at age 40 in London, England.

February 11, 2017

At the 2018 Winter Olympics, Adam Rippon wins a bronze medal as part of the figure skating team event, thus becoming the first openly gay U.S. male athlete to win a medal at the Winter Olympics.

---○---

February 12, 1929

Actor, screenwriter, and prolific low-budget filmmaker Andy Milligan (*Bloodthirsty Butchers*, *Blood Rites*, *The Rats are Coming! The Werewolves Are Here!*, *Carnage*) - is born in St. Paul, MN.

February 12, 1936

Actor Paul Shenar (*Scarface*, *Raw Deal*, *The Big Blue*, *Rage of Angels: The Story Continues*) is born in Milwaukee, WI.

February 12, 1942

Artist Grant Wood (*Self-Portrait*, *The Midnight Ride of Paul Revere*, *Iowa Cornfield*) - best known for the iconic painting *American Gothic* - dies at age 50 in Iowa City, IA.

February 12, 1976

Actor Sal Mineo (*Rebel Without a Cause*, *Exodus*, *The Gene Krupa Story*) - nominated for two Oscars and winner of a Golden Globe Award - is murdered in West Hollywood, CA.

February 12, 1982

The mainstream 20th Century Fox film *Making Love* is released about a man coming to terms with his homosexuality. The film stars Michael Ontkean, Kate Jackson, and Harry Hamlin.

February 12, 1997

Lawyer and gay rights advocate Thomas Stoddard - executive director of Lambda Legal Defense and Education Fund from 1986-1992 - dies at age 48 of an AIDS-related illness in Manhattan, N.Y.

February 12, 2007

Jazz saxophonist and bandleader Peggy Gilbert (Peggy Gilbert and the Dixie Belles, Peggy Gilbert and Her Metro Goldwyn Orchestra) - subject of the documentary film *Peggy Gilbert and Her All Girl Band* - dies at age 102 in Burbank, CA.

February 13, 1891

Artist Grant Wood (*Self-Portrait, The Midnight Ride of Paul Revere, Iowa Cornfield*) - best known for the iconic painting *American Gothic* - is born in Anamosa, IA.

February 13, 1964

Activist and founder of Sexual Minorities Uganda (SMUG) David Kato - often described as "Uganda's first openly gay man" after he came out publicly at the nation's first gay rights news conference - is born in the Mukono District, Uganda.

February 13, 1994

Biologist, activist, and important AIDS researcher Bruce Voeller - who helped found the National Gay Task Force and served as its executive director for five years; and who later campaigned for condom use to prevent the spread of STDs - dies of an AIDS-related illness at age 59 in Topanga, CA.

February 13, 2009

The ABC soap opera, *All My Children*, features daytime TV's first lesbian wedding with the union of Bianca Montgomery (Eden Riegel) and Reese Williams (Tamara Braun).

———————————◯———————————

February 14, 1921

Lesbian co-editors – and accused purveyors of obscenity – Margaret C. Anderson and Jane Heap go on trial for publishing excerpts from James Joyce's *Ulysses* in their arts and literary magazine *The Little Review*.

February 14, 1962

Make-up artist and photographer Kevin Aucoin (*Making Faces, Face Forward*) is born in Shreveport, LA.

February 14, 1993

AMBi (The Alliance of Multi-Cultural Bisexuals) organizes Washington DC's first Bi Visibility Day.

February 14, 1995

BAFTA Award winning director/producer Nigel Finch (*Stonewall, Arena: Did You Miss Me?, The Lost Language of Cranes, Kenneth Anger, The Errand*) dies at age 45 of an AIDS-related illness in London, England.

February 14, 1997

A key figure in the early gay movement, Don Slater - editor of *ONE Magazine* and co-founder of ONE Inc. and who later chaired the organization the Homosexual Information Center - dies of a heart attack at age 73 in Los Angeles, CA.

———————————————— ○ ————————————————

February 15, 1902

Fay Jackson Robinson the journalism pioneer who was the first person to found a black news magazine on the West Coast and the first black Hollywood correspondent for the Associated Negro Press, is born in Dallas, TX.

February 15, 1907

Prolific actor Cesar Romero (*Week-End in Havana, The Thin Man, Ocean's 11*) - perhaps best known for his role as The Joker on the television series *Batman* - is born in New York City.

———————————————— ○ ————————————————

February 16, 1893

Theatrical legend and Tony Award winning actress Katharine Cornell (*The Barretts of Wimpole Street, Romeo and Juliet, Candida, The Green Hat, The Age of Innocence*) - often called "The First Lady of the Theater" - is born in Berlin, Germany.

February 16, 1926

Film director John Schlesinger (*Darling, Sunday Bloody*

Sunday, Yanks, Marathon Man) - who won an Academy Award for his direction of *Midnight Cowboy* - is born in London, England.

February 16, 1931

Photographer Wilhelm von Gloeden - known primarily for his 20th century pastoral postcards of the men and boys of Sicily, mostly nudes and/or adorned in classical robes or garlands - dies at age 74 in Taormina, Sicily.

February 16, 1990

Artist and activist Keith Haring (*Radiant Baby*, *Three-Eyed Face*, *Stop AIDS*, *Barking Dogs*, *Safe Sex*) - the man whose graffiti-influenced, tribal, and patterned artwork helped define the AIDS era - dies at age 31 in New York City from complications due to AIDS.

February 16, 2015

Singer, songwriter, activist Lesley Gore (*It's My Party, You Don't Own Me, Judy's Turn to Cry)* dies of lung cancer at age 68 in Manhattan.

———————————○———————————

February 17, 1934

Oscar nominated actor Alan Bates (*Georgy Girl*, *Women in Love*, *King of Hearts*, *Gosford Park*) - who also won two Tony Awards and one BAFTA Award - is born in Allestree, England.

February 17, 1974

Jack Cole (*Gilda, Gentleman Prefer Blondes, On the Riviera, Man of La Mancha*) - dancer, choreographer and theater director who was called "the father of theatrical jazz dance" - dies at age 62 in Hollywood, CA.

February 17, 1981

Novelist, memoirist, editor, and publisher David Garnett (*Aspects of Love, The Sailor's Return, Lady into Fox*) dies at age 88 in Montcug, France. Garnett was a member of the Bloomsbury Group where he was known as "Bunny" and also co-founded Nonesuch Press.

February 17, 1994

Award winning author and journalist Randy Shilts (*And The Band Played On, Conduct Unbecoming, The Mayor of Castro Street*) - who became the first full-time openly gay journalist to cover gay politics for the mainstream U.S. press when he was hired in 1981 by *The San Francisco Chronicle* - dies at age 42 of an AIDS-related illness in Guerneville, CA.

―――――――――○―――――――――

February 18, 1564

Artist, sculptor, poet and engineer Michelangelo di Lodovico Buonarroti Simoni aka Michelangelo (*The Pieta, David,* Ceiling of the Sistine Chapel, *The Creation of Adam,* Dome of St. Peter's Basilica) dies at age 88 in Rome, Italy.

February 18, 1876

Stage actress Charlotte Cushman – acclaimed for playing both male and female roles interchangeably, and at one time acknowledged as the greatest living actress – dies of breast cancer at age 59 in Boston, MA.

February 18, 1934

Poet, essayist, educator, and activist Audre Lorde (*Zami: A New Spelling of My Name*, *From a Land Where Other People Live*, *Sister Outsider*, *The Black Unicorn*, *The Cancer Journals*) - founding influence of Kitchen Table, Women of Color Press - is born in New York City.

February 18, 2007

Key early gay and lesbian rights activist Barbara Gittings dies of breast cancer at age 74 in Kennett Square, PA. Gittings organized the New York chapter of the Daughters of Bilitis was editor of the DOB's magazine *The Ladder*, co-founded the National Gay Task Force, and helped form the first gay caucus within an organization (with the American Library Association) which helped promote positive gay and lesbian literature. Gittings was also a major influence in having homosexuality removed from the American Psychiatric Association's list of mental illnesses.

February 19, 1902

Scholar, educator, and critic F.O. Matthiessen (*American Renaissance: Art and Expression in the Age of Emerson and Whitman, Sarah Orne Jewett, From the Heart of Europe*) - an outspoken advocate of Christian socialism - is born in Pasadena, CA.

February 19, 1917

Southern gothic writer Carson McCullers (*The Heart is a Lonely Hunter, The Member of the Wedding, The Ballad of the Sad Cafe, Reflections in a Golden Eye*) - winner of a New York Drama Critics Circle Award - is born in Columbus, GA.

February 19, 1923

After playing at the Provincetown Playhouse and the Greenwich Village Theatre, *The God of Vengeance* by Sholom Ash, which features lesbianism as a large part of the plot, opens at the Apollo Theatre on Broadway where it will run for 133 performances.

February 19, 1927

French journalist, gay rights activist, author, and publisher of early LGBT magazines in the 1960s/1970s, Pierre Guenin is born in Etampes, France. He was also the founder of the LGBT film awards in France.

February 19, 1941

Warhol drag superstar of the youth-quaking underground film world Jackie Curtis (*Flesh, Women in Revolt*) is born in New York City.

February 19, 1951

Writer Andre Gide (*The Counterfeiters*, *Corydon*, *Lafcadio's Adventures*, *The Immoralist*) - winner of the Nobel Prize in Literature - dies at age 81 in Paris, France.

February 19, 1961

Soccer player Justin Fashanu - a forward for several teams and the first professional footballer to come out publicly - is born in London, England.

February 19, 1994

Filmmaker, designer, diarist Derek Jarman (*Edward II*, *Aria*, *Wittgenstein*, *Caravaggio*) - who was awarded a BAFTA Award and directed three videos for the rock band The Smiths - dies at age 52 of an AIDS-related illness in London, England.

February 19, 2002

Early transgender activist Sylvia Rivera - who was a member of the Gay Activists Alliance and the Gay Liberation Front but who was outspoken about the place transgender people had in the early gay rights movement and who later helped found S.T.A.R. (Street Transgender Action Revolutionaries) with Marsha P. Johnson - dies of complications from liver cancer at age 50 in New York City.

February 20, 2002

Activist and author John Paul Hudson - on the founding
committee of New York City's first Gay Pride Parade
(Christopher Street Liberation Day Parade), an early member
the Gay Activist Alliance, and author of such books as *The Gay
Insider* and *Superstar Murder* - dies at age 73 in Honesdale,
PA.

February 21, 1801

Cardinal John Henry Newman (*Apologia Pro Vita Sua, Loss
and Gain*) – who was Beatified by the Catholic Church in 2010
– is born in London, England.

February 21, 1903

Author, artist. and popular diarist Anais Nin (*Delta of Venus,
Little Birds*) - who enjoyed living on the artistic edge for five
decades and also helped establish the publishing house Siana
Editions when no one would publish her oftentimes intimate
and erotic work - is born in Neuilly-sur-Seine, France.

February 21, 1903

The New York police conduct the first recorded U.S. raid on
a bathhouse, the Ariston Hotel Baths. Twenty-six men are
arrested and 12 are brought to trial on sodomy charges.

February 21, 1907

Poet W.H. Auden (*Collected Poems, Tell Me the Truth About*

Love) - who among other honors won the Pulitzer Prize for Poetry, The National Book Award for Poetry, and the Bollingen Prize - is born in York, England.

February 21, 1908

Neoclassical sculptress and designer Harriet Hosmer (*Zenobia in Chains, The Sleeping Faun, Daphne, Beatrice Cenci, The Mermaid's Cradle*) - the foremost American female sculptor of her time - dies at age 77 in Watertown, MA.

February 21, 1919

Mary Edwards Walker, surgeon, abolitionist, activist, field service doctor during the Civil War, and the first woman, and to this date the only woman, to win the Medal of Honor, dies at age 86 in Oswego, NY.

February 21, 1936

U.S. Congresswoman Barbara Jordan is born in Houston, TX. Jordan was the first African American woman to be elected to Congress from a Southern state and the first to deliver the keynote address at a national presidential convention (1976).

February 21, 1940

Stage and film actor Keith Prentice (*The Boys in the Band, Dark Shadows, Cruising*) is born in Dayton, OH.

February 21, 1954

Award-winning poet and educator Francisco Xavier Alarcon (*Iguanas in the Snow and Other Winter Poems, From the Other Side of Night, Snake Poems, Body in Flames*) is born in Wilmington, CA.

February 21, 1955

Astrologer and member of the Sisters of Perpetual Indulgence, Sister Boom Boom (aka Jack Fertig) is born in Chicago, IL.

February 21, 2019

The body of pioneering trans soul singer Jackie Shane (*Any Other Way*) is discovered in Nashville, TN. Shane was 78 years old.

February 22, 1892

Poet and playwright Edna St. Vincent Millay (*Collected Sonnets, The Ballad of the Harp Weaver, First Fig and Other Poems*) - cultural idol from the heyday of Greenwich Village, winner of the Pulitzer Prize for Poetry in 1923, and winner of the Robert Frost Medal in 1943 - is born in Rockland, ME.

February 22, 1917

Writer and playwright Jane Bowles (*Two Serious Ladies, In the Summer House*) - who was married to writer/composer Paul Bowles but who also had several affairs with women - is born in New York City.

February 22, 1942

Activist and journalist Lige Clark - who wrote *The Homosexual Citizen* column in *Screw Magazine* in 1968, as well as the books *Men's Liberation, I Have More Fun With You Than Anybody* and *Roommates Can't Always Be Lovers*, with his partner Jack Nichols - is born in southeastern Kentucky.

February 22, 1964

The Canadian publication *Maclean's* publishes a two-part piece entitled *The Homosexual Next Door: A Sober Appraisal of a New Social Phenomenon* - considered the first mainstream Canadian piece to take a positive view of homosexuality. The second installment of the article is published on March 7.

February 22, 1971

Activist Frank Kameny files his papers to represent Washington DC in a special election that would give the district a representative - the first time an openly gay person declared their intentions to run for Congress.

February 22, 1987

Artist, filmmaker, underground icon, and self-marketing genius Andy Warhol (*Campbell's Soup Cans*, *Trash*, *Chelsea Girls*, *Eight Elvises*) - a leading figure in the Pop Art movement - dies at age 58 following gallbladder surgery in New York City.

February 22, 2015

Neil Patrick Harris becomes the first openly gay man to host the Academy Awards. The 87th annual Oscar contest was held at the Dolby Theatre in Los Angeles.

February 23, 1933

Three and a half weeks after Adolf Hitler became the
Chancellor of Germany on January 30th, the Nazi Party
(National Socialist German Workers Part) issues a decree
outlawing all homosexual rights organizations and clubs as
well as all pornography.

February 23, 1943

Carl Wittman - activist, early proponent of the Radical Faeries,
author of *Amerika: A Gay Manifesto* (originally published by
the Red Butterfly cell of the Gay Liberation Front in January,
1970) and member of the national council of the Students for a
Democratic Society (SDS) - is born in Hackensack, N.J.

February 23, 1999

The British television series *Queer As Folk* (later adapted for
the U.S.) debuts on Channel 4. The series, about three gay men
living in Manchester, will run for a year.

February 24, 1890

Oscar nominated actress Marjorie Main (*Ma Kettle, Meet Me in
St. Louis, The Women, The Egg and I*) - longtime companion of
actress Spring Byington - is born in Acton, IN.

February 24, 1941

Travel writer, architecture critic, and historian Robert Byron
(*The Road to Oxiana, The Byzantine Achievement, The Station*)

dies at age 35 off Cape Wrath, Scotland when his ship is torpedoed by a German submarine in the North Atlantic.

February 24, 1990

Singer Johnny Ray (*Cry*, *Just Walking in the Rain*, *The Little White Cloud That Cried*) - who was known as "Mr. Emotion" for his uninhibited vocal delivery and who also appeared in the film *There's No Business Like Show Business* - dies of liver failure at age 63 in Los Angeles, CA. after being in a coma for several days.

February 24, 2004

President George W. Bush calls on Congress to prepare a constitutional amendment to protect the sanctity of marriage and ban same-sex marriage by defining marriage as "the union of a man and woman as husband and wife."

February 24, 2006

Science fiction writer Octavia Butler (*Kindred*, *Wild Seed*, *Parable of the Sower*, *Bloodchild*, *Parable of the Talents*) - winner of two Hugo Awards as well as two Nebula Awards for excellence in fantasy/science fiction writing - dies at age 58 following a fall outside her Lake Forest Park, WA. home.

February 25, 1937

Playwright, poet, critic, visual artist, and author Severo Sarduy (*For Voice*, *Beach Birds*, *Colibri*, *From Cuba With a Song*) - known for his extreme and unpredictable plots as well as experimental style - is born in Camaguey, Cuba.

February 25, 1939

Playwright, director, activist, and gay/queer theater pioneer Doric Wilson (*And He Made a Her*, *The West Street Gang*, *Pretty People*, *Now She Dances!*) - a mainstay in the Off Off Broadway and gay theater movements, a founding member of the Circle Repertory Theater; and who also began Tosos, often cited as perhaps the first professional theater company to deal openly with the gay experience - is born in Los Angeles, CA.

February 25, 1983

Writer Tennessee Williams (*Cat on a Hot Tin Roof*, *Sweet Bird of Youth*, *Suddenly, Last Summer*, *The Rose Tattoo*, *The Night of the Iguana*, *The Glass Menagerie*, *A Streetcar Named Desire*) - whose many honors and awards include two Pulitzer Prizes, two Tony Awards, and a New York Drama Critics' Circle Award - chokes to death on the cap from a bottle of eye drops at age 71 in New York City.

February 25, 2002

Comic, actress, and talk show host Rosie O'Donnell officially comes out on stage at Caroline's Comedy Club in New York City stating "I'm a dyke!" during a comedy benefit for Ovarian Cancer Research Fund (OCRF). O'Donnell has since said her primary reason for doing so was to bring attention to the issue of gay adoption.

February 25, 2007

Ellen DeGeneres becomes the first open lesbian to host the Academy Awards when she takes on the task at the 79th annual Oscars. DeGeneres will host the prestigious award show broadcast again in 2014.

---○---

February 26, 1564

Playwright and poet Christopher Marlowe (*Doctor Faustus*, *Edward II*, *Tamburlaine*, *The Jew of Malta*) is baptized as an infant in Canterbury, England. His exact date of birth is unknown.

February 26, 1905

Travel writer, architecture critic, and historian Robert Byron (*The Road to Oxiana*, *The Byzantine Achievement*, *The Station*) is born in Middlesex, England.

February 26, 1955

Playwright and novelist Harry Kondoleon (*Diary of a Lost Boy*, *Zero Positive*, *Saved or Destroyed*, *The Houseguests*) - who won two Obie Awards, given for Off and Off-Off Broadway productions - is born in Queens, N.Y.

---○---

February 27, 1880

Poet, playwright, journalist, author, and educator Angelina Weld Grimke - who was part of the Harlem Renaissance and whose popular three-act play *Rachel* was staged as a vehicle for NAACP rallies against the effects of the film *Birth of a Nation* - is born in Boston, MA.

February 27, 1925

Actress, comedienne, and storyteller Pat Bond (*Gerty Gerty Gerty Stein is Back Back Back*, *Murder in the WAC, Lorena Hickok and Eleanor Roosevelt: A Love Story, Word is Out, Designing Women*) is born in Chicago, IL.

February 27, 1964

Fashion designer Orry-Kelly (Orry George Kelly) - winner of three Academy Awards for Best Costumes for *An American in Paris, Les Girls*, and *Some Like it Hot* - dies of liver cancer at age 66 in Los Angeles, CA.

February 27, 1970

The first issue of the feminist lesbian magazine – *off our backs* – is published.

February 27, 1994

Historian, writer and scholar Harold Acton (*The Villas of Tuscany, The Last Medici, The Bourbons of Naples*) - and an inspiration for Evelyn Waugh's classic novel *Brideshead Revisited* - dies at age 89 in Florence, Italy.

February 27, 2011

Educator James Gruber – a gay activist and early member of the Mattachine Society who also founded a motorcycle group called The Satyrs – dies at age 82 in Santa Clara, CA.

February 27, 2013

Pianist Van Cliburn – who won the first quadrennial

International Tchaikovsky Piano Competition in Moscow – dies of bone cancer at age 78 in Fort Worth, TX.

———————————○———————————

February 28, 1797

Educator, Women's Rights Activist, and first president of Mount Holyoke College, Mary Lyon is born in Buckland, MA.

February 28, 1909

Poet, essayist, educator, and novelist Sir Stephen Spender (*World Within World, The Temple, Vienna, Selected Poems*) - whose work centered on social issues and the class struggle and who was the only non-U.S. citizen (to date) to serve as U.S. Poet Laureate - is born in London, England.

———————————○———————————

February 29, 1948

Fashion designer Willi Smith - founder of the company WilliWear Limited (which featured inexpensive sportswear) and recipient of the American Fashion Critics' Coty Award in 1983 - is born in Philadelphia, PA.

February 29, 1972

Reality television star Pedro Zamora (*The Real World: San Francisco*) is born in Havana, Cuba.

MARCH

March 1972

The New Republic publishes the article "The Gay Vote" which discusses the Gay Activists Alliance and the emergence of gays and lesbians as a political force.

March 1

Zero Discrimination Day is observed join together against discrimination and inequality in health care, including fighting stigma regarding HIV/AIDS.

March 1, 1896

Conductor and composer Dimitri Mitropoulos - conductor at both the New York Philharmonic (where he greatly expanded the repertoire) as well as The Metropolitan Opera - is born in Athens, Greece.

March 1, 1893

Eccentric poet, playwright, and novelist Mercedes de Acosta (*Here Lies the Heart*) - whose lovers included Alla Nazimova, Isadora Duncan, and Greta Garbo and whose personal wardrobe became the start of the Costume Institute at the Metropolitan Museum of Art - is born in New York City.

March 1, 1936

Mikhail Kuzmin, author of *Wings* (1906) – the first Russian novel to not only center on homosexuality, but to deal with it openly and sympathetically – dies at age 61 in Saint Petersburg, Russia.

March 1, 1994

The "Don't Ask, Don't Tell" episode of the ABC sitcom *Roseanne* [Season 6, Episode 18] airs in which Roseanne (Roseanne Barr) goes to a gay bar with her sister Jackie and co-worker Nancy and is kissed by another woman, played by Mariel Hemingway as Sharon. Initially ABC refuses to air the episode until Barr demands that it be shown.

March 1, 2017

French journalist, gay rights activist, author, and publisher of early LGBT magazines in the 1960s/1970s, Pierre Guenin dies at age 90 in Paris. He was also the founder of the LGBT film awards in France.

———————————⊖———————————

March 2, 1942

Musician, singer, songwriter Lou Reed (The Velvet Underground, *Transformer*, *Walk on the Wild Side, Coney Island Baby*) is born in Brooklyn.

March 2, 1982

Wisconsin becomes the first state in the U.S. to ban discrimination based on sexual orientation.

March 2, 1987

Screen actor and top 10 film box office draw, Randolph Scott (*Ride the High Country*, *The Tall T*, *My Favorite Wife*) dies of heart and lung ailments at age 89 in Beverly Hills, CA.

March 2, 1991

Louis Sullivan (transgender activist, author of one of the first guidebooks for FTM persons - *Information for the Female to Male Cross Dresser and Transsexual* – and founder of FTM International, the first FTM organization) dies of an AIDS-related illness at age 39 in San Francisco, CA.

March 2, 1992

Winner of two Tony Awards and an Oscar, actress Sandy Dennis (*The Out of Towners*, *Who's Afraid of Virginia Woolf?*, *Up the Down Staircase*, *The Fox*, *Sweet November*, *Come Back to the Five and Dime, Jimmy Dean, Jimmy Dean*) dies of ovarian cancer at age 54 in Westport. CT.

March 2, 1999

Singer Dusty Springfield (*Son of a Preacher Man*, *The Look of Love*, *You Don't Have to Say You Love Me*, *The Windmills of Your Mind*) - who charted 18 singles on the Billboard Hot 100 - dies at age 59 of breast cancer at Henley-on-Thames, Oxfordshire, England.

---○---

March 3, 1756

Actress and beauty Mlle Francoise Raucourt (*Gaston et Bayard, Henriette*) - who also led la Secte Androgyne, a lesbian society in Paris - is born in Nancy, France.

March 3, 1849

Educator, Women's Rights Activist, and first president of Mount Holyoke College, Mary Lyon is dies at age 52 South Hadley, MA.

March 3, 1903

Adrian aka Adrian Adolph Greenberg – one of Hollywood's premier costume designers whose film credits include *The Women*, *The Wizard of Oz*, *Camille*, *Dinner at Eight* and *The Great Ziegfeld* – is born in Naugatuck, CT.

March 3, 1926

Poet and writer James Merrill (*The Changing Light at Sandover*, *Divine Comedies*, *Nights and Days*, *Mirabell: Books of Numbers*, *A Scattering of Salts*) - whose many honors and awards include two National Book Awards, the National Book Critics Circle Award, and the Pulitzer Prize - is born in New York City.

March 3, 1940

Fashion designer Perry Ellis – who built an empire on contemporary sportswear – is born in Portsmouth, VA.

March 3, 1972

Singer and television personality Yasmine - whose albums include *Vandaag, Licht Ontvlambaar* and who after coming out in 1996 became an established icon for Dutch and Flemish LGBT youth - is born in Antwerp, Belgium.

March 3, 2001

Actor Louis Edmonds (*All My Children*, Roger Collins in the daytime series *Dark Shadows*) - who came out publicly in his biography *Big Lou* - dies of respiratory failure at age 77 in Port Jefferson, N.Y.

March 3, 2017

Singer songwriter and pop star Tommy Page (*I'll Be Your Everything, A Shoulder to Cry On, When I Dreamed of You*) commits suicide at age 46 in East Stroudsburg, PA.

March 4, 1852

Writer Nikolai Gogol (*Dead Souls, Taras Bulba*) dies at age 42 in Moscow, Russia.

March 4, 1992

Cinematographer Nestor Almendros (*Sophie's Choice, Kramer vs. Kramer, The Last Metro, Places in the Heart, The Blue Lagoon*) - who won an Oscar for *Days of Heaven* and who also co-directed *Improper Conduct* in 1984 about the persecution of gays in Cuba - dies of an AIDS-related illness at age 61 in New York City.

March 4, 1993

Miguel de Molina – Flamenco dancer, singer, and friend of Eva "Evita" Perón – dies at age 85 in Buenos Aires, Argentina.

March 4, 1995

Activist Martin Block dies at age 75 in West Hollywood, CA. He was the first chairman of ONE Inc., which he co-founded with William Dale Jennings and Antonio Sanchez (aka Don Slater), and also served as the first editor of *ONE Magazine*.

March 4, 2001

Glenn M. Hughes – who portrayed "the biker" in the musical group The Village People (*YMCA, In the Navy, Go West*) – dies of lung cancer at age 50 in New York City.

March 4, 2018

Daniela Vega, star of *A Fantastic Woman*, becomes the first openly transgender presenter at the Academy Awards.

―――――――――○―――――――――

March 5, 1922

Controversial film director, poet, and novelist Pier Paolo Pasolini (*Salo, or the 120 Days of Sodom, Il Decameron, The Gospel According to St. Matthew*) - who was expelled from the Italian Community Party because of his homosexuality - is born in Bologna, Italy.

March 6, 1475

Artist, sculptor, poet and engineer Michelangelo di Lodovico Buonarroti Simoni aka Michelangelo (*The Pieta*, *David*, Ceiling of the Sistine Chapel, *The Creation of Adam*, Dome of St. Peter's Basilica) is born in present day Tuscany, Italy.

March 6, 1951

Singer, songwriter and actor Ivor Novello (*Keep The Home Fires Burning*, *The Lodger*, *The White Rose*) - a force in the entertainment field for thirty-five years and until the advent of Andrew Lloyd Webber the most consistently successful composer of British musicals - dies at age 58 from a coronary thrombosis in London, England. Over 10,000 fans line the streets of London for his funeral service which was broadcast live on radio.

March 6, 2017

Film historian, author, actor columnist, and Turner Movie Channel film host Robert Osborne, dies at age 84 in New York City.

March 7, 1893

Journalist and author Lorena Hickok – the public relations official known for her very close relationship with Eleanor Roosevelt – is born in East Troy, WI.

March 7, 1926

Actor and comic Alan Sues - best remembered for his work as a regular on *Rowan & Martin's Laugh-In* 1968-1972 - is born in Ross, CA.

March 7, 1935

Lucille Bogan records the song *B.D. Woman's Blues* (the B.D. meaning bull dyke or bull dagger, colloquialisms for butch lesbian) under the pseudonym Bessie Jackson.

March 7, 1941

Popular stage actor, silent film actor and female impersonator Julian Eltinge (*The Fascinating Widow*, *The Crinoline Girl*, *The Isle of Love*) - who even had the Eltinge Theater on 42nd Street named in his honor - dies of a cerebral hemorrhage at age 59 in New York City.

March 7, 1967

Alice B. Toklas – U.S. expatriate based in France, longtime partner of Gertrude Stein, and author of *The Alice B. Toklas Cookbook* – dies at age 89 in Paris, France.

March 7, 1967

CBS airs "The Homosexuals" episode of the one-hour documentary series *CBS Reports*. Though it increases visibility, the Mike Wallace anchored, co-written, and narrated episode is filled with broad generalizations. It is the first network documentary dealing with the topic of homosexuality, though public television in San Francisco had aired a show on the topic six years earlier called *The Rejected*.

March 7, 1972

The East Lansing Michigan City Council votes to "employ the best applicant for each vacancy on the basis of his qualifications for the job and without regard to race, color, creed, national origin, sex or homosexuality" – thus leading the U.S. in protecting gay employees from job discrimination.

March 7, 1988

Underground and cult film legend Divine aka Harris Glenn Milstead (*Pink Flamingos, Polyester, Lust in the Dust, Female Trouble, Hairspray*) - as well as a popular disco/dance and nightclub entertainer - dies at age 42 of an enlarged heart and sleep apnea in Los Angeles, CA.

March 7, 2004

Academy Award nominated Actor Paul Winfield (*Sounder, The Terminator, The Serpent and the Rainbow*) dies at age 64 of a heart attack in Los Angeles, CA.

March 7, 2004

With his investiture ceremony at St. Paul's Church in Concord, N.H., Gene Robinson becomes the first openly gay bishop in the Episcopal Church.

March 8, 1929

Poet, essayist, and photographer Jonathan Williams (*Jubilant Thicket, An Ear in Bartram's Tree*) – founder of Jargon Society Press – is born in Asheville, N.C.

March 8, 2007

Actor John Inman - best known for his role as Mr. Humphries on the British sitcom *Are You Being Served?* and who was named BBC TV personality of the year in 1976 - dies of hepatitis at age 71 in London, England.

———————————○———————————

March 9, 1806

Shakespearean stage actor Edwin Forrest (*Hamlet, Macbeth, Othello, Spartacus*) - a top money earning actor of the 1800s - is born in Philadelphia, PA.

March 9, 1892

Author and gardener Vita Sackville-West (*The Edwardians, All Passion Spent, In Your Garden Again*) is born at Knole House in Kent, England.

March 9, 1892

Novelist, memoirist, editor, and publisher David Garnett (*Aspects of Love, The Sailor's Return, Lady into Fox*) is born in Brighton, England. Garnett was a member of the Bloomsbury Group where he was known as "Bunny", and also co-founded Nonesuch Press.

March 9, 1895

Author, publisher, and literary expatriate Robert McAlmon (*Village: It Happened Through a Fifteen Year Period, A Hasty Bunch, Not Alone Lost, A Scarlet Pansy, McAlmon and the Lost Generation: A Self-Portrait*) is born in Clifton, KS.

March 9, 1902

Actor Will Geer (Grandpa on *The Waltons*, *Jeremiah Johnson*, *Winchester '73*) - one time lover of Harry Hay and eight time Emmy Award nominee (with one win) - is born in Frankfort, IN.

March 9, 1950

Lambda Award winning author and health care analyst Mark Merlis (*American Studies, An Arrow's Flight, JD: A Novel, Man About Town*) is born in Framingham, MA.

March 9, 1989

Photographer Robert Mapplethorpe (*The Black Book*, *Some Women, Mapplethorpe: Portraits, Flowers*) - known for his stark, elegant style and controversial subject matter - dies of an AIDS-related illness at age 42 in Boston, MA.

March 10, 1924

Transgender composer Angela Morley (*The Little Prince*, *The Slipper and the Rose, Watership Down, Julie Andrews: The Sound of Christmas, Dallas*) - who was nominated for two Oscars and won three Emmy Awards for her scores - is born Walter Stott in Leeds, England.

March 10, 1987

The AIDS Coalition to Unleash Power (ACT-UP) is formed at the Lesbian and Gay Community Services Center in New York when speaker Larry Kramer attacks the political ineffectiveness of the Gay Men's Health Crisis (GMHC) and asks "Do we want to start a new organization devoted to political action?" Approximately 300 people met two days later to officially launch ACT-UP.

March 10, 1996

Film producer Ross Hunter (*Pillow Talk, Airport, Madame X, Thoroughly Modern Millie, Back Street, Portrait in Black, Imitation of Life*) - known primarily for his glossy productions and melodramas; life partner of producer/set decorator Jacques Mapes - dies at age 75 in Los Angeles, CA.

March 11, 222 AD

Elagabalus, the Roman emperor/empress from 218-222 who has been characterized as being trans, is assassinated in Rome at age 18.

March 11, 1897

Innovative avant-garde composer, pianist, and musical theorist Henry Cowell *(The Banshee, Exultation, Suite for Violin and Piano)* - who founded and edited the *New Music Quarterly* and who spent four years in San Quentin (1936-1940) for homosexual conduct - is born in Menlo Park, CA.

March 11, 1931

Hugely influential German silent film director F.W. Murnau (*Nosferatu, Sunrise, Faust*) - whose films have withstood the test of time - dies in an auto accident at age 42 in Santa Barbara, CA.

March 11, 1941

Multi-medium artist, designer, poet, and writer Joe Brainard - a master of collage and whose work includes the memoir *I Remember* - is born in Salem, AR.

March 11, 1957

The Lady Chablis, the trans star of the book and later the film *Midnight in the Garden of Good and Evil,* dies at age 59 in Savannah, GA.

March 11, 1990

Less than one month after his death on February 24th, billionaire Malcolm Forbes is posthumously outed in the weekly gay magazine *Outweek.*

March 12, 1883

Physician Ethel Collins Dunham, the first female member of the American Pediatric Society and recipient of the organization's most prestigious award, the John Howland Medal, is born in Hartford, CT.

March 12, 1890

Dancer and choreographer Vaslav Nijinski (*Scheherazade, The Talisman, Giselle, Swan Lake, Sleeping Beauty*) - often called the greatest male dancer of the early 20th century - is born in Kiev, Russia.

March 12, 1928

Tony Award winning playwright Edward Albee (*The Sandbox, Who's Afraid of Virginia Woolf?, The Zoo Story, Three Tall Women; The Goat, or Who is Sylvia?*) is born in Virginia.

March 12, 1989

Trained stage and film actor Maurice Evans (*Richard II, Batman, Rosemary's Baby, Planet of the Apes*) – best known for appearing as Samantha Stevens' father in the 1960s sitcom *Bewitched* – dies of cancer at age 88 in Rottingdean, East Sussex, England.

———————————————○———————————————

March 13, 1884

Prolific novelist and writer Sir Hugh Walpole (*The Dark Forest, The Secret City, The Cathedral*) is born in Auckland, New Zealand.

March 13, 1892

Influential journalist and writer Janet Flanner - Paris correspondent for *The New Yorker* from 1925-1975 and winner of the National Book Award - is born in Indianapolis, IN.

March 13, 1981

Novelist, playwright, and non-fiction writer Robin Maugham (*The Servant*, *The Wrong People*, *Escape From the Shadows*) aka 2nd Viscount Maugham of Hartfield - whose frequently homosexual themed work scandalized his family - dies of several ailments, complicated by diabetes and alcohol abuse, at age 64 in Brighton, England.

March 13, 2009

Writer James Purdy (*On Glory's Course*, *Malcolm*, *Eustice Chisholm and the Works*, *Narrow Rooms*, *Jeremy's Version*) - who was nominated for the National Book Award as well as the Pen/Faulkner Award for Fiction - dies at age 94 in Englewood, N.J.

———————————————○———————————————

March 14, 1887

Sylvia Beach – expatriate, bookseller, publisher, founder of the Paris bookstore Shakespeare and Company, and the first publisher of James Joyce's groundbreaking novel *Ulysses* – is born in Baltimore, MD.

March 14, 1989

Theater actor Timothy Meyers – who won fame and received a Tony nomination as the original Kenickie in the Broadway production of *Grease*, and was featured in numerous other shows – dies of an AIDS-related illness at age 43 in New York City.

March 14, 2016

Composer and conductor Sir Peter Maxwell Davies (*Eight Songs for a Mad King, Kommilitonen, Caroline Mathilde, The Doctor of Myddfai*), dies at age 81 in the Orkney Islands.

March 14, 2018

Politician, feminist, and activist Marielle Franco (Socialism and Liberty Party/PSOL) is assassinated at age 38 in Rio de Janeiro, Brazil.

———————————◯———————————

March 15, 1905

Poet and journalist Brian Howard (*God Save the King*) - a key figure among England's "Bright Young Things", a group of wealthy, talented, and often hard partying artists - is born in Surrey, England.

March 15, 1926

Ruth Simpson – former president of the Daughters of Bilitis, founder of the first lesbian community center in the U.S, and author of *From the Closets to the Courts* – is born in Cleveland, OH.

———————————◯———————————

March 16, 1822

Animalier artist Rosa Bonheur (*The Horse Fair, Ploughing the Nivernais*) - the most famous female artist of the 19th century - is born in Bordeaux, France.

March 16, 1898

Art Nouveau illustrator and author Aubrey Beardsley - the controversial artist known primarily for his unique, decadent, and dramatic black ink drawings - dies of tuberculosis at age 25 in Menton, France.

March 16, 1938

Activist and writer Jack Nichols (co-founder of the Washington, DC branch of The Mattachine Society and author of *The Tomcat Chronicles*) - who wrote *The Homosexual Citizen* column in *Screw Magazine* in 1968, as well as the books *Men's Liberation, I Have More Fun With You Than Anybody* and *Roommates Can't Always Be Lovers*, with his partner Lige Clarke - is born in Washington, DC.

March 16, 1940

Author and educator Selma Lagerlof (*The Wonderful Adventures of Nils, Gosta Berlings Saga*) - the first female writer to win the Nobel Prize in Literature (1909) - dies at age 81 in Varmland, Sweden.

March 16, 1994

Playwright and novelist Harry Kondoleon (*Diary of a Lost Boy, Zero Positive, Saved or Destroyed, The Houseguests*) - who won two Obie Awards, given for Off and Off-Off Broadway productions - dies of an AIDS-related illness at age 39 in New York City.

March 16, 2008

Poet, essayist, and photographer Jonathan Williams (*Jubilant Thicket, An Ear in Bartram's Tree*) – founder of Jargon Society Press – dies at age 79 of pneumonia in Highlands, N.C.

March 17, 1886

Prolific photographer Alice Austen - known for her images of her lover as well as lesbian friends and women workers - is born in Staten Island, N.Y.

March 17, 1912

Civil Rights activist and pioneer Bayard Rustin - a leading proponent of non-violent protest – is born in West Chester, PA. A political advisor and strategist, Rustin was the architect of the 1963 March on Washington for Jobs and Freedom, where Dr. Martin Luther King Jr. delivered his famous *I Have a Dream* speech.

March 17, 1938

Ballet dancer, choreographer, film star and media personality Rudolf Nureyev *(Romeo and Juliet, Sleeping Beauty, Swan Lake)* - the first dancer to defect from the Soviet Union and who appeared with over 30 ballet and modern dance companies - is born in Irkutsk, Russia.

March 17, 1968

More than 200 people turn out to the protest ongoing LAPD harassment by attending a St. Patrick's Day party hosted by drag queens The Princess and The Duchess in the popular cruising spot known as Griffith Park.

March 17, 1969

Innovative fashion designer Alexander McQueen - four time winner of the British Designer of the Year award as well being named International Designer of the Year at the Council of Fashion Designers Awards - is born in London, England.

March 17, 1970

The film version of *The Boys in the Band* premieres – directed by William Friedkin from a screenplay written by Mart Crowley, based on his Off-Broadway play.

March 17, 1972

The film which launched John Waters' career - the twisted and outrageous camp classic *Pink Flamingos* opens in theaters.

March 17, 1976

Oscar nominated film, theater, and opera director as well as screenwriter Luchino Visconti (*The Leopard*, *The Damned*, *Death in Venice*) dies of a stroke at age 69 in Rome, Italy.

March 17, 1976

Stephen Gately, one of the two lead singers of the group Boyzone (*Working My Way Back To You*, *Love Me for a Reason*, *Words*, *Father and Son*) is born in Dublin, Ireland.

March 17, 1989

Actor Merritt Butrick (*Square Pegs, Zapped!, Fright Night Part II*) - probably best remembered as David, the son of Admiral James T. Kirk in *Star Trek II : The Wrath of Khan* and *Star Trek III: The Search for Spock* - dies of complications from AIDS at age 29 in Los Angeles, CA.

March 17, 1996

Perry Watkins - who, in 1990, was one of the first U.S. soldiers to challenge the ban on gays in the U.S. military and have some success with the issue before the Supreme Court - dies at age 47 of an AIDS-related illness in Tacoma, WA.

March 17, 1997

Singer and songwriter Jermaine Stewart (*We Don't Have to Take Our Clothes Off, The Word is Out, Say It Again*) dies of AIDS-related liver cancer at age 39 in Homewood, IL.

March 18, 1886

Character actor Edward Everett Horton (*Shall We Dance, Arsenic and Old Lace, Ziegfeld Girl, Lost Horizon, Springtime in the Rockies, Here Comes Mr. Jordan, F Troop*) - narrator of the *Fractured Fairy Tales* cartoon on *The Rocky and Bullwinkle Show* - is born in Brooklyn, N.Y.

March 18, 1980

Art Deco painter Tamara de Lempicka (*Young Lady with Gloves, The Musician, Andromeda*) - popular for her portraits and nudes; her work has been featured in several Madonna videos - dies at age 81 in Cuernavaca, Mexico.

March 18, 2001

Paris, France elects an openly gay mayor, Bertrand Delanoe of the Socialist Party.

March 18, 2014

Gay liberation pioneer, women's rights activist, community pioneer, restaurateur, and writer (*Sweet Sixteen*) Vernita Gray dies of cancer at age 65 in Chicago, IL.

March 19, 1894

Stand-up comedian Jackie "Moms" Mabley (*Amazing Grace, Killer Diller*) is born in Brevard, N.C. In a career that spanned six decades, Mabley originally found fame touring the Black vaudeville circuit, working her way up to the Cotton Club, Carnegie Hall in 1962, then expanding to television, comedy albums, and film.

March 19, 1953

Ricky Wilson - original guitarist for the band The B52s who helped give the group their early signature sound, and brother of band member Cindy Wilson - is born in Athens, GA.

March 19, 1973

Opera singer, Wagnerian heroic tenor, Lauritz Melchior (*Tristan und Isolde, Parsifal, Tannhauser*) who also became a popular film star at MGM (*Thrill of a Romance, Luxury Liner*) dies following emergency gall bladder surgery one day shy of his 83rd birthday in Santa Monica, CA.

March 19, 2008

Science fiction writer and inventor Arthur C. Clarke (*2001: A Space Odyssey, Rendezvous With Rama, The Fountains of Paradise, A Fall of Moondust, 2010: Odyssey Two*) - winner of multiple Huge and Nebula Awards for fantasy/science fiction writing - dies of respiratory failure in Colombo, Sri Lanka at age 90.

March 19, 2013

A team of volunteers paint Equality House, across from the Westboro Baptist Church in Topeka, KS., to duplicate the colors of the Gay Rainbow Flag, in anticipation of turning it into an anti-bullying sanctuary and gay history museum.

March 20, 203 AD

Elagabalus, the Roman emperor/empress from 218-222 who has been characterized as being trans, is born in Syria.

March 20, 1890

Opera singer, Wagnerian heroic tenor, Lauritz Melchior (*Tristan und Isolde, Parsifal, Tannhauser*) who also became a popular film star at MGM (*Thrill of a Romance*, *Luxury Liner*) is born in Copenhagen, Denmark.

March 20, 1891

Director, screenwriter, playwright, and actor Edmund Goulding (*Grand Hotel*, *Dark Victory*, *White Banners*, *The Razor's Edge*, *The Great Lie*, *Nightmare Alley*, *The Old Maid*) is born in Feltham, Middlesex, England.

March 20, 1945

Lord Alfred Douglas – author, and the lover for whom Oscar Wilde stood trial and went to prison – dies of congestive heart failure at age 74 in Lancing, England.

March 20, 1947

Historian and writer John Boswell (*Christianity, Social Tolerance, and Homosexuality*, *Same Sex Unions in Premodern Europe*, *The Kindness of Strangers*) - winner of the American Book Award and Stonewall Book Award as well as Lambda Literary Award nominee - is born in Boston, MA.

March 20, 1990

The group Queer Nation is formed in New York City by several members of ACT-UP. Using confrontational tactics to focus on LGBT visibility, the group sought to combat homophobia by raising the public's awareness of sexual minorities.

March 20, 2017

George Weinberg, author *(Society and the Healthy Homosexual)* and psychotherapist who coined the word 'Homophobia,' dies of cancer at age 87 in Manhattan.

———————————○———————————

March 21, 1903

Popular tenor Vadim Kozin (*Nishchaya, Druzhba*) - who in 1944 was jailed for five years in Stalin's Russia as part of the repression campaign against prominent Soviet performers - is born in Saint Petersburg in the Russian Empire.

March 21, 1934

Actress Lilyan Tashman (*So This is Paris, Manhandled, Bulldog Drummond, Girl About Town, Gold Diggers of Broadway, No, No, Nanette*) - a silent film actress who successfully made the transition to sound films - dies at age 37 of abdominal cancer in New York City.

March 21, 1974

Warhol drag superstar of the youth-quaking underground film world Candy Darling (*Flesh, Women in Revolt, Some of My Best Friends Are*) - who is immortalized in rock songs by Lou Reed and the Rolling Stones - dies at age 29 from lymphoma in New York City.

March 21, 1994

Popular television actor Dack Rambo - Jack Ewing on *Dallas*, Jeff Sonnett on *The Guns of Will Sonnett*, Steve Jacobi on

All My Children - dies of an AIDS-related illness at age 52 in Delano, CA.

———————○———————

March 22, 1932

Mister Marcus (Hernandez) - longtime social columnist for the *Bay Area Reporter* and also referred to as the "Dean of Leather Columnists" - is born in Los Angeles, CA.

March 22, 1943

Lambda Literary Award nominated playwright, journalist, composer, and educator Robert Chesley (*Jerker*) - and whose play *Night Sweat* was one of the first produced full-length plays to deal with the AIDS epidemic - is born in Jersey City, N.J.

March 22, 1975

Legal and social justice advocate Pearl M. Hart, known for her work defending oppressed minority groups – especially gay men who were victims of entrapment – dies at age 84 in Chicago, IL.

March 22, 1994

Singer, songwriter, and music producer Dan Hartman (*I Can Dream About You, Instant Reply, Relight My Fire*) dies at age 43 of an AIDS-related brain tumor in Westport, CT.

March 22, 2004

John Burlingame Whyte – male model turned real estate entrepreneur who helped develop the Fire Island Pines – dies at age 75 of prostate cancer in Dana Point, CA.

———————⊖———————

March 23, 1874

Illustrator J.C. Leyendecker – who popularized The Arrow Collar Man, created the popular imagery of Baby New Year and Mrs. Santa Claus, and did numerous covers for *The Saturday Evening Post* – is born in Montabaur, Rhine Province, German Empire.

March 23, 1972

Cristobel Balenciaga, fashion designer and founder of the Balenciaga fashion house, dies at age 77 in Valencia, Spain.

March 23, 1994

Actress, writer, playwright Nancy Cardenas (*The Empty Pitcher, Sexualidades, The Day We Walked on the Moon)*, one of the first Mexican celebrities to publicly declare they were a homosexual, dies of breast cancer at age 59 in Mexico City, Mexico.

———————⊖———————

March 24, 1930

Stage and film actor Kenneth Nelson (*The Boys in the Band, The Aldrich Family, Lovely Ladies, Kind Gentleman*) is born in Rocky Mount, N.C.

March 24, 1986

William Hurt wins the Best Actor Oscar for *Kiss of the Spider Woman,* becoming the first actor to win an Academy Award for portraying an openly gay character.

March 24, 1988

In the first of several demonstrations by the AIDS activist group ACT-UP targeting Wall Street, 250 ACT-UP members protest to demand greater access to experimental drugs to fight the disease as well as a more unified effort to find a cure. Seventeen are arrested.

March 24, 2011

Playwright Lanford Wilson (*Balm in Gilead, Hot L Baltimore, Talley's Folly, Fifth of July, Burn This*) - who emerged as a playwright in New York's Caffe Cino in the mid 1960s and won the Pulitzer Prize for Drama in 1980 - dies at age 73 of complications from pneumonia in Wayne, N.J.

March 24, 2011

The Book of Mormon, by *South Park*'s Trey Parker and Matt Stone, opens on Broadway at the Eugene O'Neill Theatre and will go on to win nine Tony Awards.

March 25, 1922

Artist, anthropologist and AIDS activist Tobias Schneebaum (*Keep the River on Your Right: A Modern Cannibal Tale*) - who lived for a time with the cannibals of the Amazon - is born in New York City.

March 25, 1985

The 1984 documentary, *The Times of Harvey Milk*, wins the Oscar for best feature documentary film.

March 25, 1988

Dancer and choreographer Robert Joffrey, co-founder and artistic director of the Joffrey Ballet - which he began in 1956 and which often brought ballet to people for the first time - dies at age 57 in New York City.

March 25, 1989

Several members of the previous Washington DC bisexual organization Bi-Ways (1985-89) form the BiWomen's and BiMen's Network (soon renamed the BiNetwork).

March 25, 2018

The revival of Tony's Kushner's award winning play, *Angels in America: Millennium Approaches* and *Angels in America: Perestroika* opens at the Neil Simon Theatre and will go on to win 3 Tony Awards including Best Revival and acting honors for Andrew Garfield and Nathan Lane.

March 26, 1859

Poet, professor, and classicist A.E. Housman (*A Shropshire Lad*, *Fragment of a Greek Tragedy*, *Last Poems*, *The Classical Papers of A.E. Housman*) is born in Bromsgrove, Worcestershire, England.

March 26, 1892

Vastly influential poet Walt Whitman (*Leaves of Grass*, *Song of Myself*, *I Hear America Singing*) - a key figure in U.S. literary history - dies at age 72 from bronchial pneumonia in Camden N.J.

March 26, 1911

Writer Tennessee Williams (*Cat on a Hot Tin Roof*, *Sweet Bird of Youth*, *Suddenly, Last Summer*, *The Rose Tattoo*, *The Night of the Iguana*, *The Glass Menagerie*, *A Streetcar Named Desire*) - whose many honors and awards include two Pulitzer Prizes, two Tony Awards, and a New York Drama Critics' Circle Award - is born in Columbus, MS.

March 26, 1923

Actress Sarah Bernhardt (*Le Passant*, *Zaire*, *Hamlet*, *La Tosca*, *Phedre*, *The Lady of the Camellias*) dies from uremia at age 78 in Paris, France. Often called "The Divine Sarah", Bernhardt was considered the greatest stage actress of her time. She named a Paris theater in her honor and dabbled in early films.

March 26, 1961

Influential performance artist, fashion designer, and club personality Leigh Bowery is born in Sunshire, Australia.

March 26, 1973

English playwright, composer, director, actor, and singer Noel Coward (*Private Lives*, *Hay Fever, Easy Virtue*, *Blithe Spirit*, *Design for Living, Quadrille*) - whose many honors include a special Tony Award (1970) for his contributions to the theater and induction into the Songwriters Hall of Fame - dies at age 73 in Blue Harbor, Jamaica.

March 26, 1973

Approximately 20 people attend the first formal meeting of PFLAG (Parents and Friends of Lesbians and Gays) at the Metropolitan-Duane Methodist Church in Greenwich Village – just months after the organization was founded by Jeanne Manford while marching with her son, Monty, in New York's Christopher Street Liberation Day March.

March 26, 1979

Abstract Expressionist painter Beauford Delaney – a France-based U.S. expatriate, often associated with the Harlem Renaissance – dies at age 77 at St. Anne's Hospital for the Insane in Paris, France.

March 26, 1990

Iconic fashion designer Halston - whose sexy and elegant clothes reached their greatest popularity during the disco era - dies at age 57 of an AIDS-related cancer in San Francisco, CA.

March 26, 1990

Common Threads: Stories from the Quilt - a collection of profiles of those honored in the AIDS Memorial Quilt –

receives the Oscar for Best Documentary Feature at the 62nd annual Academy Awards.

March 26, 1990

Trans actress (*Q & A, How To Pick Up Girls!*) and entertainer International Chrysis, who was also a protégé of Salvador Dali's, dies at age 39.

───────────○───────────

March 27, 1922

Bob Mizer – beefcake photographer, filmmaker, and founder of the Athletic Model Guild – is born in Hailey, ID.

March 27, 1926

Poet Frank O'Hara (*Lunch Poems, Love Poems, The Selected Poems of Frank O'Hara*) - who worked at the Museum of Modern Art, was a member of the New York School of poets, and was the posthumous winner of the National Book Award for Poetry - is born in Baltimore, MD.

March 27, 1952

Actress Maria Schneider (*Last Tango in Paris, The Passenger*) is born in Paris, France.

March 27, 1988

Actor and best-selling gay author Gordon Merrick (*The Lord Won't Mind, The Great Urge Downward, One for the Gods*) dies at age 71 in Colombo, Sri Lanka.

March 27, 2011

Actor Farley Granger (*Strangers on a Train*, *Rope*, *Hans Christian Anderson*, *One Life to Live*) - who also wrote the 2007 memoir *Include Me Out: My Life from Goldwyn to Broadway* - dies at age 85 in New York City.

March 27, 2011

Figurative painter George Tooker (*Subway*, *Waiting Room*, *Government Bureau*) - awarded the National Medal of Arts and elected to the National Academy of Design - dies of kidney failure at age 90 in Hartland, VT.

March 27, 2012

Poet, essayist, and feminist Adrienne Rich (*Diving in the Wreck*, *Of Woman Born*, *What is Found There*, *The Fact of a Doorframe*, *A Wild Patience Has Taken Me This Far*) - whose numerous awards and honors include The National Book Award for Poetry, The Lambda Literary Award, The Bollingen Prize, and The National Book Critics' Circle Award - dies at age 82 in Santa Cruz, CA.

March 28, 1921

Actor Sir Dirk Bogarde (*Death in Venice*, *The Night Porter*, *The Damned*, *Darling*, *The Servant*) - whose honors include two BAFTA film awards - is born in London, England.

March 28, 1929

America the Beautiful author and the woman who popularized

Mrs. Santa Claus - Katharine Lee Bates dies at age 69 in Wellesley, MA.

March 28, 1931

Author and educator Jane Rule (*Desert of the Heart*, *After the Fire*, *One Another's Arms*) is born in Plainfield, N.J.

March 28, 1941

Modernist literary legend Virginia Woolf (*Mrs Dalloway*, *A Room of One's Own*, *The Waves*, *To the Lighthouse*, *Orlando*) commits suicide at age 59 by filling her coat pockets with stones and walking into the River Ouse near Lewes, England.

March 28, 1971

Over 200 people attend the first National Gay Liberation Conference which takes place in Austin, TX, and is organized by the Gay Liberation Front.

―――――――――――○―――――――――――

March 29, 1915

Author and painter Denton Welch (*In Youth is Pleasure*, *Brave and Cruel*, *Maiden Voyage*, *A Voice Through a Cloud*) is born in Shanghai, China.

March 29, 1985

Jeanne Deckers aka The Singing Nun - who became a recording sensation with her song *Dominique* which led to the highly fictionalized filming of her story, *The Singing Nun* - commits suicide at age 51, with her partner Annie Pescher, in Wavre, Brabant, Belgium.

March 29, 1993

Baritone William Parker, creator of the *AIDS Quilt Songbook*, dies at age 49 of an AIDS-related-illness in Manhattan, N.Y.

March 30, 1844

Poet Paul Verlaine (*Sagasse, Selected Poems*), associated with the Symbolist movement - which sought to express states of mind rather than objective reality through the power of words and images - is born in Metz, France. His torrid affair with poet Arthur Rimbaud ended in disaster.

March 30, 1903

Countee Cullen – poet (*Color, Copper Sun*), playwright (*St. Louis Woman*), and leading figure of the Harlem Renaissance – is born in New York City.

March 30, 1973

Jill Johnston's book of essays *Lesbian Nation* is published which calls for a lesbian movement separate from the gay rights movement, an important factor in evolving ideology and practice of lesbian separatism.

March 30, 1988

Photographer and choreographer Arnie Zane - co-founder and co-artistic director of the postmodernist Bill T. Jones/Arnie Zane Dance Company and whose honors include a New York Dance Performance Award - dies at age 39 of AIDS-related lymphoma in Valley Cottage, N.Y.

March 30, 2003

Primetime Emmy Award winning actor Michael Jeter (*Evening Shade*, *Grand Hotel: The Musical*, *The Green Mile*) dies of an epileptic seizure/asphyxiation at age 50 in Los Angeles, CA.

———————————◯———————————

March 31

International Transgender Day of Visibility is celebrated. A day dedicated to raising trans awareness as well as celebrating the accomplishments and victories of transgender and gender non-conforming people.

March 31, 1809

Writer Nikolai Gogol (*Dead Souls*, *Taras Bulba*) is born in the Ukrainian village of Sorochyntsi.

March 31, 1872

Ballet impresario Sergei Diaghliev - founder of the Ballet Russes in 1909 which toured worldwide and eventually became the catalyst for the Royal Ballet - is born in Selishchi, Russia.

March 31, 1937

Newspaper columnist, essayist, and activist Jon-Henri Damski (*Angels into Dust*, *Damski-To-Go*) - who at the time of his death was the longest running columnist published in the U.S. gay and lesbian press - is born in Seattle, WA.

March 31, 1974

The Lesbian Herstory Archives is founded by Joan Nestle and Deborah Edel - and the other members of the Lesbian Academic Union - with a mission of gathering and preserving lesbian materials that will help reveal the richness of lesbian lives to future generations. The archives were housed for a number of years in Nestle's Upper West Side apartment before moving to a fouristory brownstone at 484 14th Street in Brooklyn, N.Y. in 1990.

March 31, 1993

Angie Xtravaganza, trans performer, underground superstar, and founding member of the House of Xtravaganza and star of the 1990 documentary *Paris is Burning*, dies of AIDS related liver disease at age 28 in New York City.

March 31, 2014

Frankie Knuckles, the Grammy Award winning DJ, record producer, and re-mixer known as "The Godfather of House Music," dies in Chicago of complications from diabetes at age 59.

March 31, 2017

Gay rights activist Gilbert Baker, who designed the rainbow flag in 1978, dies at age 65 in New York City.

APRIL

April 1964

ASK (The Association for Social Knowledge) the first homophile organization in Canada is officially formed. It was heavily influenced by the Mattachine Society in the U.S. and also published a newsletter. The group disbanded in 1969.

April 1, 1884

Actress Laurette Taylor (*One Night in Rome, Happiness*) - the original Amanda Wingfield in the Broadway production of *The Glass Menagerie* - is born in New York City.

April 1, 1895

Blues singer, songwriter and nurse Alberta Hunter (*Nobody Knows You When You're Down and Out, The Darktown Strutters' Ball*) - a member of the Blues Hall of Fame - is born in Memphis, TN.

April 1, 1896

The first journal on homosexuality, the Berlin based periodical *Der Eigene*, is published. *Der Eigene (*which vaguely translated means "self-ownership") began as an anarchist journal, but as early as 1898 until it ceased publication in 1932, despite censorship and legal interventions, it published what could be defined as gay literature.

April 1, 1950

Scholar, educator, and critic F.O. Matthiessen (*American Renaissance: Art and Expression in the Age of Emerson and Whitman, Sarah Orne Jewett, From the Heart of Europe*) - an outspoken advocate of Christian socialism - commits suicide at age 48 in Boston, MA.

April 1, 1971

The Bay Area Reporter is founded in San Francisco, CA.

April 1, 1974

Kathy Kozachenko wins a seat on the Ann Arbor, Michigan City Council, becoming the first openly LGBT candidate to win elected office in the United States.

April 1, 2003

Singer and actor Leslie Cheung (*A Better Tomorrow, Farewell My Concubine*) - considered one of the founders of "Cantopop" - commits suicide at age 46 by leaping from his hotel window in Central Hong Kong.

April 1, 2007

Steve Ginsburg - who in 1966 founded the early gay rights organization Personal Rights in Defense and Education (P.R.I.D.E.), in response to police raids on a gay bar - dies of respiratory failure in Ukiah, CA.

———————◯———————

April 2, 1805

Author Hans Christian Andersen (*The Snow Queen, The Red Shoes, The Ugly Duckling, The Little Match Girl, The Emperor's New Clothes, The Little Mermaid, The Princess and the Pea*) - is born in Odense, Denmark. Though the writer of books, plays, and poems, Anderson is primarily remembered for over 160 fairy tales.

April 2, 1867

The Father of Modern Bodybuilding and Victorian era strongman, the great Eugen Sandow, is born in Prussia.

April 2, 1914

Oscar winning actor Sir Alec Guinness (*The Bridge on the River Kwai, Star Wars, Dr. Zhivago, Kind Hearts and Coronets*) is born in London

April 2, 1949

Actor Ron Palillo - best known for his role as Arnold Horshack on the ABC sitcom *Welcome Back, Kotter* - is born in New Haven, CT.

April 2, 1956

Eccentric avant-garde painter Filippo De Pisis (*Still Life With Apple, Street Scene in Italy, Reclining Male Nude, Paesaggio di Cadore*) - who frequently painted nudes and cityscapes - dies at age 59 in Milan, Italy.

April 2, 1967

Theatrical producer Joe Cino - who in 1958 opened of Caffe Cino in Greenwich Village, cited as the birthplace of Off-Off Broadway and gay theater - dies at age 35 from self-inflicted stab wounds from an incident which occurred on March 30.

———————————————○———————————————

April 3, 1791

Landowner, diarist, and business woman Anne Lister – whose encoded diaries were deciphered to reveal intricate details about lesbian life in 19th century Europe – is born in Halifax, United Kingdom.

April 3, 2000

Journalist Evelyn Irons, the first female war correspondent to be decorated with the French Croix de Guerre and who had a romance with the Bloomsbury novelist and poet Vita Sackville-West, dies at age 99 in Brewster, NY.

April 3, 1986

Tenor and organist Sir Peter Pears - who sang regularly at Covent Garden in London, was a guest performer at venues worldwide, and was the longtime partner of composer Benjamin Britten - dies of a heart attack at age 75 in Aldeburgh, England. Many of Britten's works included parts specifically written for Pears such as *Peter Grimes*.

———————————⊖———————————

April 4, 1932

Oscar nominated actor Anthony Perkins (*Fear Strikes Out, Friendly Persuasion, The Black Hole*) - best known as Norman Bates in *Psycho* and who also won Best Actor at the Cannes Film Festival in 1961 - is born in New York City.

April 4, 1958

Best selling Brazilian rock singer and composer Cazuza - who gained fame as the lead singer of the group Barao Vermelho and later recorded solo - is born in Rio de Janiero, Brazil.

April 4, 1975

Photographer Herbert List (*Junge Manner, Italy, Photographs 1930-1970, Portraits*) - known for his magazine work with periodicals such as *Vogue* and *Harper's Bazaar* - dies at age 71 in Munich, Germany.

April 4, 2013

Kinky Boots (with Book by Harvey Fierstein and Music and Lyrics by Cyndi Lauper) opens on Broadway at the Al Hirschfeld Theatre and will go on to win six Tony Awards.

April 4, 2017

The 7th Circuit Court of Appeals rules that the Civil Rights Act prohibits workplace discrimination against LGBT employees.

---○---

April 5, 1929

Oscar nominated actor Nigel Hawthorne (*Amistad, The Madness of King George, Demolition Man*) - who won six BAFTA Awards - is born in Coventry, England.

April 5, 1994

Filmmaker, activist, and educator Marlon Riggs (*Tongues Untied, Color Adjustment, Ethnic Notions*) - who won an Emmy and a Peabody Award for his documentary work - dies of an AIDS-related illness at age 37 in Oakland, CA.

April 5, 1997

Poet and leading figure of the Beat Generation, Allen Ginsberg (*Howl and Other Poems, Kaddish, The Fall of America: Poems of These States, Reality Sandwiches*) - whose numerous awards and honors include a National Book Award for Poetry - dies at age 70 from liver cancer in New York City.

April 5, 2014

Berlin, Germany opens Europe's first cemetery exclusively for lesbians, a scenic 4,300 square foot section inside the Lutheran Georgen Parochial Cemetery.

---○---

April 6, 1528

Graphic artist, printmaker, engraver, and painter Albrecht Durer (*Men's Bath, Saint Jerome in His Study, Adam and Eve, The Green Passion* series) dies at age 56 in Nuremberg, Germany.

April 6, 1815

Activist, liveryman, Freemason, and patriot George Middleton - leader of the Bucks of America, an all Black regiment that fought against the British during the Revolutionary War and a leader in the African-American community in post-colonial Boston - dies at age 80. For years, Middleton shared his Beacon Hill home with hairdresser, Louis Glapion.

April 6, 1908

Writer Gale Wilhelm - whose novels included the early lesbian themed romances *We Too Are Drifting* (1935) and *Torchlight to Valhalla* (1938) - is born in Eugene, OR.

April 6, 2001

Civil rights activist Robert Sloane Basker - founder of Mattachine Midwest in 1965 as well as the founder of Chicago's first gay and lesbian hotline - dies of heart failure at age 82.

April 7, 1890

Legal and social justice advocate Pearl M. Hart, known for her work defending oppressed minority groups – especially gay men who were victims of entrapment – is born in Traverse City, MI.

April 7, 1889

Poet and diplomat Gabriela Mistral, the first Spanish American author to receive the Nobel Prize in Literature, is born in Vicuna, Chile.

April 7, 1912

Activist Harry Hay (*Radically Gay*), often called "The Father of the Modern Gay Movement" for being founder of the Mattachine Society and also a founding member of the Radical Faeries - is born in Worthing, England.

April 7, 1941

Actor and singer Gorden Kaye (*'Allo 'Allo, Brazil, Born and Bred, Coronation Street*) is born in Yorkshire, England.

―――――――――○―――――――――

April 8, 1918

Trans race car driver and WWII fighter pilot Roberta Cowell, who was also the first British trans woman to undergo gender confirmation surgery, is born Robert Cowell in London.

April 8, 1943

Innovative musical theater director and choreographer Michael Bennett (*Follies, A Chorus Line, Dreamgirls, Ballroom*) - who received Tony nominations for every musical he was associated with and won a total of eight awards - is born in Buffalo, N.Y.

April 8, 1950

Dancer and choreographer Vaslav Nijinski (*Scheherazade, The Talisman, Giselle, Swan Lake, Sleeping Beauty*) - often called the greatest male dancer of the early 20th century - dies at age 61 in London, England.

April 8, 1987

Britain's Princess Diana gains worldwide attention when she is photographed comforting and shaking the hand of an AIDS patient without wearing gloves while visiting the opening of the HIV ward at Middlesex Hospital in London. Her gesture contributes greatly to calming some of the hysteria regarding the illness as well as ending some of the misconceptions prevalent at the time, such as that AIDS could be transmitted through casual touch.

April 8, 1997

Trail blazing singer and songwriter Laura Nyro (*Stoned Soul Picnic, Stoney End, Eli's Coming, Wedding Bell Blues, And When I Die*) - a trained pianist who often blended musical styles in her work - dies of ovarian cancer at age 49 in Danbury, CT.

April 9, 1626

Sir Francis Bacon - statesman and philosopher who served as both Attorney General and Lord Chancellor of England - dies of pneumonia at age 65 in London. He also developed the scientific method in which natural laws or theories are reached though observation.

April 9, 2005

Feminist and writer Andrea Dworkin (*Pornography: Men Possessing Women, Intercourse, Life and Death: Unapologetic Writings on the Continuing War on Women*) - best known for her strong stance against pornography and winner of the American Book Award in 2001 - dies at age 58 of myocarditis in Washington, DC.

April 10, 1880

Frances Perkins – economist, social worker, and the first woman appointed to a U.S. Cabinet post, as FDR's Secretary of Labor from 1933-1945 – is born in Boston, MA. Eager to help people during the Great Depression, Perkins is credited with the passage of the Social Security Act and the Fair Labor Standards Act as well as things such as child labor laws, the first minimum wage, overtime restrictions, and the 40 hour work week.

April 10, 1908

Miguel de Molina – Flamenco dancer, singer, and friend of Eva "Evita" Perón – is born in Frias near Malaga, Spain.

April 10, 1941

Witty socialite Dorothy "Dolly" Wilde - niece of Oscar Wilde and a lover of Natalie Clifford Barney who also had an affair with Alla Nazimova - dies in England at age 45 of cancer and/ or a drug overdose.

April 10, 1963

Poet Reginald Shepherd (*Otherhood, Fata Morgana, Some Are Drowning, Angel, Interrupted*) - who was nominated for a National Book Critics Circle Award and a Lambda Literary Award - is born in New York City

April 10, 1966

Author Evelyn Waugh (*Brideshead Revisited, Scoop, A Handful of Dust, Vile Bodies, Decline and Fall*) dies of heart failure at age 62 in Combe Florey, Somerset, England

April 10, 1975

Oscar nominated actress Marjorie Main (*Ma Kettle, Meet Me in St. Louis, The Women, The Egg and I*) - longtime companion of actress Spring Byington - dies of lung cancer at age 85 in Los Angeles, CA.

April 11, 1955

Activist, actor, singer, and songwriter Michael Callen (*Zero Patience, Surviving AIDS*) - a founding member of the gay male a cappella singing group The Flirtations - is born in Rising Sun, IN.

April 12, 1939

Groundbreaking playwright, editor, and director William M. Hoffman, author of *As Is*, one of the first AIDS plays, is born in New York City.

April 12, 1943

Actor, playwright, and director Charles Ludlam (*The Mystery of Irma Vep, The Artificial Jungle, Camille, Stage Blood, The Ventriloquist's Wife, Eunuchs of the Forbidden City*) - who established the Ridiculous Theatrical Company in 1967 - is born in Floral Park, N.Y.

April 12, 1975

Actress, singer, and dancer Josephine Baker (whose films include *Zouzou* and *Princess Tam Tam*) dies at age 68 following a cerebral hemorrhage in Paris, France. Baker came to fame with her "banana dance" at the Folies Bergere and soon became the toast of Paris. Later in life she received France's highest award, The Legion of Honor.

April 12, 2007

Film actor James Lyons (*Poison, I Shot Andy Warhol* - in which he played Billy Name, *Swoon, Safe*) editor (*Far From Heaven, Velvet Goldmine, The Virgin Suicides*), and also an activist and writer - dies at age 46 from AIDS-related squamous cell cancer in New York City.

---○---

April 13, 1937

Playwright Lanford Wilson (*Balm in Gilead, Hot L Baltimore, Talley's Folly, Fifth of July, Burn This*) - who emerged as a playwright in New York's Caffe Cino in the mid 1960s and won the Pulitzer Prize for Drama in 1980 - is born in Lebanon, MO.

---○---

April 14, 1904

Actor of stage, screen, and television, Sir John Gielgud (*Arthur, Becket, Chariots of Fire, The Elephant Man*) - winner of an Oscar, an Emmy, two Golden Globes, three BAFTAs, and three Tony Awards; and who has been called "the greatest Hamlet of the 20th century" - is born in South Kensington, London, England.

April 14, 1964

Conservationist, marine biologist, and author Rachel Carson (*Silent Spring, The Edge of the Sea, The Sea Around Us*) - a harsh early critic of the overuse of pesticides and fertilizers, the recipient of the Presidential Medal of Freedom, the National Book Award for Nonfiction, and a charter inductee into the Ecology Hall of Fame - dies at age 56 in Silver Spring, MD.

April 14, 1968

Mart Crowley's play *The Boys in the Band* opens at Theater Four in New York City. The production will be adapted into a film directed by William Friedkin two years later. The play was revived on Broadway fifty years later.

April 14, 1988

Militant gay political activist Daniel Guerin (*Anarchism: From Theory to Practice*) - who was also key in the French labor and socialist movements - dies at age 83 in the suburbs of Paris, France.

April 14, 1997

Ellen DeGeneres appears on the cover of *TIME Magazine* along with the headline, 'Yep, I'm Gay.' Her character on her TV sitcom comes out soon after.

April 15, 1542

Painter, inventor, architect, scientist Leonardo da Vinci (*Mona Lisa, The Last Supper, The Vitruvian Man*) - often cited as the ultimate Renaissance man and whose inventions include things from the armored car to the parachute - is born in Vinci, Italy.

April 15, 1894

Blues singer Bessie Smith (*Nobody Knows You When You're Down and Out, St. Louis Blues, A Good Man is Hard to Find, I Need a Little Sugar in My Bowl*) - "The Empress of the Blues" - is born in Chattanooga, TN.

April 15, 1907

Commercial and figure photographer George Platt Lynes (*George Platt Lynes: The Male Nudes, When We Were Three, George Platt Lynes: Photographs from the Kinsey Institute*) is born in East Orange, N.J.

April 15, 1979

The Liberace Museum is opened by Liberace in Las Vegas, NV.

April 15, 1979

On Easter Sunday, The Sisters of Perpetual Indulgence - a performance order of queer nuns dedicated to community service, entertainment, ministry, respect for diversity, and promoting human rights - make their first appearance in San Francisco, CA.

April 15-17, 1985

The U.S. Department of Health and Human Resources and the World Health Organization host the first International AIDS Conference in Atlanta, GA.

April 15, 1986

Novelist, playwright, and activist Jean Genet (*Querelle*, *The Thief's Journal*, *Our Lady of the Flowers*, *The Balcony*, *The Blacks, The Maids*) – who was suffering from throat cancer – dies in Paris at age 75 following what may have been a fall in his room.

April 15, 1990

Actress and international film icon Greta Garbo (*Camille*, *Ninotchka*, *Grand Hotel*, *Queen Christina, Anna Karenina*) - who was nominated for four Oscars - dies at age 84 in New York City.

April 15, 1994

Figure skater John Curry (1976 Olympic and World Champion) dies of an AIDS-related heart attack at age 44 in Binton, England.

———————————◯———————————

April 16, 1919

Dancer and contemporary choreographer Merce Cunningham (*Ocean, Biped, Rainforest, Second Hand*) - winner of numerous awards and honors such as being named a "Living Legend" by the Library of Congress - is born in Centralia, WA.

April 16, 1939

Singer Dusty Springfield (*Son of a Preacher Man, The Look of Love, You Don't Have to Say You Love Me, The Windmills of Your Mind*) - who charted 18 singles on the Billboard Hot 100 - is born in London, England.

April 16, 1957

Poet, performance artist, and activist Essex Hemphill (*Ceremonies, Brother to Brother, Tongues Untied, Black Is... Black Ain't*) is born in Chicago, IL.

April 16, 2000

The Transgender flag, created by trans woman Monica Helms in 1999, is first revealed publicly at the Phoenix, Arizona pride parade in 2000. The flag represents the transgender community and consists of five horizontal stripes: two light blue, two pink stripes, and a white one in the center.

April 16, 2004

The episode of *Oprah* entitled "A Secret Sex World: Living on the Down Low" airs. Winfrey and several interview subjects discuss the practice of closeted gay Black men to have wives and girlfriends but still secretly have sex with men (known as being or living on the "down low") and the threat it poses to the spread of HIV in the African American community.

April 17, 1695

Nun, poet, feminist, and scholar Sor Juana Ines de la Cruz dies in Mexico City from The Plague at age 46 after ministering to others. Sor Juana had a reputation as one of the leading lyric poets of her era, but was censured when she confronted the church about keeping women uneducated. She is currently pictured on Mexico's 200-peso note.

April 17, 1897

Playwright and novelist Thornton Wilder (*The Skin of Our Teeth*, *Our Town*, *The Eighth Day*, *The Bridge of San Luis Rey*) - whose many honors and awards include Pulitzer Prizes both for Fiction as well as Drama and a National Book Award - is born in Madison, WI.

April 17, 1955

Bisexual punk rock icon, singer, songwriter, guitarist Pete Shelley, front man of the Buzzcocks, is born in Lancashire, England.

April 17, 1965

Homophile activists (from Mattachine Society chapters out of New York and Washington DC as well as Philadelphia's Janus Society and the New York chapter of Daughters of Bilitis) picket in front of the White House to protest the U.S. policies toward homosexuals with signs saying such things as *Homosexuals Are U.S. Citizens Too!*

April 17, 1987

Fashion designer Willi Smith - founder of the company WilliWear Limited (which featured inexpensive sportswear) and recipient of the American Fashion Critics' Coty Award in 1983 - dies at age 39 of an AIDS-related illness in New York City.

April 18, 1925

Professor, author, activist, and editor of *the Journal of Homosexuality* from 1975-2009, John Paul De Cecco, is born in Erie, PA.

April 18, 1926

Long-time Chicago activist and attorney Renee Hanover - who opened what is often cited as the first law office in the U.S. to focus on women's issues and who was also believed to be the first "out" lesbian attorney in the county - is born Renee Marcus in New York City, NY.

April 18, 1947

Experimental postmodern writer and performance artist Kathy Acker (*My Mother Demonology, Blood and Guts in High School, Pussycat Fever, Literal Madness*) is born in New York City.

April 18, 1965

After picketing in front of the White House in Washington, DC the day before, homophile activists (from Mattachine Society chapters out of New York and Washington, DC as well as Philadelphia's Janus Society and the New York chapter of Daughters of Bilitis) picket in front of the United Nations in New York City after learning that Cuba was placing homosexuals in forced labor camps.

April 19, 1689

Queen Christina of Sweden, who ruled as Queen from 1632 until her abdication in 1654, and who was famous portrayed on film in *Queen Christina* by Greta Garbo, dies at age 62 in Rome, Italy.

April 19, 1824

Poet George Gordon Byron, who later became known as Lord Byron (*Don Juan, The Corsair, Childe Harold's Pilgrimage*) and was a leading figure of the Romantic Movement - dies from a fever resulting from sepsis at age 36 in Missolonghi in the Ottoman Empire.

April 19, 1893

Essayist, poet, translator, biographer, memoirist, and literary critic John Addington Symonds (*Memoirs, The Renaissance in Italy* - 7 volumes, *Walt Whitman, Beast 666, The Life of Michelangelo Buonarroti, A Problem in Modern Ethics, Memoirs*) - best known as a cultural historian of the Italian Renaissance - dies at age 52 in Rome, Italy.

April 19, 1930

Actor Dick Sargent *(Operation Petticoat, The Ghost and Mr. Chicken)* - and best known as the second Darrin Stephens on *Bewitched* - is born in Carmel-by-the-Sea, CA.

April 19, 1967

The Student Homophile League at Columbia University (now the Columbia Queer Alliance) is officially granted its charter, becoming the oldest gay campus organization in the U.S.

April 19, 1989

Playwright and writer George Whitmore (*The Confessions of Danny Slocum, Nebraska, Someone Was Here: Profiles in the AIDS Epidemic*) - a member of the gay men's writing group the Violet Quill which included Robert Ferro, Edmund White, Felice Picano, and Andrew Holleran among others - dies at age 43 from an AIDS-related illness in New York City.

April 19, 2009

Lighting designer Tharon Musser - who was nominated for ten Tony Awards and won three times for her work on the Broadway productions *Follies*, *A Chorus Line*, and *Dreamgirls*

- dies at age 84 from complications of Alzheimer's disease in Newtown, CT.

April 19, 2015

Fun Home, the first Broadway musical with a lesbian protagonist, premieres on Broadway and will go on to win five Tony Awards. Based on Alison Bechdel's graphic memoir of the same name, the show had previously been off-Broadway since 2013.

April 20, 1921

Influential honky-tonk pianist, singer, and composer Tony Jackson (*Pretty Baby, Michigan Water Blues, The Naked Dance*) - a pioneer in ragtime music - dies of syphilis at age 44 in Chicago, IL.

April 20, 1943

Actor and comedian Michael Greer who played the prison drag queen in the stage and film versions *Fortune and Men's Eyes* and whose best known comedy bit was a monologue as *Mona Lisa* while holding a gilded frame - is born in Galesburg, IL.

April 20, 1951

Singer, songwriter, record producer Luther Vandross (*Here and Now, A House is Not a Home, Never Too Much*) - who won eight Grammy Awards and had every one of his 14 albums go either platinum or multi-platinum - is born in New York City.

April 20, 1984

Celebrated cabaret and jazz singer singer Mabel Mercer, recipient of the Presidential Medal of Freedom and whose notable recordings include *From This Moment On* and *Just One of Those Things*, dies at age 84 in Pittsfield, MA.

April 20, 2001

The Chinese Psychiatric Association removes homosexuality from its list of mental disorders.

April 20, 2010

Writer Sanford Friedman (*Totempole, Still Life: Two Short Novels, A Haunted Woman*) dies of a heart attack at age 81 in Manhattan, N.Y.

―――――――――○―――――――――

April 21, 1924

Internationally known stage actress Eleonora Duse (*La Dame aux Camelias, Francesca da Rimini, La Citta Morta*) - noted for her roles in the works of Henrik Ibsen - dies of pneumonia at age 65 in Pittsburgh, PA.

April 21, 1946

Economist John Maynard Keynes (*Essays in Persuasion, The Economic Consequences of the Peace, General Theory of Employment Interest and Money*) – founder of the International Monetary Fund and the World Bank – dies at age 62 in Firle, East Sussex, England.

April 21, 1966

Members of the Mattachine Society stage a "sip-in" at the Julius Bar in Greenwich Village to protest a recent ruling by the New York Liquor Authority which prohibited gays from being served liquor in bars on the grounds that they are disorderly.

April 21, 1985

Rudi Gernreich – a fashion designer (the topless monokini), activist, and core Mattachine Society member (with Harry Hay, Chuck Rowland, Bob Hull, and William Dale Jennings) – dies at age 62 in Los Angeles, CA.

April 21, 1985

The original production of Larry Kramer's play *The Normal Heart*, about the AIDS epidemic in New York City from 1981-1984, opens at The Public Theater in New York City.

April 21, 1989

Tony Award winning playwright, author, and actor James Kirkwood (*P.S. Your Cat is Dead, A Chorus Line, Diary of a Mad Playwright: Perilous Adventures on the Road with Mary Martin and Carol Channing*) dies of spinal cancer at age 64 in New York City.

April 21, 1990

Art Deco artist and designer Erte aka Romain de Tirtoff (*Things I Remember: An Autobiography*) dies at age 97 in Paris, France.

------------------------------○------------------------------

April 22, 835

Monk, artist, and scholar Kukai – founder of the Shingon or "True Word" school of Buddhism – dies at age 61 at Mount Koya, Japan.

April 22, 1891

Photographer Laura Gilpin (*The Pueblos: A Camera Chronicle, The Enduring Navajo, The Rio Grande*) - known for her pictures of Native Americans - is born in Austin Bluffs, CO.

April 22, 1978

Actor Will Geer (Grandpa on *The Waltons, Jeremiah Johnson, Winchester '73*) - one time lover of Harry Hay and eight time Emmy Award nominee (with one win) - dies of respiratory failure at age 76 in Los Angeles, CA.

------------------------------○------------------------------

April 23, 1858

Composer and suffragette Dame Ethel Mary Smyth (*Mass in D, String Quartet in E Minor, Der Wald, The Wreckers*) - who also composed *The March of the Women*, the anthem of the women's suffrage movement in the U.K. - is born in London, England.

April 23, 1872

Violet Gordon-Woodhouse, keyboard player who specialized in the harpsichord (*The Harpsichord Virtuoso*) and clavichord, was the first person to record the harpsichord, and the first to broadcast harpsichord music, is born in Maryleborn, England.

April 23, 1909

Pioneering gay author Charles Warren Stoddard (*For the Pleasure of His Company*, *Summer Cruising in the South Seas*, *In the Footprints of the Padres*) dies at age 65 in Monterey, CA.

April 23, 1932

Iconic fashion designer Halston - whose sexy and elegant clothes reached their greatest popularity during the disco era - is born in Des Moines, IA.

April 23, 1956

Actor and stand-up comedian Kevin Meaney (*30 Rock, Uncle Buck, Plump Fiction, Big*) is born in White Plains, NY.

April 23, 2003

The daytime ABC soap opera, *All My Children*, features the first lesbian kiss on daytime TV when Lena Kundera (Olga Sosnovska) and Bianca Montgomery (Eden Riegel) kiss.

April 24, 1947

Pulitzer Prize winning writer Willa Cather (*My Antonia, O Pioneers!, Death Comes for the Archbishop*) dies of a cerebral hemorrhage at age 73 in New York City.

April 24, 1980

San Francisco resident Ken Horne – aka Patient Zero – the first AIDS case in the United States to be recognized at the time – is reported to the Center for Disease Control with Kaposi's sarcoma.

April 24, 2009

A statue is dedicated to the memory of Congresswoman Barbara Jordan at the University of Texas at Austin. Jordan was the first African American woman to be elected to congress from a southern state, and the first to deliver the keynote address at a national presidential convention (1976).

April 24, 2015

In the ABC news program *20/20,* in an interview with Diane Sawyer, Bruce/Caitlin Jenner comes out as trans with the statement "I am a woman."

April 25, 1284

King Edward II of England aka Edward of Caernarfon - who ruled England from 1307-1327 and whose widely documented relationship with lover Piers Gaveston was one of the earliest examples of Medieval Europe's religion-based same-sex joining ritual known as Wedded Brotherhood - is born at Caernarfon Castle.

April 25, 1928

Artist Cy Twombly (*Leaving Paphos Ringed With Waves,*

Lepanto, Scent of Madness) - primarily known for his large, scribbled, and graffiti-like paintings - is born in Lexington City, VA.

April 25, 1933

Adventurer, educator, paleontologist, and Transylvanian baron Franz Nopcsa - who discovered some of the first dinosaurs from central Europe and became a member of the Royal Geological Society in London - kills his lover and then himself at age 55 in Vienna, Austria.

April 25, 1953

Activist, poet, writer, and journalist Michiyo Fukaya (*Lesbian Lyrics, A Fire is Burning It is in Me: The Life and Writings of Michiyo Fukaya*) - is born in Japan. As the representative of the Lesbian and Gay Asian Collective which formed during the First National Third World Lesbian and Gay Conference during the 1979 March on Washington - Fukaya gave the eloquent speech "Living in Asia America: An Asian American Lesbian's Address Before the Washington Monument."

April 25, 1965

An estimated 150 people participate in a sit-in at Dewey's restaurant in Philadelphia after management refuses to serve several people because he thought they looked gay. Four people are arrested, including Janus Society president Clark Polak, and charged with disorderly conduct.

April 25, 1993

800,000 people attend the National March for Lesbian, Gay, and Bi Equal Rights and Liberation in Washington, DC – one of the largest demonstrations in U.S history.

April 25, 2004

Lambda Literary Award winning poet Thom Gunn (*The Man with Night Sweats*, *Boss Cupid*) dies of acute polysubstance abuse at age 74 in San Francisco, CA.

———————————⊖———————————

April 26

Lesbian Visibility Day is a day that celebrates lesbian role models throughout history as well as lesbian life and culture.

April 26, 1886

Blues singer Ma Rainey (*Ma Rainey's Black Bottom*, *See See Rider Blues*, *Bo-Weavil Blues*) - one of the earliest known professional blues singers - is born in Columbus, GA.

April 26, 1889

Philosopher Ludwig Wittgenstein (*Tractus Logico-Philosophicus*, *Remarks on the Foundations of Mathematics*) - who explored the relationship of language to the world and was a major influence in the realm of logic - is born in Vienna, Austria.

April 26, 1977

Disco, nightclub, and rich and famous playground, Studio 54, has it's grand opening.

April 26, 1995

Frieda Belinfante – cellist, conductor and member of the Dutch Resistance during WWII – who also conducted the Orange County Philharmonic in the 1950s - dies of cancer at age 90 in Santa Fe, N.M.

April 26, 2000

Vermont becomes the first state in the U.S. to legalize civil unions between same-sex couples.

―――――――――――⊖―――――――――――

April 27

Day of Silence, a student-led national event where people take a vow of silence to highlight the silencing of LGBTQ people at school, is celebrated.

April 27, 1917

Writer, painter, and activist Mary Meigs (*The Medusa Head, Lily Briscoe: A Self-Portrait*) - who became a spokesperson for elderly lesbians - is born in Philadelphia, PA.

April 27, 1932

While cruising in the Gulf of Mexico off the coast of Florida, poet Hart Crane (*The Bridge, White Buildings*) jumps overboard from the deck of a steamship and drowns at age 32.

April 27, 1937

Winner of two Tony Awards and an Oscar, actress Sandy Dennis (*The Out of Towners, Who's Afraid of Virginia Woolf?, Up the Down Staircase, The Fox, Sweet November, Come Back to the Five and Dime, Jimmy Dean, Jimmy Dean*) is born in Hastings, NE.

April 27, 1953

President Dwight D. Eisenhower signs Executive Order 10450 banning homosexuals from working for the federal government or any of its private contractors.

April 27, 2011

A revival of Larry Kramer's 1985 Off-Broadway play *The Normal Heart* opens at the John GoldenTheatre, The play will go on to win three Tony Awards including Best Revival of a Play as well as Tony Awards for John Benjamin Hickey and Ellen Barkin for Best Featured Actor and Featured Actress in a Play.

April 28, 1929

Activist and author John Paul Hudson - on the founding committee of New York City's first Gay Pride Parade

(Christopher Street Liberation Day Parade), an early member the Gay Activist Alliance, and author of such books as *The Gay Insider* and *Superstar Murder* - is born.

April 28, 1988

Author Michael Grumley (*After Midnight*, *Hard Corps: Studies in Leather and Sadomasochism*, *Life Drawing*) - a founding member of the gay men's writing group The Violet Quill which included Edmund White, Andrew Holleran, Felice Picano, and Grumley's partner, Robert Ferro - dies at age 46 in New York City of an AIDS-related illness.

April 28, 1992

Painter Francis Bacon (*Three Studies for Figures at the Base of a Crucifixion*, *Head I*, *Painting*, *Study for the Head of George Dyer*) - whose work often depicted brutal and gruesome scenes - dies of cardiac arrest at age 80 in Madrid, Spain.

April 28, 1994

Author and editor John Preston (*Mr. Benson*, *I Once Had a Master*, *Franny the Queen of Provincetown*, *Hometowns*) - winner of a Lambda Literary Award as well as the American Library Association's Stonewall Book Award - dies at age 48 of an AIDS-related illness in Portland, ME.

---○---

April 29, 1863

Poet Constantine Cavafy (*The Unfinished Poems, Before Time Could Change Them*) - perhaps the most original and influential Greek poet of the 20th century - is born in Alexandria, Egypt.

April 29, 1911

Jack Cole (*Gilda, Gentleman Prefer Blondes, On the Riviera, Man of La Mancha*) - dancer, choreographer and theater director who was called "the father of theatrical jazz dance" - is born in East Brunswick, N.J.

April 29, 1933

Poet Constantine Cavafy (*The Unfinished Poems, Before Time Could Change Them*) - perhaps the most original and influential Greek poet of the 20th century - dies of larynx cancer on his 70th birthday in Alexandria, Egypt.

April 29, 1951

Philosopher Ludwig Wittgenstein (*Tractus Logico-Philosophicus, Remarks on the Foundations of Mathematics*) - who explored the relationship of language to the world and was a major influence in the realm of logic - dies of prostate cancer at age 62 in Cambridge, England.

April 29, 1983

The film *The Hunger* debuts - the plot entails a love triangle between two vampires (Catherine Deneuve and David Bowie) and a doctor (Susan Sarandon). The film develops a large lesbian following for scenes with Deneuve and Sarandon.

April 29, 1987

The FDA (U.S. Food and Drug Administration) approves the first Western blot blood test for detecting the HIV virus or serodiagnosis. It is a more specific test than the ELISA test which had been in use since 1985.

April 29, 1992

The original production of *Falsettos* by Willian Finn and James Lapine opens on Broadway at the John Golden Theater.

April 29, 1996

Rent (Book, Music and Lyrics by Jonathan Larson) opens on Broadway at the Nederlander Theatre and will go on to win ten Tony Awards.

April 29, 2013

Washington Wizards center Jason Collins becomes the first NBA player to come out as gay while still actively playing the sport.

April 29, 2016

Cartoonist Jok Church (*Beakman's World, You Can With Beakman and Jax*) dies of a heart attack at age 66 in San Francisco, CA.

April 29, 2017

Groundbreaking playwright, editor, and director William M. Hoffman, author of *As Is*, one of the first AIDS plays, dies of a heart attack at age 78 in the Bronx.

―――――――――――――○―――――――――――――

April 30, 1877

Alice B. Toklas – longtime partner of Gertrude Stein and author of *The Alice B. Toklas Cookbook* – is born in San Francisco, CA.

April 30, 1936

Poet, professor, and classicist A.E. Housman (*A Shropshire Lad, Fragment of a Greek Tragedy, Last Poems, The Classical Papers of A.E. Housman*) dies at age 77 in Cambridge, England.

April 30, 1974

Actress Agnes Moorehead (*The Magnificent Ambersons, Pollyanna, Citizen Kane, Journey Into Fear, Hush Hush Sweet Charlotte*) – nominated for four Oscars and best known for appearing as Samantha Stevens' mother Endora in the 1960s sitcom *Bewitched* –dies of uterine cancer at age 73 in Rochester, MN.

April 30, 1997

"The Puppy Episode" of the sitcom *Ellen* [Season 4, Episode 22/23] airs in which the main character Ellen Morgan, played by Ellen DeGeneres, comes out to her therapist, played by Oprah Winfrey.

MAY

May 1959

Cooper's Donuts in Los Angeles was a hangout for the trans and hustler crowd. One night in May, police entered and asked for I.D.'s. Fed up with ongoing harassment, patrons bombard the cops with donuts and coffee cups, causing officers to retreat. The incident spills into the street with rioters dancing on cars, lighting fires, and wreaking havoc. The police return with backup and several rioters are beaten and arrested – turning an isolated incident of harassment into what would be remembered as The Cooper's Donuts Riot. It is one of a number of events foreshadowing the Stonewall Riot a decade later.

May 1968

The first issue of the entertainment and lifestyle magazine *After Dark,* which had a decidedly gay slant, is published. The magazine will eventually end in December 1982.

May 1, 1874

Painter Romaine Brooks (*The Cross of France*, *White Azaleas*) - who specialized in portraiture with a somber and subdued color palette and who was also the one-time lover of Natalie Clifford Barney - is born in Rome, Italy.

May 1, 1881

Racy and frank memoir writer Mary MacLane (*The Story of Mary MacLane*, *Men Who Have Made Love To Me*, *Tender Darkness*) - known as "the Wild Woman of Butte" - is born in Winnipeg, Manitoba, Canada.

May 1, 1915

Merchant marine, physician and transgender pioneer Dr. Michael Dillon - the first female-to-male trans person to undergo phalloplasty and author of the groundbreaking book *Self: A Study in Endocrinology and Ethics* - is born Laura Maud Dillon in London, England.

May 1, 1962

Bob Hull (core Mattachine Society member with Harry Hay, Chuck Rowland, William Dale Jennings, and Rudi Gernreich) kills himself at age 43.

May 1, 1968

Journalist and author Lorena Hickok – the public relations official known for her very close relationship with Eleanor Roosevelt – dies from complications due to diabetes at age 75 in Hyde Park, N.Y.

May 1, 1968

Harold Nicholson – diplomat, diarist, and author (*Public Faces*) – whose marriage to Vita Sackville-West was chronicled by their son in *Portrait of a Marriage* – dies at age 81 following a stroke at Sissinghurst Castle, Kent, England.

May 1, 1970

The Second Congress to Unite Women meets in New York City but excludes lesbian issues. In response, the lesbian feminist group –The Lavender Menace – organizes and confronts Betty Friedan and NOW.

───────────○───────────

May 2, 1519

Painter, inventor, architect, and scientist Leonardo da Vinci (*Mona Lisa, The Last Supper, The Vitruvian Man*) - often cited as the ultimate Renaissance man and whose inventions include things from the armored car to the parachute - dies at age 67 in Amboise, France.

May 2, 1844

William Beckford, art collector, politician, and writer (*Vathek, Memoirs of Extraordinary Painters*) - who chose self-exile after his affair with William Courtney was revealed - dies at age 83 in Bath, England.

May 2, 1895

Lyricist Lorenz Hart (*Blue Moon, The Lady is a Tramp, My Funny Valentine, It Never Entered My Mind, I Could Write a Book, Bewitched, Bothered and Bewildered*) - the lyricist half of Rogers and Hart, a member of the Songwriters Hall of Fame, and commemorated on a postage stamp - is born in New York City.

May 2, 1902

Dancer and activist Mabel Hampton - active during the Harlem Renaissance and who appeared in the documentary *Before Stonewall* - is born in Winston-Salem, N.C.

May 2, 1946

Singer, songwriter, activist Lesley Gore (*It's My Party, You Don't Own Me, Judy's Turn to Cry*) is born in Brooklyn, NY.

May 2, 1998

Soccer player Justin Fashanu – a forward for several teams and the first professional footballer to come out publicly – hangs himself at age 37 in London, England.

May 2, 2005

Activist and writer Jack Nichols (co-founder of the Washington, DC branch of The Mattachine Society and author of *The Tomcat Chronicles*) - who wrote *The Homosexual Citizen* column in *Screw Magazine* in 1968, as well as the books *Men's Liberation, I Have More Fun With You Than Anybody* and *Roommates Can't Always Be Lovers*, with his partner Lige Clarke - dies of cancer at age 67 in Cocoa Beach, FL.

May 3, 1877

Adventurer, educator, paleontologist, and baron Franz Nopcsa - who discovered some of the first dinosaurs from central Europe and became a member of the Royal Geological Society in London - is born in Deva, Transylvania.

May 3, 1912

Writer May Sarton (*Mrs. Stevens Hears the Mermaids Singing, As We Are Now, Journal of a Solitude*) - well-known for her published journals - is born in Wondelgem, Belgium.

May 3, 1932

Film historian, author, actor columnist, and Turner Movie Channel film host Robert Osborne, is born in Colfax, WA.

May 3, 1989

Transgender spokesperson and entertainer Christine Jorgensen -the first person to become a celebrity in the United States for having gender confirmation surgery - dies of cancer at age 62 in San Clemente, CA.

May 4, 1907

Lincoln Kirstein – writer (*Flesh is Heir, Mosaic, Quarry*), critic, and co-founder of the New York City Ballet - whose numerous awards include the American Guild of Musical Artists Award, the Distinguished Service Award from the National Institute of Arts and Letters, and who was also nominated for a National Book Award – is born in Rochester, NY.

May 4, 1937

Transgender ventriloquist and magician Terri Rogers - who created several popular illusions still in use today - is born Ivan Southgate in Ipswich, England.

May 4, 1945

Dancer, choreographer, and co-founder of the Louis Falco Dance Company, Juan Antonio - who later became the co-director of Le Ballet Jazz de Montreal and subsequently founded the dance company Confidanse - is born in Mexico City.

May 4, 1958

Artist and activist Keith Haring (*Radiant Baby*, *Three-Eyed Face*, *Stop AIDS*, *Barking Dogs*, *Safe Sex*) - the man whose graffiti-influenced, tribal, and patterned artwork helped define the AIDS era - is born in Reading, PA.

May 4, 1963

Singer, songwriter, musician, writer Vange Leonel (*Esse Mundo, Noite Preta, Madame Oraculo*) is born in Sao Paulo, Brazil.

May 4, 1969

Novelist, poet, memoirist, and essayist Sir Francis Osbert Sitwell, 5th Baronet (*Open the Door, Those Were the Days, Great Morning!, Laughter in the Next Room, Before the Bombardment*) dies from complications due to advanced Parkinson's Disease at age 76 near Florence, Italy.

May 4, 1973

Writer and playwright Jane Bowles (*Two Serious Ladies, In the Summer House*) who was married to writer/composer Paul Bowles but also had several affairs with women, dies at age 56 in Malaga, Spain.

May 4, 1993

After 20 previews Tony Kushner's play *Angels in America: Millennium Approaches* opens at the Walter Kerr Theatre on Broadway. It will play 367 performances and will be in repertory with *Angels in America: Perestroika*, which will open on November 23, 1993 and play for 217 performances.

May 4, 2002

Film set decorator and producer Jacques Mapes (*Singing in the Rain, Arthur Hailey's The Moneychangers, Airport, The Loretta Young Show*) - the life partner of film producer Ross Hunter - dies at age 88 in Beverly Hills, CA.

―――――――――○―――――――――

May 5, 1921

Activist and Daughters of Bilitis co-founder Del Martin (*Lesbian/Woman, Lesbian Love and Liberation*) is born in San Francisco, CA. In addition to starting the Daughters of Bilitis in 1955, Martin and partner Phyllis Lyon also were one of the first lesbian couples to join the National Organization for Women and worked to form the Council on Religion and the Homosexual to help unite churches and gays.

May 5, 2011

Playwright, stage director, and screenwriter Arthur Laurents (*West Side Story*, *Gypsy*, *Rope*, *The Way We Were*) - winner of two Tony Awards and nominated for two Oscars - dies from complications due to pneumonia at age 93 in Manhattan, N.Y.

May 6, 1829

Christian Universalist minister Phebe Hanaford, active in championing universal suffrage and women's rights, the first woman ordained as a Universalist minister in New England, and the first woman to serve as chaplain to the Connecticut state legislature, is born in Nantucket, MA.

May 6, 1895

Silent screen actor, and film icon Rudolph Valentino *(The Four Horseman of the Apocalypse, Camille, Cobra, The Hooded Falcon, The Sheik, Son of the Sheik, Blood and Sand)* - known as "The Sheik" and "The Latin Lover" and many times considered the first male sex symbol of the movies - is born in Castellaneta, Italy.

May 6, 1920

Film producer Ross Hunter (*Pillow Talk*, *Airport*, *Madame X*, *Thoroughly Modern Millie*, *Back Street*, *Portrait in Black*, *Imitation of Life*) - known primarily for his glossy productions and melodramas; life partner of producer/set decorator Jacques Mapes- is born in Cleveland, OH.

May 6, 1982

Hibiscus - founding member and creative director of the gay liberation theater and performance collective The Cockettes - dies at age 33 in New York City, NY of an AIDS-related illness when AIDS was still being called GRID (Gay Related Immune Deficiency).

May 6, 1992

Oscar nominated actress and entertainment legend Marlene Dietrich (*Morocco, Destry Rides Again, The Blue Angel, Blonde Venus, Shanghai Express, A Foreign Affair, A Touch of Evil, Judgment at Nuremberg, Witness for the Prosecution*) - who won a special Tony Award as well as the U.S. War Department's Medal of Freedom for her WWII work entertaining troops - dies at age 90 of renal failure in Paris, France.

May 6, 2013

The *Sports Illustrated* magazine issue featuring newly out NBA player Jason Collins (center for the Washington Wizards) on the cover – under the headline *The Gay Athlete* – appears on the newsstands.

May 7, 1840

Composer and conductor Pyotr Ilyich Tchaikovsky (*The Nutcracker, Swan Lake, The 1812 Overture, Romeo and Juliet*) - creator of some of the most popular of the world's orchestrations; his work includes concertos, symphonies, ballets, and operas - is born in Votkinsk, Russia.

May 7, 2002

Make-up artist and photographer Kevin Aucoin (*Making Faces, Face Forward*) dies at age 40 of kidney and liver failure due to acetaminophen toxicity in Valhalla, N.Y.

May 7, 2011

Playwright, director, activist, and gay/queer theater pioneer Doric Wilson (*And He Made a Her*, *The West Street Gang*, *Pretty People*, *Now She Dances!*) - a mainstay in the Off Off Broadway and gay theater movements, a founding member of the Circle Repertory Theater; and who also began Tosos, often cited as perhaps the first professional theater company to deal openly with the gay experience - dies at age 72 in Manhattan, N.Y.

May 8, 1920

Prolific artist Touko Laaksonen aka Tom of Finland - known for his stylized and sexually charged homoerotic art which has had a deep and lasting impact on gay iconography - is born in Kaarina, Finland.

May 8, 1944

British composer and suffragette Dame Ethel Mary Smyth (*Mass in D*, *String Quartet in E Minor*, *Der Wald*, *The Wreckers*) - who also composed *The March of the Women*, the anthem of the women's suffrage movement in the U.K. dies at age 86 in Woking, England.

May 8, 1978

Painter and designer Duncan Grant (*Garden Path in Spring, Self-Portrait, Vanessa Bell in Armchair, Paul Roche, Girl at the Piano, George Mallory*) - a member of the Bloomsbury Group and whose lovers included Maynard Keynes and David Garnett - dies at age 93.

May 8, 1999

Actor Sir Dirk Bogarde (*Death in Venice, The Night Porter, The Damned, Darling, The Servant*) - whose honors include two BAFTA film awards - dies of a heart attack at age 78 in London, England.

May 8, 2008

Ruth Simpson – former president of the Daughters of Bilitis, founder of the first lesbian community center in the U.S, and author of *From the Closets to the Courts* – dies at age 82 after a series of illnesses in Woodstock, N.Y.

May 8, 2012

Artist, illustrator and writer Maurice Sendak (*Where the Wild Things Are, Outside Over There, The Nutshell Library, In the Night Kitchen*) - winner of the 1964 Caldecott Medal which is awarded annually for excellence in children's picture books - dies of complications from a stroke at age 83 in Danbury, CT.

May 8, 2013

Writer, performer, beatnik, and eventually underground film actor Taylor Mead (*Lonesome Cowboys*, *Imitation of Christ*, *The Nude Restaurant*) - often associated with Andy Warhol and The Factory - dies at age 88 in Colorado.

———————————○———————————

May 9, 1943

AIDS and civil rights activist Kiyoshi Kuromiya – editor of the seminal *ACT-UP Standard of Care* health guide – is born in Heart Mountain War Relocation Center in Heart Mountain, WY.

May 9, 1968

Eccentric poet, playwright, and novelist Mercedes de Acosta (*Here Lies the Heart*) - whose lovers included Alla Nazimova, Isadora Duncan, and Greta Garbo and whose personal wardrobe became the start of the Costume Institute at the Metropolitan Museum of Art - dies at age 75 in New York City.

May 9, 2012

President Barack Obama personally endorses same sex marriage in an ABC News interview.

———————————○———————————

May 10, 1904

Frieda Belinafante – cellist, conductor and member of the Dutch Resistance during WWII who also conducted the Orange

County Philharmonic in the 1950s – is born in Amsterdam, Netherlands.

May 10, 2000

AIDS and civil rights activist Kiyoshi Kuromiya – editor of the seminal *ACT-UP Standard of Care* health guide – dies at age 57 from an AIDS-related illness in Philadelphia, PA.

May 11, 1896

Eccentric avant-garde painter Filippo De Pisis (*Still Life With Apple*, *Street Scene in Italy*, *Reclining Male Nude*, *Paesaggio di Cadore*) - who frequently painted nudes and cityscapes - is born in Ferrara, Italy.

May 11, 1933

New York Fire Department Chaplain Father Mychal F. Judge – who was designated the solemn honor of Victim 0001 during the September 11th terrorist attacks – is born in Brooklyn, N.Y.

May 11, 1935

Gay rights pioneer and activist Dick Leitsch, who led the 1966 'Sip In' an early act of civil disobedience to protest gay patrons not being allowed to be served in bars, is born in Louisville, KY.

May 11, 2000

Writer and activist William Dale Jennings - core Mattachine Society member (along with Harry Hay, Chuck Rowland, Bob Hull, and Rudi Gernreich) and later a founding member of the early homophile organization ONE, Inc. - dies at age 82 in La Miranda, CA.

―――――――――○―――――――――

May 12, 1925

Poet Amy Lowell (*Pictures of the Floating World, The Complete Poetical Works of Amy Lowell*) - who was posthumously awarded the Pulitzer Prize for Poetry in 1926 for *What's O'clock* - dies of a cerebral hemorrhage at age 51 in Brookline, MA.

May 12, 1934

Biologist, activist, and important AIDS researcher Bruce Voeller - who helped found the National Gay Task Force and served as its executive director for five years; and who later campaigned for condom use to prevent the spread of STDs - is born in Minneapolis, MN.

May 12, 1937

Gerry Studds - the first openly gay member of Congress and Massachusetts Democratic Congressman from 1973-1997 and who was an inspiration for many by winning re-election after coming out as gay - is born in Mineola, N.Y.

May 12, 1958

The Homosexual Law Reform Society is founded in the United Kingdom to lobby the government to implement the *Wolfenden Report* which recommended the decriminalization of homosexual behavior between consenting adults over the age of 21.

May 12, 1992

Bob Mizer – beefcake photographer, filmmaker, and founder of the Athletic Model Guild – dies at age 70.

May 12, 1992

Actor Robert Reed (*The Defenders, Mannix*) - best known as Mike Brady on *The Brady Bunch* - dies of intestinal cancer and complications from AIDS at age 59 in Pasadena, CA.

May 12, 1995

TV and film director/producer Arthur Lubin (*Buck Privates, Francis, Hold That Ghost, The Incredible Mr. Limpet*) - and creator of the television sitcom *Mr. Ed* - dies at age 96 in Glendale, CA.

May 12, 2008

Influential multi-medium artist Robert Rauschenberg (*White Paintings, Black Paintings, Combine, Monogram, Stoned Moon*) - who liked to incorporate materials typically outside the artist's mode into his work - dies of heart failure at age 82 in Captiva Island, FL.

May 12, 2012

President Obama says he personally endorses Same-sex marriage in an ABC News interview.

———————⊖———————

May 13, 1940

Novelist, adventurer, and travel writer Bruce Chatwin (*The Songlines, In Patagonia, Utz, The Viceroy of Ouidah*) is born in Sheffield, England.

May 13, 2000

Actor and cult film director Paul Bartel (*Eating Raoul, Lust in the Dust, Death Race 2000, Rock 'n' Roll High School*) dies of a heart attack after being diagnosed with liver cancer in New York, N.Y.

———————⊖———————

May 14, 1868

Physician and sexologist Magnus Hirschfeld, who founded the Scientific Humanitarian Committee – which has been called "the first advocacy for homosexual and transgender rights" – is born in Kolberg, Prussia.

May 14, 1881

Popular stage actor, silent film actor and female impersonator Julian Eltinge (*The Fascinating Widow, The Crinoline Girl, The Isle of Love*) - who even had the Eltinge Theater on 42nd Street named in his honor - is born in Newtonville, MA.

May 14, 1917

Prolific composer, conductor, musician and environmentalist Lou Harrison (*Suite for Percussion*, *Young Caesar*, *Elegiac Symphony*) - who had over 300 diverse compositions to his credit and was known for his synthesis of styles - is born in Portland, OR.

May 14, 1921

Popular supporting comic actor Richard Deacon - well known for his regular television sitcom roles which included Mel Cooley on *The Dick Van Dyke Show*, Fred Rutherford on *Leave It to Beaver*, and Roger Buell on *The Mothers-In-Law* - is born in Philadelphia, PA.

May 14, 1928

The first issue of the German lesbian magazine *Die Freundin* is published.

May 14, 1935

Physician and sexologist Magnus Hirschfeld, who founded the Scientific Humanitarian Committee – which has been called "the first advocacy for homosexual and transgender rights" – dies of a heart attack in Nice, France on his 67th birthday.

May 14, 1965

Frances Perkins – economist, social worker, and the first woman appointed to a U.S. Cabinet post, as FDR's Secretary of Labor from 1933-1945 – dies at age 85 in New York City. Eager to help people during the Great Depression, Perkins is credited with the passage of the Social Security Act and the Fair Labor Standards Act as well as things such as child labor laws, the first minimum wage, overtime restrictions, and the 40 hour work week.

―――――――――――○―――――――――――

May 15, 1940

Pioneering trans soul singer Jackie Shane (*Any Other Way*) is born in Nashville, TN.

May 15, 1962

Merchant marine, physician and trans pioneer Dr. Michael Dillon - the first female-to-male trans person to undergo phalloplasty and author of the groundbreaking book *Self: A Study in Endocrinology and Ethics* - dies at age 47 in Dalhousie, Punjab, India.

May 15, 1985

Warhol drag superstar of the youth-quaking underground film world Jackie Curtis (*Flesh*, *Women in Revolt*) dies of a heroin overdose in New York City, NY at age 38.

May 15, 2004

Chicana and feminist writer/theorist Gloria Anzaldua

(*Borderlands/La Frontera: The New Mestiza*) - winner of an American Book Award as well as a Lambda Literary Award and who also co-edited *This Bridge Called My Back: Writings By Radical Women of Color* - dies from complications due to diabetes at age 61 in Santa Cruz, CA.

May 16, 1898

Art Deco painter Tamara de Lempicka (*Young Lady with Gloves*, *The Musician*, *Andromeda*) - popular for her portraits and nudes; her work has been featured in several Madonna videos - is born Maria Gorska in Warsaw, Poland.

May 16, 1919

Pianist, personality, and flamboyantly dressed showman Liberace (*The Loved One*, *A Liberace Christmas*, *Sincerely Yours, The Liberace Show*) - whose many awards include two Emmys and six gold records - is born in West Allis, WI.

May 16, 1929

Poet, essayist, and feminist Adrienne Rich (*Diving in the Wreck*, *Of Woman Born*, *What is Found There*, *The Fact of a Doorframe*, *A Wild Patience Has Taken Me This Far*) - whose numerous awards and honors include The National Book Award for Poetry, The Lambda Literary Award, The Bollingen Prize, and The National Book Critics' Circle Award - is born in Baltimore, MD.

May 17

International Day Against Homophobia, Transphobia and Biphobia, created to draw attention to the violence and discrimination experienced by LGBTQ people, is observed.

May 17, 1916

Novelist, playwright, and non-fiction writer Robin Maugham (*The Servant*, *The Wrong People*, *Escape From the Shadows*) aka 2nd Viscount Maugham of Hartfield - whose frequently homosexual themed work scandalized his family - is born in England.

May 17, 1929

Feminist author, cultural critic, and journalist Jill Johnston (*Lesbian Nation: The Feminist Solution*, *The Village Voice*, *Admission Accomplished: The Lesbian Nation Years 1970-75*) - who championed the lesbian separatist movement of the 1970s - is born in London, England.

May 17, 1929

George Weinberg, author (*Society and the Healthy Homosexual*) and psychotherapist who coined the word 'Homophobia,' is born in New York City.

May 17, 1999

Poet, filmmaker, Radical Faerie, and member of the Sisters of Perpetual Indulgence, James Broughton (*Packing Up for Paradise: Selected Poems 1946-1996*, *Coming Unbuttoned*, H*ymns to Hermes*) dies of heart failure at age 85 in Port Townsend, WA.

May 17, 2004

Massachusetts legalizes gay marriage and becomes the first state in the U.S. to allow same sex couples to marry.

May 17, 2004

The board of the International Olympic Committee rules that transsexuals will be allowed to compete for the first time in the Olympics and that the ruling will go into effect at the 2004 Athens Summer Olympic Games. The ruling allows for both FTM and MTF individuals to compete.

May 17, 2015

William B. Kelley, longtime gay activist and an important figure in the early LGBT rights movement, dies of a heart attack at age 72 in Chicago, IL.

May 17, 2016

The Senate confirms Eric Fanning as Secretary of the Army, making him the first openly gay secretary of a US military branch.

―――――――――○―――――――――

May 18, 1921

Author Patrick Dennis (*Auntie Mame*, *Little Me*) – the first author to have three books on *The New York Times* Bestseller list simultaneously – is born Edward Everett Tanner III in Evanston, IL.

May 18, 1988

Actor Anthony Forwood *(The Story of Robin Hood and His Merrie Men, Knights of the Round Table)* and later manager of his partner Sir Dirk Bogarde -dies at age 72 of bowel cancer and Parkinson's disease in London, England.

May 18, 2008

Multiple Emmy-winning TV sitcom *Will and Grace* ends its 8 season run on NBC as the first successful U.S. sitcom featuring gay main characters. The series will be resurrected in 2017.

May 19, 1897

Oscar Wilde is released from Reading Prison after two years of hard labor for his conviction of "gross indecency between males."

May 19, 1904

Militant gay political activist Daniel Guerin *(Anarchism: From Theory to Practice)* – who was also key in the French labor and socialist movements – is born in Paris, France.

May 19, 1930

Essayist, playwright, activist, and editor Lorraine Hansberry *(A Raisin in the Sun, To Be Young, Gifted and Black)* - winner of the New York Critics' Circle Award and whose play *A Raisin in the Sun* ran 530 performances and was the first play produced on Broadway written by an African-American woman - is born in Chicago, IL.

May 19, 1935

Colonel T.E. Lawrence aka Lawrence of Arabia (*The Seven Pillars of Wisdom*) - best known for his war activities in the Middle East during WWI - dies at age 46 from injuries sustained in a motorcycle accident in Dorset, England.

May 19, 1987

The FDA (The U.S. Food and Drug Administration) approves AZT, the first drug for use in the treatment of AIDS.

May 19, 2009

The FOX series *Glee* premieres. The groundbreaking series had storylines of acceptance and sexuality and featured a cast of openly gay and trans characters.

May 20, 1849

Actress and sensation of the French stage Marie Dorval (*Chatterton, Lucrèce, Marie-Jeanne*) - who was also rumored to be a lover of female writer George Sand - dies at age 51 in Paris, France.

May 20, 1979

Twelve contestants compete in the first International Mr. Leather contest held in the Grand Ballroom of the Radisson Hotel in Chicago, IL.

May 20, 1996

In a 5-4 ruling which restores Colorado's existing gay rights laws, the U.S. Supreme Court strikes down Amendment 2 – asserting for the first time that homosexuals were a *class of persons* – a critical legal distinction which will have a significant impact on future cases pertaining to the civil rights and legal status of LGBT people.

———————————○———————————

May 21, 1471

Graphic artist, printmaker, engraver, and painter Albrecht Durer (*Men's Bath, Saint Jerome in His Study, Adam and Eve, The Green Passion* series) is born in Nuremberg, Germany.

May 21, 1810

Diplomat, spy, and soldier Chevalier d'Eon - who lived his first 49 years as a man and her next 33 as a woman - dies in London at age 82.

May 21, 1917

Actor Raymond Burr (*Perry Mason, Ironside, Rear Window*) - who was nominated for eight primetime Emmy Awards and won twice - is born in New Westminster, British Columbia, Canada.

May 21, 1925

Key gay rights activist and pioneer Frank Kameny - who believed "Gay is Good" despite the institutionalized homophobia in place at the time, and resolved to transform the way gay people were treated in society - is born in New York City. Among his many accomplishments, the tireless Kameny was co-founder of the Washington, DC chapter of the Mattachine Society, championed to remove homosexuality from the American Psychiatric Association's list of mental disorders, and was the first openly gay person to run for Congress.

May 21, 1926

Author Ronald Firbank (*Five Novels*, *The Flower Beneath the Foot*) - whose novels were greatly inspired by the society aesthetes - dies of lung disease at age 40 in Rome, Italy.

May 21, 1935

Hull House founder, social welfare advocate, and Nobel Peace Prize recipient - Jane Addams (*Newer Ideals of Peace*, *Peace and Bread in a Time of War*) dies at age 74 in Chicago, IL.

May 21, 1949

Writer Klaus Mann (*Mephisto*, *Der Vulkan*, *The Turning Point*) and son of writer Thomas Mann, dies of an overdose of sleeping pills at age 42 in Cannes, France.

May 21, 1966

On Armed Forces Day – to protest the exclusion of homosexuals from the U.S. armed forces – homophile groups in five cities nationwide organize demonstrations which include a 15 car motorcade in Los Angeles, CA.

May 21, 1979

Convicted of voluntary manslaughter, Dan White receives a seven-year sentence for the premeditated assassination of San Francisco Supervisor Harvey Milk and Mayor George Moscone – triggering the White Night riots by outraged protestors at San Francisco City Hall and elsewhere. White's status as a former police officer intensified the community's anger at the SFPD. After the riots, the police made a retaliatory raid on a Castro gay bar. Many patrons were beaten and two dozen were arrested. This galvanized political power within the gay community, culminating in the election of Mayor Dianne Feinstein.

May 21, 2000

Actor of stage, screen, and television, Sir John Gielgud (*Arthur*, *Becket*, *Chariots of Fire*, *The Elephant Man*) - winner of an Oscar, an Emmy, two Golden Globes, three BAFTAs, and three Tony Awards; and who has been called "the greatest Hamlet of the 20th century" - dies of a respiratory infection at age 96 in Wotton Underwood, Buckinghamshire, England.

May 22, 1907

Noted film actor Sir Laurence Olivier (*Rebecca*, *The Entertainer*, *Wuthering Heights*, *Spartacus*, *Marathon Man*, *Hamlet*, *Sleuth*), is born in Surry, England.

May 22, 1928

John Burlingame Whyte – male model turned real estate entrepreneur who helped develop the Fire Island Pines – is born in Milwaukee, WI.

May 22, 1930

Iconic politician Harvey Milk – one of the first openly gay people to be elected to public office when he won a seat on the San Francisco Board of Supervisors and who was posthumously awarded the Presidential Medal of Freedom – is born in Woodmere, N.Y.

May 22, 1939

Academy Award nominated Actor Paul Winfield (*Sounder, The Terminator, The Serpent and the Rainbow*) is born in Los Angeles, CA.

May 22, 1949

Writer and poet Claude McKay (*Home to Harlem, Banjo, Banana Bottom, Harlem: Negro Metropolis*) – a key figure in the Harlem Renaissance – dies of a heart attack at age 59 in Chicago, IL.

May 22, 1967

Poet, writer and activist Langston Hughes (*The Ways of White Folks, Not Without Laughter, The Selected Poems of Langston Hughes*) – known for his work during the Harlem Renaissance – dies in New York City at age 65 following complications from abdominal surgery related to prostate cancer.

May 22, 1970

Public relations executive Mark Bingham - one of four who attempted to take control of ill-fated United Airlines Flight 93 from terrorist hijackers on September 11 – is born in Phoenix, AZ.

May 22, 1989

Pilot Karen Ulane - whose successful suit against Eastern Airlines in the wake of being dismissed after her 1980 transition set a legal precedent for transgender status - dies at age 47 in a plane crash near DeKalb, IL.

May 22, 2005

Author Bertha Harris (*Lover*, *Catching Saradove*, *Confessions of Cherubino*, *Gertrude Stein*) - who also co-authored *The Joy of Lesbian Sex* - dies at age 67 in New York City.

May 22, 2014

The official first-day-of-issue ceremony of the U.S. Postal Service Harvey Milk Forever Stamp takes place. Milk's stamp becomes the first U.S. postage stamp to commemorate an open LGBT political official.

May 23, 1904

Torch singer and stage actress Libby Holman (*The Garrick Gaieties*, *The Little Show*, *You Never Know*, *Greenwich Village Follies*) - who introduced the standard *Body and Soul* and whose signature song was *Moanin' Low* - is born in Cincinnati, OH.

May 23, 1910

Beloved bisexual children's book author Margaret Wise Brown (*Goodnight Moon, The Runaway Bunny*) is born in Brooklyn, N.Y.

May 23, 1955

Author and AIDS educator Allen Barnett - whose collection of stories *The Body and Its Dangers and Other Stories* was the winner of the PEN/Ernest Hemingway Citation and who helped establish the Gay and Lesbian Alliance Against Defamation (GLAAD) - is born near Joliet, IL.

May 23, 1975

Stand-up comedian Jackie "Moms" Mabley (*Amazing Grace, Killer Diller*) dies of heart failure at age 81 in White Plains, N.Y. In a career that spanned six decades Mabley originally found fame touring the Black vaudeville circuit, working her way up to the Cotton Club, Carnegie Hall in 1962, then expanding to television, comedy albums, and film.

———————⊖———————

May 24

Pansexual and Panromantic Awareness and Visibility Day, which promotes visibility and awareness of pansexual and panromantic identities, is celebrated.

May 24, 1494

Painter Jacopo Pontormo aka Pontormo (*The Deposition from the Cross, The Visitation, Madonna with Child and Saints*) - an early Mannerist painter from the Florentine School who focused primarily on religious subjects with some portraiture work - is born in Empoli, Italy.

May 24, 1962

Actor Gene Anthony Ray - best known for his role as Leroy Johnson in the film and television series *Fame* - is born in New York City.

May 24, 1970

Singer songwriter and pop star Tommy Page *(I'll Be Your Everything, A Shoulder to Cry On, When I Think of You)* is born in Glen Ridge, NJ.

May 24, 1976

Armistead Maupin publishes the first of his humorous "Tales of the City" columns in *The San Francisco Chronicle* - the popularity of the newspaper series eventually prompts a highly successful *Tales of the City* book followed by several best-selling sequels including *More Tales of the City, Further Tales of the City, Babycakes,* and *Significant Others.*

May 24, 1990

Dancer, choreographer, and co-founder of the Louis Falco Dance Company, Juan Antonio - who later became the co-director of Le Ballet Jazz de Montreal and subsequently founded the dance company Confidanse - dies of an AIDS-related illness at age 45 in Toronto, Canada.

May 24, 1996

Theater and film director Norman Rene (*Longtime Companion*, *Prelude to a Kiss*, *Reckless*) dies of complications due to AIDS at age 44 in New York City.

May 24, 2000

In the "True Love" episode [Season 3, Episode 23] of the WB show *Dawson's Creek* Jack and Ethan kiss - making it the first romantic on-screen kiss between two males on a primetime network drama series.

May 24, 2002

Civil rights leader Dr. Antonia Pantoja - recipient of the Presidential Medal of Freedom and founder of the Puerto Rican Forum and ASPIRA (Spanish for "Aspire", this not-for-profit group emphasizes pride, education, and commitment to community) - dies at age 79 in San Juan, Puerto Rico.

May 24, 2006

Fred 'Fritz' Klein – activist, sex researcher, inventor of the *Klein Sexual Orientation Grid*, and author (*The Bisexual Option*, *Bisexualities: Theory and Research*, *Bisexual and Gay Husbands*) and founder of the *Journal of Bisexuality* - dies at age 73 of cardiac arrest in San Diego, CA.

May 24, 2008

Robert Calhoun – Emmy Award winning TV producer of *As the World Turns*, *Another World*, *Guiding Light* and life partner of Farley Granger – dies at age 77 of lung cancer in New York City, NY.

May 25, 1895

Oscar Wilde is convicted of "gross indecency between males" at the conclusion of his second famous London trial over "the love that dare not speak its name."

May 25, 1899

Animalier artist Rosa Bonheur (*The Horse Fair*, *Ploughing the Nivernais*) - the most famous female artist of the 19th century - dies at age 77 in Thomery, France.

May 25, 1913

Alfred Redl – the head of Austro-Hungarian Intelligence – commits suicide after being identified as a Russian double-agent and outed as a homosexual. This widely publicized case was a primary reason homosexuals were regarded as security risks for decades to come.

May 25, 1994

Multi-medium artist, designer, poet, and writer Joe Brainard - a master of collage and whose work includes the memoir *I Remember* - dies of AIDS-related pneumonia in New York City.

May 25, 2005

Film producer Ismael Merchant (*A Room with a View*, *Maurice*, *Howard's End*) - who was nominated for four Oscars - dies at age 68 following surgery for abdominal ulcers in London, England.

May 25, 2007

TV and stage actor Charles Nelson Reilly (*The Ghost & Mrs. Muir*, *Match Game*) - who also won a Tony Award in 1962 as Best Featured Actor in a Musical for *How to Succeed in Business Without Really Trying* - dies of complications from pneumonia at age 76 in Beverly Hills, CA.

―――――――――――――○―――――――――――――

May 26, 1835

William "Kitty" Courtenay, 9th Earl of Devon - who became infamous in England for his homosexuality and was subsequently exiled - dies at age 66 in Paris, France.

May 26, 1918

Stage and film actor John Dall (*Gun Crazy*, *Another Part of the Forest*, *Spartacus*) - who was nominated for a Best Supporting Actor Oscar for his role in the 1945 film *The Corn is Green* but is best remembered as one of the two prep school killers in Alfred Hitchcock's *Rope* - is born in New York City.

May 26, 1925

Out film and stage actor Sir Alex McCowen (*Henry V, Frenzy, Travels With My Aunt, Never Say Never Again, Waiting for Godot, Caesar and Cleopatra*), is born in Kent, England.

May 26, 1951

Physicist, educator, and astronaut Sally Ride - a member of NASA's class of 1978 (the first to include women) - who in 1983 became the first woman to enter into low Earth orbit - is born in Encino, CA. Among her many honors and awards, Ride received the NASA Space Flight Medal twice, was inducted into The Aviation Hall of Fame, The National Women's Hall of Fame, and was posthumously awarded The General James E. Hill Lifetime Space Achievement Award.

May 26, 1991

Playwright, lyricist, writer and director Tom Eyen (*Dreamgirls, Women Behind Bars, The Neon Woman, Ol' Red Hair is Back*) dies at age 50 of an AIDS-related illness in Palm Beach, CA.

May 27, 1907

Conservationist, marine biologist, and author Rachel Carson (*Silent Spring, The Edge of the Sea, The Sea Around Us*) - a harsh early critic of the overuse of pesticides and fertilizers, the recipient of the Presidential Medal of Freedom, the National Book Award for Nonfiction, and a charter inductee into the Ecology Hall of Fame - is born in Springdale, PA.

May 27, 1912

Writer and educator John Cheever (*The Short Stories of John Cheever*, *The Wapshot Chronicle*, *Falconer*) - whose many awards and honors include the Pulitzer Prize for Fiction, The National Book Award for Fiction, the National Book Critics Circle Award for Fiction - is born in Quincy, MA.

May 27, 1937

Allan Carr - producer of such films as *Grease*, *Can't Stop the Music* and *Where the Boys Are '84* and the stage musical *La Cage aux Folles* (for which he won a Tony Award) - is born in Chicago, IL.

May 27, 1987

Harlem Renaissance writer and painter Richard Bruce Nugent – whose short story *Smoke, Lillies and Jade* (1926) is regarded by many to be the first publication by an African-American author to openly depict homosexuality – dies at age 80 in Hoboken, N.J.

May 27, 1993

Author and journalist Bo Huston and journalist (*Horse and Other Stories*, *The Listener*, *The Dream Life*) dies of an AIDS-related illness at age 33 in San Francisco, CA.

―――――――――――○―――――――――――

May 28, 1912

Novelist, poet, playwright, and essayist Patrick White (*Voss, The Eye of the Storm, The Twyborn Affair, Riders in the Chariot*) - who in 1973 won the Nobel Prize in Literature and was named Australian of the Year - is born in London, England.

May 28, 1913

Award-winning poet May Swenson (*Dear Elizabeth, New and Selected Things Taking Place, Nature: Poems Old and New*) - whose many awards and honors include a Bollingen Prize, a nomination for The National Book Award, and a fellowship from the MacArthur Foundation - is born in Logan, UT.

May 28, 1919

The first pro-gay film – a German silent feature entitled *Anders als die Andern* (*"Different From the Others"*) – is released featuring German sex-researcher Magnus Hirchsfeld in a series of soliloquies intended to encourage audience sympathy for the challenges facing the film's gay protagonists.

May 28, 1956

Author Paul Reed - who wrote one of the first AIDS novels in 1984, *Facing It: A Novel of AIDS*, as well as books such as *Vertical Intercourse* and *Longing* - is born in San Diego, CA.

May 28 1987

Actor, playwright, and director Charles Ludlam (*The Mystery of Irma Vep, The Artificial Jungle, Camille, Stage Blood, The Ventriloquist's Wife, Eunuchs of the Forbidden City*) - who established the Ridiculous Theatrical Company in 1967 - dies of an AIDS-related illness at age 44 in New York City.

May 28, 1989

The Leather Pride Flag, designed by Tony DeBlase, is presented at International Mr. Leather in Chicago, IL.

May 29, 1927

Benjamin Henry Jesse Francis Shepard aka Francis Gierson, composer, pianist, author, and spiritualist (*The Valley of Shadows, Lincoln, the Practical Mystic, Modern Mysticism*) dies while giving a piano performance in Los Angeles, CA.

May 29, 1934

Actress, writer, playwright Nancy Cardenas (*The Empty Pitcher, Sexualidades, The Day We Walked on the Moon*), one of the first Mexican celebrities to publicly declare they were a homosexual, is born in Parras, Mexico.

May 29, 1947

Educator and author Geoff Mains (*Urban Aboriginals: A Celebration of Leather Sexuality, Gentle Warriors*) is born in England.

May 29, 1950

Author, educator, and translator Melvin Dixon (*Vanishing Rooms, Trouble the Water*) - who was nominated for a Lambda Literary Award - is born in Stamford, CT.

May 29, 1957

Unique and highly stylized film director James Whale (*Frankenstein, The Bride of Frankenstein, The Invisible Man, The Old Dark House*) commits suicide by drowning in his pool at age 67 in Hollywood, CA.

May 29, 2008

Writer and activist Paula Gunn Allen (*The Sacred Hoop, Spider Woman's Granddaughters*) - whose book *Studies in American Indian Literature: Critical Essays and Course Designs* is considered a landmark in Native American literary criticism - dies of lung cancer at age 68 in Fort Bragg, CA.

―――――――――――○―――――――――――

May 30, 1593

Playwright and poet Christopher Marlowe (*Doctor Faustus, Edward II, Tamburlaine, The Jew of Malta*) is stabbed to death at age 29 in Deptford, England.

May 30, 1926

Transgender spokesperson and entertainer Christine Jorgensen - the first person to become a celebrity in the United States for having gender confirmation surgery - is born George William Jorgensen Jr. in the Bronx, N.Y.

May 30, 1968

Several homophile groups organize a "gay-in" in Griffith Park in Los Angeles, CA.

May 30, 1986

Fashion designer Perry Ellis – who built an empire on contemporary sportswear – dies at age 46 of an AIDS-related viral encephalitis in New York City, NY.

May 30, 1995

Major League Baseball player Glenn Burke, one of the first professional athletes to come out of the closet while still actively playing and who played for the Los Angeles Dodgers and Oakland Athletics from 1976-1979 – dies at age 42 of an AIDS-related illness in San Leandro, CA. He is credited with popularizing the High-Five.

May 30, 1999

Transgender ventriloquist and magician Terri Rogers - who created several popular illusions still in use today - dies in London England following a series of strokes.

May 30, 2010

Peter Orlovsky, actor, poet (*Leper's Cry*, *Clean Asshole Poems and Smiling Vegetable Songs*, *Straight Hearts Delight*) – and partner of Allen Ginsberg – dies of lung cancer at age 76 in Williston, VT.

May 30, 2013

Award-winning film director, writer and actor Rituparno Ghosh (*Chitrangada, Raincoat, Unishe April, Chokher Bali, The Last Lear*), dies of a heart attack at age 49 in West Bengal, India.

May 31, 1819

Vastly influential poet Walt Whitman (*Leaves of Grass*, *Song of Myself*, *I Hear America Singing*) - a key figure in U.S. literary history - is born on Long Island, N.Y.

May 31, 1918

Bob Hull - core Mattachine Society member (along with Harry Hay, Chuck Rowland, William Dale Jennings, and Rudi Gernreich) - is born in St. Louis Park, MN.

May 31, 1922

Actor Denholm Elliott (*Indiana Jones*, *A Room with a View*, *Trading Places*) - who was nominated for an Oscar and won four BAFTA Awards - is born in London, England.

May 31, 1923

Painter, sculptor, and printmaker Ellsworth Kelly (*Houston Triptych*, *Black Ripe*, *Sculpture for a Large Wall*, *Red Curves*, *Red Blue Green*) is born in Newburgh, NY.

May 31, 1945

Film director Rainer Werner Fassbinder (*The Marriage of Maria Braun*, *Querelle*, *Veronica Voss*, *Lola*, *Lili Marleen*) - the prolific "enfant terrible" of 1970s cinema whose awards include Germany's Golden Bear and is considered most representative of the New German Cinema - is born in Bad Worishofen, Germany.

May 31, 1963

Educator, classicist and author Edith Hamilton - whose books on mythology (*Mythology*, *The Greek Way*, *The Roman Way*) have become staples in education - dies at age 95 in Washington, DC.

May 31, 1967

Jazz composer and pianist Billy Strayhorn (*Lush Life*, *Take the A Train*, *Satin Doll*) – the frequently unheralded collaborator with Duke Ellington – dies of esophageal cancer at age 51 in New York City, NY.

May 31, 1978

Dada artist of the Weimar Period, Hannah Hoch (*Cut With a Dada Knife Through the Last Weimar Beer Belly*, *The Puppet Balsamine*, *Dada Panorama*, *The Staircase*) - known for her photomontages - dies at age 88 in Berlin, Germany.

May 31, 1991

Author Sir Angus Wilson (*The Middle Age of Mrs. Eliot*, *The Old Men at the Zoo*, *A Bit Off the Map*) dies following a stroke at age 77 in Bury St. Edmunds, Suffolk, England.

May 31, 1992

The activist group The Lesbian Avengers is founded in New York City by a group of women from ACT-UP with a purpose of promoting lesbian issues.

May 31, 1999

Comic, actor, and one of the 20th century's foremost female impersonators, Charles Pierce – who did impressions of screen divas and actresses from Joan Crawford to Bette Davis to Carol Channing – dies of cancer at age 72 in Toluca Lake, CA.

May 31, 2010

Lambda Literary Award winning novelist and memoirist Donald Windham (*Lost Friendships*, *The Dog Star*, *The Hero Continues*, *Tanaquil*, *Two People*) - an intimate friend of Tennessee Williams, Lincoln Kirstein, Paul Cadmus, and Truman Capote - dies at age 89 in New York City.

May 31, 2018

A remounting of Matt Crowley's groundbreaking 1968 play *The Boys in the Band* opens fifty years later at the Booth Theatre with a cast that includes Jim Parsons, Matt Bomer, and Zachary Quinto.

JUNE

June 1, 1930

Actor, singer, comedian Jim Nabors (*Gomer Pyle, U.S.M.C., The Andy Griffith Show, The Best Little Whorehouse in Texas*) is born in Sylacauga, AL.

June 1, 1941

Prolific novelist and writer Sir Hugh Walpole (*The Dark Forest*, T*he Secret City, The Cathedral)* dies of a heart attack at age 57 near Keswick, England.

June 1, 1947

The first known U.S. periodical published especially for lesbians –*Vice Versa* magazine – is published by Edith Eyde under the pseudonym Lisa Ben (an anagram for lesbian). Nine issues of *Vice Versa* will be printed before it ceases publication in February 1948.

June 1, 1950

Author and screenwriter Michael McDowell (*The Amulet, Blackwater, The Elementals, Tales From the Darkside, Beetlejuice, The Nightmare Before Christmas*) aka gay mystery writer Nathan Aldyne (*Cobalt, Vermilion, Canary*) is born in Enterprise, AL.

June 1, 1981

The groundbreaking collection, *This Bridge Called My Back: Writings By Radical Women of Color* edited by Cherrie Moraga and Gloria Anzaldua, is published by Persephone Press. The second edition will be published in 1984 by Kitchen Table: Women of Color Press.

June 1, 1991

The first "Gay Day" for LGBT people, their families and supporters is held at Walt Disney World in Florida.

June 1, 1992

Trans gospel quartet singer and soloist Willmer "Little Ax" Broadnax dies at age 75 in Philadelphia.

June 1, 2007

The Midwest's leading and most comprehensive LGBT community center - the 55,000 square foot the Center on Halsted, at 3656 N. Halsted in Chicago, Ill. - opens its doors.

June 1, 2008

Designer Yves Saint Laurent - whose collections revolutionized the world of fashion and who was the first living fashion designer to be given a solo exhibition at the Metropolitan Museum of Art - dies of brain cancer at age 71 in Paris, France.

───────────────○───────────────

June 2, 1921

Christian Universalist minister Phebe Hanaford, active in championing universal suffrage and women's rights, the first woman ordained as a Universalist minister in New England, and the first woman to serve as chaplain to the Connecticut state legislature, dies at age 92 in Rochester, NY.

June 2, 1951

Gay rights activist Gilbert Baker, who designed the rainbow flag in 1978, is born in Chanute, KS.

June 2, 1962

Author and gardener Vita Sackville-West (*The Edwardians, All Passion Spent, In Your Garden Again*) dies at age 70 in Sissington Castle, Kent, England.

June 2, 1984

Arthur Bell dies at age 51 from complications due to diabetes in New York City. Bell was an activist, journalist, an early member of the Gay Liberation Front, a founding member of the Gay Activists Alliance, a columnist for *The Village Voice,* and the author of *Dancing the Gay Lib Blues* and *Kings Don't Mean a Thing.*

June 2, 1989

The first annual Lambda Literary Awards, celebrating excellence in gay and lesbian writing and publishing for 1988, are held at the Hyatt Regency in Washington, DC.

June 2, 1991

The Red AIDS Ribbon – created by the Visual AIDS Artists' Caucus – makes its public debut at the 1991 Tony Awards when Broadway Cares/Equity Fights AIDS distributes the ribbons to guests and presenters. The first celebrity to be seen wearing the ribbon was co-host Jeremy Irons.

June 2, 1997

Helen Jacobs, winner of nine Grand Slam tennis titles including five for singles and the first female tennis player named the *Associated Press* Female Athlete of the Year, dies at age 88 in East Hampton, NY.

―――――――――○―――――――――

June 3, 1879

Stage and silent film actress and producer Alla Nazimova (*Salome, Camille, Blood and Sand, The Red Lantern*) – a central figure in Hollywood's early lesbian scene, whose grand home The Garden of Allah was hotspot for Hollywood's elite, and who was also the godmother of former First Lady Nancy Reagan – is born in Yalta in the Ukraine.

June 3, 1901

Trained stage and film actor Maurice Evans (*Richard II, Batman, Rosemary's Baby, Planet of the Apes*) – best known for appearing as Samantha Stevens' father in the 1960s sitcom *Bewitched* – is born in Dorchester, Dorset, England.

June 3, 1902

Pioneering artist George Quaintance – known for his idealized and strongly homoerotic work and whose art was used for the first cover of *Physique Pictorial* – is born in Page County, VA.

June 3, 1906

Actress, singer and dancer Josephine Baker (whose films include *Zouzou* and *Princess Tam Tam*) is born in St. Louis, MO. Baker came to fame with her "banana dance" at the Folies Bergere and soon became the toast of Paris. Later in life she received France's highest award, The Legion of Honor.

June 3, 1926

Poet and leading figure of the Beat Generation, Allen Ginsberg (*Howl and Other Poems*, *Kaddish*, *The Fall of America: Poems of These States*, *Reality Sandwiches*) - whose numerous awards and honors include a National Book Award for Poetry - is born in Newark, N.J.

June 3, 1986

Actor Robert La Tourneaux (who played the likable but dim hustler in both the Off-Broadway production and film versions of *The Boys in the Band)* dies at age 41 in New York City from an AIDS-related illness.

June 3, 1991

Stage actress Eva Le Gallienne - recipient of a Tony Award in 1964 for her body of work (*The Swan*, *Resurrection*, *Alison's House*, *To Grandmother's House We Go*, *Peter Pan*) - dies at age 92 in Weston, CT.

June 3, 1991

Actor, screenwriter, and prolific low-budget filmmaker Andy Milligan (*Bloodthirsty Butchers, Blood Rites, The Rats are Coming! The Werewolves Are Here!, Carnage*) dies of an AIDS-related illness at age 62 in Los Angeles, CA.

June 3, 2018

Pose, the Ryan Murphy created TV series set in 1987–88 and looks at the juxtaposition of several segments of life and society in New York including the African-American and Latino ball culture world and the downtown social and literary scene, premieres on FX.

June 4, 1967

Writer and literary editor J.R. Ackerley (*My Father and Myself, Hindoo Holiday, We Think The World of You, My Dog Tulip*) dies at age 70 of a coronary thrombosis in London, England.

June 4, 1998

Actress Josephine Hutchinson (*North By Northwest, Son of Frankenstein, The Story of Louis Pasteur*) dies at age 94 in New York City.

June 5, 1876

Influential honky-tonk pianist, singer and composer Tony Jackson (*Pretty Baby, Michigan Water Blues, The Naked*

Dance) - a pioneer in ragtime music - is born in New Orleans, LA.

June 5, 1883

Economist John Maynard Keynes (*Essays in Persuasion, The Economic Consequences of the Peace, General Theory of Employment Interest and Money*) – founder of the International Monetary Fund and the World Bank – is born Cambridge, England.

June 5, 1887

Anthropologist and educator Ruth Benedict (*The Chrysanthemum and the Sword, Patterns of Culture*) – partner of Margaret Mead and president of the American Anthropological Association – is born in New York City.

June 5, 1898

Poet and dramatist Federico Garcia Lorca (*The House of Bernarda Alba, Blood Wedding, Yerma, The Sonnets of Dark Love*) - who was lionized as The Finest Poet of Imperial Spain as well as a member of the avant-garde artists' group the Generation of '27 - is born in Fuente Vauqeros, Granada, Spain.

June 5, 1928

British new wave film director and winner of two Oscars, Tony Richardson (*Tom Jones, A Taste of Honey, Look Back in Anger, The Loneliness of the Long Distance Runner, Blue Sky*) - father of Natasha and Joely Richardson with Vanessa Redgrave - is born in Shipley, Yorkshire, England.

June 5, 1953

Tennis great Bill Tilden – the world's number one player for seven years in the 1920s and the winner of seven United States championships – dies of a stroke at age 60 in Los Angeles, CA.

June 5, 1966

Set and costume designer, screenwriter, and dancer Natacha Rambova - remembered as one time wife of Rudolph Valentino and for her Art Deco and Art Nouveau sets and lavish costumes of Alla Nazimova's silent films *Camille* and *Salome* - dies of a heart attack brought on by anorexia nervosa at age 69 in Pasadena, CA.

June 5, 1981

The CDC (Center for Disease Control) identifies Pneumocystis Carinii Pneumonia (PCP) – a rare infection – in five previously healthy gay men in Los Angeles, CA. who are also suffering from other opportunistic infections, indicating to doctors that their immune systems are not working.

June 5, 1983

In his acceptance speech at the Tony Awards - after *Torch Song Trilogy* wins for Best Play – producer John Glines becomes the first person ever to acknowledge a same-sex partner on a major televised awards show in the U.S.

---○---

June 6, 1962

Advice & Consent, the first mainstream film from a major studio with a scene that takes place in a gay bar, is released.

June 6, 2006

Grammy Award winning recording artist, songwriter, and musician Billy Preston (*Will It Go Round in Circles*, *Nothing From Nothing*) dies at age 59 of complications from malignant hypertension leading to kidney disease in Scottsdale, AZ.

---○---

June 7, 1954

British mathematician, scientist, logician, and naval cryptologist Alan Turing commits suicide at age 41 in Wilmslow, Cheshire, England. For having broken the Nazi Enigma Code and formulating the test for Artificial Intelligence he is considered the Father of Computer Science.

June 7, 1970

Novelist and author E.M. Forster (*Howards End*, *A Passage to India*, *Where Angels Fear to Tread*, *Maurice*, *A Room with a View*) dies at age 91 of an apparent stroke in Coventry, Warwickshire, England.

June 7, 1977

Anita Bryant – former Miss America, singer and orange juice industry spokesperson turned politically conservative activist – leads a successful campaign with the Save Our Children Crusade to repeal a gay rights ordinance in Dade County, FL. Bryant will succeed in spreading her campaign before suffering a severe backlash which galvanizes the community. Gay rights supporters nationwide organize fundraisers, events and protests in response.

———————————————⊖———————————————

June 8, 1768

Art historian and archeologist Johann Joachim Winckelmann *(Reflections on the Painting and Sculpture of the Greeks, History of the Art of Antiquity)* - known as "the founder of modern archeology" - is murdered at age 50 in Trieste, Italy. He was the first to differentiate Roman, Greek, and Greco-Roman art and the first to apply scientific archeology to art history

June 8, 1876

Novelist, feminist writer, and bohemian memoirist George Sand, the pen name of Armandine Aurore Lucille Dudevant *(Indiana, Consuelo, Mauprat, Marianne, Valentine)* - best known for her rustic novels of love and class - dies at age 71 in Nohant, France.

June 8, 1903

Writer Marguerite Yourcenar *(Memoirs of Hadrian, Oriental Tales)* - who was the first woman to be elected to the Académie Française - is born in Brussels, Belgium.

June 8, 1904

Angus McBean – mask maker and photographer of celebrities such as Vivien Leigh, Audrey Hepburn, and Agatha Christie – and The Beatles' first album cover – is born in South Wales.

June 8, 1979

Fashion designer Norman Bishop Hartnell - who was appointed as dressmaker to Britain's Royal Family in 1938 and whose designs included Princess Elizabeth's 1947 wedding dress and later Queen Elizabeth's II 1953 coronation gown - dies at age 77 in Windsor, England.

June 8, 1993

Playwright, poet, critic, visual artist, and author Severo Sarduy (*For Voice, Beach Birds, Colibri, From Cuba With a Song*) - known for his extreme and unpredictable plots as well as experimental style - dies at age 56 of an AIDS-related illness in Paris, France.

June 9, 1891

Composer, songwriter, and Broadway legend Cole Porter (*Love For Sale, Can-Can, Silk Stockings, Anything Goes, I Get a Kick out of You, Night and Day, Begin the Beguine, So in Love*) is born in Peru, IN. Porter is considered one of the principle contributors of the *Great American Songbook* with over 900 songs attributed to him. He was nominated for four Oscars, won one Grammy, won two Tony Awards (for *Kiss Me Kate*), and was inducted into the Songwriters Hall of Fame.

June 9, 1952

Prolific photographer Alice Austen - known for her images of her lover as well as lesbian friends and women workers - dies at age 86 in Staten Island, N.Y.

June 9, 1954

Alain Locke – writer (*The Negro in America*), philosopher, educator and "Dean" of the Harlem Renaissance who also edited several collections including *The New Negro: An Interpretation* – dies at age 68 in New York City.

June 9, 1974

Theatrical legend and Tony Award winning actress Katharine Cornell (*The Barretts of Wimpole Street, Romeo and Juliet, Candida, The Green Hat, The Age of Innocence*) - often called "The First Lady of the Theater" - dies of pneumonia at age 81 in Vineyard Haven, MA.

June 9, 1990

Angus McBean – mask maker and photographer of celebrities as Vivien Leigh, Audrey Hepburn, and Agatha Christie – and The Beatles' first album cover – dies the day after his 86th birthday.

———————————○———————————

June 10/11, 323 BC

Alexander III of Macedonia, better known as Alexander the Great – who, by age 30 had created one of the largest empires in the ancient world and was undefeated in battle – dies in Babylon at age 32 of a mysterious illness just 8 months after the death of his lover, General Hephaestion.

June 10, 1928

Artist, illustrator and writer Maurice Sendak (*Where the Wild Things Are*, *Outside Over There*, *The Nutshell Library*, *In the Night Kitchen*) - winner of the 1964 Caldecott Medal which is awarded annually for excellence in children's picture books - is born in Brooklyn, N.Y.

June 10, 1944

German-Hungarian novelist, playwright and sculptor Christa Winsloe (*Madchen in Uniform/Girls in Uniform*, *Life Begins*, *Half the Violin*) - who boldly explored lesbian and gay themes in her writing during the 1930s and was one time lover of American journalist Dorothy Thompson - is shot to death in Cluny, France.

June 10, 1958

Poet, playwright, journalist, author, and educator Angelina Weld Grimke - who was part of the Harlem Renaissance and whose popular three-act play *Rachel* was staged as a vehicle for NAACP rallies against the effects of the film *Birth of a Nation* - dies at age 78 in New York City.

June 10, 1959

Author and journalist Bo Huston and journalist (*Horse and Other Stories*, *The Listener*, *The Dream Life*) is born.

June 10, 1982

Film director Rainer Werner Fassbinder (*The Marriage of Maria Braun, Querelle, Veronica Voss, Lola, Lili Marleen*) - the prolific "enfant terrible" of 1970s cinema whose awards include Germany's Golden Bear and is considered most representative of the New German Cinema - dies at age 37 of a myocardial infarction in Munich, Germany.

June 10, 1983

The play *Torch Song Trilogy* opens on Broadway at the Little Theatre. Written by and starring Harvey Fierstein, the play will go on to win Tony Awards for Best Play and Best Actor in a Play (Fierstein) and will run almost three years.

June 11, 1877

Belle Epoque poet Renee Vivien (*Roses Rising, The Touch, Prolong the Night*) - who counted Natalie Clifford Barney and Baroness Heléne de Zuylen de Nyevelt among her lovers - is born in London, England.

June 11, 1923

Screenwriter and crime fiction novelist George Baxt - best known for creating the gay black detective Pharaoh Love in a series of five books (*A Queer Kind of Death, Swing Low Sweet Harriet, A Queer Kind of Love,* etc.) as well as a series of 13 celebrity murder novels (*The Tallulah Bankhead Murder Case, The Dorothy Parker Murder Case*, etc.) - is born in Brooklyn, N.Y.

June 11, 1928

Writer Sanford Friedman (*Totempole*, *Still Life: Two Short Novels*, *A Haunted Woman*) is born in New York City.

June 11, 1939

Country western singer Wilma Burgess (*Don't Touch Me*, *Fifteen Days*, *Tear Time*, *Baby*, *Misty Blue*) - who had 15 singles from 1965-1975 on the Billboard Country and Western chart - is born in Orlando, FL.

June 11, 2009

Chastity Bono, daughter of Sonny and Cher, announces that she plans to undergo gender confirmation surgery and afterwards go by the name Chaz.

June 12, 1892

Modernist writer Djuna Barnes (*Nightwood* - which is considered her masterpiece, *Ladies Almanack*) - a leading figure in bohemian Paris of the 1930s and member of the group known as "The Literary Women of the Left Bank" - is born in Storm King Mountain, N.Y.

June 12, 1901

Fashion designer Norman Bishop Hartnell - who was appointed as dressmaker to Britain's Royal Family in 1938 and whose designs included Princess Elizabeth's 1947 wedding dress and later Queen Elizabeth's II 1953 coronation gown - is born in London, England.

June 12, 2002

Award-winning fashion designer Bill Blass - who expanded his label to include not only men and women's wear but also swimwear, perfume, and even chocolate - dies of cancer at age 79 in New Preston, CT.

June 12, 2016

49 people are killed and 53 are wounded in the Pulse nightclub shooting in Orlando, FL., which became the worst mass shooting in U.S. history. The shooter, Omar Mateen, was killed by police following a three-hour standoff.

June 12, 2016

Lambda Award winning author Michelle Cliff (*Free Enterprise, No Telephone to Heaven, The Land of Look Behind and Claiming, Abeng*) dies of liver failure at age 69 in Santa Cruz, CA.

June 13, 1926

Comic actor of stage, screen, and especially television, Paul Lynde (*Hollywood Squares*, Uncle Arthur on *Bewitched, Send Me No Flowers, Donny and Marie, The Paul Lynde Show, Bye Bye Birdie*) - a five time Emmy Award nominee - is born in Mount Vernon, OH.

June 13, 1984

Popular Portuguese singer, songwriter and innovative entertainer Antonio Variacoes (*Anjo de Guarda, Dar & Receber*) dies from pneumonia at age 39 in Lisbon, Portugal.

---○---

June 14, 1910

Seven time Oscar-nominated film editor William H. Reynolds - who won the award for *The Sound of Music* and *The Sting* but also edited such classics as *The Day The Earth Stood Still, Hello, Dolly!, Fanny, The Turning Point, Three Coins in the Fountain, Love is a Many Splendid Thing, The Godfather, The Sand Pebbles*, and *The Great White Hope* - is born in Elmira, N.Y.

June 14, 1913

Film set decorator and producer Jacques Mapes (*Singing in the Rain, Arthur Hailey's The Moneychangers, Airport, The Loretta Young Show*) - the life partner of film producer Ross Hunter - is born in the U.S.

June 14, 2002

Writer, poet, playwright, and activist June Jordan (*Some of Us Did Not Die, Directed By Desire: The Collected Poems of June Jordan*) - author of the *American Poetry Review* column "The Black Poet Speaks of Poetry" and regular columnist for the *Progressive* - dies of breast cancer at age 65 in Berkeley, CA.

---○---

June 15, 1936

Award winning author Patricia Nell Warren (Harlan's Race, Billy's Boy) whose novel The Front Runner was one of the first works of contemporary gay fiction to make the New York Times best seller list, is born in Helena, MT.

June 15, 2003

The world's longest rainbow flag to date, stretching from the Atlantic to the Gulf of Mexico, was unfurled as part of Key West Pride in Florida. The finished flag was 1.25 miles long and 2,000 people were needed to hold it after the unfurling.

―――――――――――○―――――――――――

June 16, 1951

Louis Sullivan, activist and author (*Information for the Female to Male Cross Dresser and Transsexual* – one of the first guidebooks for FTM persons) and founder of FTM International, the first FTM organization – is born Sheila Jean Sullivan in Milwaukee, WI.

June 16, 1961

Gay ballet dancer Rudolf Nureyev defects from the Soviet Union at Le Bourget Airport in Paris.

June 16, 1979

Oscar nominated film director and screenwriter Nicholas Ray (*Rebel Without a Cause, Johnny Guitar, 55 Days At Peking, The Savage Innocents*) dies of lung cancer at age 67 in New York City.

June 16, 2008

Daughters of Bilitis co-founders Del Martin and Phyllis Lyon are the first same-sex couple to be married in San Francisco after the California Supreme Court legalizes gay marriage.

---○---

June 17, 1880

Writer, journalist, and photographer Carl van Vechten (*Parties, Peter Whiffle, The Tattooed Countess, Sacred and Profane Memories*) - patron and unofficial publicist of the Harlem Renaissance and also known for the vast photographic portraits of his very wide circle of friends - is born in Cedar Rapids, IA.

June 17, 1900

Journalist Evelyn Irons, the first female war correspondent to be decorated with the French Croix de Guerre and who had a romance with the Bloomsbury novelist and poet Vita Sackville-West, is born in Scotland.

---○---

June 18, 1964

Jane Heap – the publisher who co-founded the art and literary magazine *The Little Review* with Margaret C. Anderson and became a pioneer of literary modernism – dies at age 80 in London, England.

June 18, 1971

Torch singer and stage actress Libby Holman (*The Garrick Gaieties, The Little Show, You Never Know, Greenwich Village Follies)* - who introduced the standard *Body and Soul* and whose signature song was *Moanin' Low* - dies at age 67 in Stamford, CT. Her death was ruled a suicide by carbon monoxide poisoning after she was found in the front seat of her Rolls Royce.

June 18, 1982

Modernist writer Djuna Barnes (*Nightwood* - which is considered her masterpiece, *Ladies Almanack*) - a leading figure in bohemian Paris of the 1930s and a member of the group known as "The Literary Women of the Left Bank" - dies in relative seclusion at age 90 in New York City.

June 18, 1982

Writer and educator John Cheever (*The Short Stories of John Cheever*, *The Wapshot Chronicle*, *Falconer*) - whose many awards and honors include the Pulitzer Prize for Fiction, The National Book Award for Fiction, the National Book Critics Circle Award for Fiction - dies of cancer at age 70 in Ossining, N.Y.

June 18, 1983

The space shuttle Challenger launches from Kennedy Space Center, Florida and Sally Ride becomes the first American woman in space.

June 18, 1992

Oscar, Grammy, and Golden Globe winning songwriter and entertainer Peter Allen (*I Go To Rio*, *Arthur's Theme*, *I Honestly Love You*) dies at age 48 from an AIDS-related illness in San Diego, CA.

June 18, 1993

Activist Craig L. Rodwell (early gay rights activist and founder of the Oscar Wilde Memorial Bookshop – the first bookstore devoted to gay and lesbian authors and literature) dies of stomach cancer in New York City.

June 18, 2012

Actor and entertainment personality Victor Spinetti (*The Taming of the Shrew, The Little Prince, Voyage of the Damned*) - whose memorable roles include the Beatles' films *A Hard Day's Night, Magical Mystery Tour,* and *Help* and who won Broadway's Tony Award in 1965 for Best Supporting of Featured Actor in a Musical for *Oh, What a Lovely War* - dies of pancreatic cancer at age 82 in Monmouth, Wales.

———————○———————

June 19, 1989

Poet, activist, and founder of the Black Women's Revolutionary Council - Pat Parker (*Jonestown & Other Madness, Child of Myself, Pit Stop, Movement in Black*) dies of breast cancer at age 45 in Oakland, CA.

———————○———————

June 20, 1906

Interior designer and antiques expert John Beresford Fowler - who specialized in wallpaper, printing, and upholstery - is born in Lingfield, Surrey, England.

June 20, 1917

Publisher and diarist Donald Vining (*A Gay Diary, How Can You Come Out If You've Never Been In?*) - who also founded Pepys Press - is born in Benton, PA.

June 20, 1929

Activist Edith "Edie" Windsor is born in Philadelphia, PA. Windsor was the primary plaintiff in the Supreme Court case United States vs. Windsor which overturned part of the Defense of Marriage Act and is considered a huge legal victory for the same sex marriage movement in the U.S.

June 20, 1940

Award winning stage, TV, and screen actor John Mahoney (*Frasier, Barton Fink, Say Anything*) is born in Lancashire, England.

June 20, 1955

One of the most successful African American authors of all time E. Lynn Harris (*Invisible Life, Just As I Am, And This Too Shall Pass*) – the Lambda Literary Award winning writer who had ten books on *The New York Times* bestseller list and was one of the first to write about men on the "down-low" – is born in Flint, MI.

June 20, 1975

The first issue of the magazine *Drummer*, which helped define leather culture, is published. The magazine will cease publication in 1999 after 214 issues.

June 20, 1980

The film *Can't Stop the Music* starring the Village People, Valerie Perrine, Steve Guttenberg, and Bruce Jenner - directed by Nancy Walker and co-written by Allan Carr - opens to resoundingly atrocious reviews.

June 21, 1891

Educator Sophia B. Packard, who would eventually cofound a school for African American women that would eventually become Spelman College, dies at age 67 in Washington D.C.

June 21, 1972

The short-lived ABC sitcom *The Corner Bar* debuts featuring the first recurring gay character on American television: Peter Panama, a flamboyant set designer played by Vincent Schiavelli.

June 21, 1989

Educator and author Geoff Mains (*Urban Aboriginals: A Celebration of Leather Sexuality, Gentle Warriors*) dies at age 42 of an AIDS-related illness in San Francisco, CA.

June 21, 1999

Transgender journalist and author Nancy Hunt Bowman (*Mirror Image: The Odyssey of a Male-to-Female Transsexual*) - who won four Associated Press Awards for her reportage during the Vietnam War under the name Ridgely Hunt and was a featured writer with the *Chicago Tribune* - dies at age 72 in Bonita Springs, FL.

June 22, 1664

Poet Katherine Philips (*Poems by the Incomparable Mrs. K.P.*, *Poems*, *Pompey: A Tragedy*) - the first British woman to find wide public acclaim as a poet during her lifetime - dies at age 32 of smallpox in London, England.

June 22, 1910

Tenor and organist Sir Peter Pears - who sang regularly at Covent Garden in London, was a guest performer at venues worldwide, and was the longtime partner of composer Benjamin Britten - is born in Farnham, England. Many of Britten's works included parts specifically written for Pears such as *Peter Grimes*.

June 22, 1922

Award-winning fashion designer Bill Blass - who expanded his label to include not only men and women's wear but also swimwear, perfume, and even chocolate - is born in Fort Wayne, IN.

June 22, 1947

Science fiction writer Octavia Butler (*Kindred*, *Wild Seed*, *Parable of the Sower*, *Bloodchild*, *Parable of the Talents*) - winner of two Hugo Awards as well as two Nebula Awards for excellence in fantasy/science fiction writing - is born in Pasadena, CA.

June 22, 1988

Vietnam Air Force Sgt. Leonard Matlovich – the first gay

service member to purposely out himself in order to challenge the military's ban on gays serving openly – dies at age 44 of an AIDS-related illness is West Hollywood, CA. Matlovich, recipient of a Purple Heart and a Bronze Star, was a veteran of three tours in Vietnam.

June 22, 2018

Gay rights pioneer and activist Dick Leitsch, who led the 1966 'Sip In' an early act of civil disobedience to protest gay patrons not being allowed to be served in bars, dies of cancer at age 83 in Manhattan.

––––––––––––––––––––⊖––––––––––––––––––––

June 23, 1894

Researcher and sexologist Dr. Alfred Kinsey (*Sexual Behavior in the Human Male*, *Sexual Behavior in the Human Female*) - founder in 1947 of the Institute for Sex Research at Indiana University - is born in Hoboken, N.J.

June 23, 1912

British mathematician, scientist, logician, and naval cryptologist Alan Turing is born in London, England. For having broken the Nazi Enigma Code and formulating the test for Artificial Intelligence he is considered the Father of Computer Science.

June 24, 1909

Writer Sarah Orne Jewett (*The Country of Pointed Fires,
A White Heron, Strangers and Wayfarers*) - known for her
realistic and regional depiction of her Maine world - dies as the
result of a stroke at age 59 in South Berwick, ME.

June 24, 1973

An arsonist fire is set at the Upstairs Lounge in New Orleans,
LA. Because of bars on the windows, 32 LGBT patrons die.
The disaster is mostly met with indifference by city residents.
Some of the bodies were never identified because families were
too ashamed to claim them.

June 24, 2012

Gad Beck - the last known gay Jewish survivor of the
Holocaust and Lambda Literary Award nominee for *An
Underground Life: Memoirs of a Gay Jew in Nazi Berlin* - dies
at age 88 in Berlin, Germany.

June 24, 2016

President Obama announces the designation of the 1st national
monument to LGBT rights. The Stonewall National Monument
will include Christopher Park, the Stonewall Inn and the
surrounding area - site of the 1969 Stonewall riots.

June 25, 1962

In MANual Enterprises v. Day, the U.S. Supreme Court

declares that magazines consisting largely of photographs of nude or mostly nude models are not obscene. The ruling opens the U.S. Mail to many magazines containing previously banned material, especially those catering to gay males.

June 25, 1963

Singer, songwriter, and record producer George Michael whose many hit records included solo work (*Faith, I Want Your Sex, One More Try*) and with the band Wham! (*Wake Me Up Before You Go-Go, Careless Whisper*) is born in London.

June 25, 1972

After coming out in the seminary two years before, William (Bill) R. Johnson is ordained into the United Church of Christ, making him the first officially out gay person to be ordained in the Christian ministry in modern times.

June 25, 1978

The original Gay Pride Flag, created by Ryan Halliday, is displayed in the San Francisco Gay Freedom Day Parade.

June 25, 1984

French philosopher, social theorist, historian of ideas, and literary critic Michel Foucault (*The History of Sexuality, Madness and Civilization, The Order of Things*) dies at age 57 of an AIDS-related illness in Paris, France.

June 25, 1992

AIDS educator and film executive Donald W. Woods (*Tongues Untied, No Regrets*) - executive director of AIDS Films, a non-profit organization producing AIDS education and prevention films - dies of cardiac arrest at age 34 in Manhattan, N.Y.

June 25, 2009

Singer and television personality Yasmine - whose albums include *Vandaag, Licht Ontvlambaar* and who after coming out in 1996 became an established icon for Dutch and Flemish LGBT youth - commits suicide at age 37 in Kontich, Belgium.

———————————◯———————————

June 26, 1890

Stage and early film actress Jeanne Eagles (*The Letter, Jealousy, Man Woman and Sin*), who in 1929 became the first actor to receive a posthumous Oscar nomination, is born in Kansas City. MO.

June 26, 1902

Hugues Cuenod, a tenor in opera, operetta, and traditional musical theater – who made his debut at the Metropolitan Opera at the age of 84 – is born in Corseaux-sur-Vevey, Switzerland.

June 26, 1951

Writer and performer Lance Loud - known primarily for his appearance on the 1973 PBS reality series *An American Family* in which he came out as a gay man - is born in La Jolla, CA.

June 26, 1964

LIFE Magazine publishes the 14 page article *Homosexuality in America.*

June 26, 1989

The first issue of *OutWeek Magazine* – a gay and lesbian activist periodical out of New York best remembered for sparking the debate about the use of 'outing' as a weapon against those perceived to be enemies of LGBT people or inhibitors of the LGBT cause – is published. It will continue to operate until June 1991.

June 26, 2003

Ruling in the case of Lawrence v. Texas, the U.S. Supreme Court declares all state sodomy laws unconstitutional, overturning the precedent it had establish 17 years earlier in Bowers v. Hardwick.

June 26, 2013

In a 5-4 vote the Supreme Court rules that the Defense of Marriage Act (DOMA) - the law which banned the U.S. federal government from recognizing same-sex marriages, legalized by various states, and thereby denying same-sex spouses benefits available to married heterosexual couples - is declared unconstitutional.

June 26, 2015

The Supreme Court finally and officially declares same-sex marriage a Constitutional right nationwide, meaning all states must allow Americans to get married, regardless of their gender or sexual orientation.

June 27, 1985

Before Stonewall, Greta Schiller's documentary about LGBT life prior to the Stonewall riots, is released.

June 27, 2001

Writer, cartoonist, comic strip author, and illustrator Tove Jansson (*The Moomins, Moominland Midwinter, The Summer Book, Sun City*) dies at age 86 in Helsinki, Finland.

June 27, 2014

In a formal ribbon cutting ceremony, the 100 block of Turk Street in San Francisco is renamed Vicki Mar Lane after community elder, drag performer extraordinaire, and activist Vicki Marlane who died in 2011.

June 27, 2017

Washington DC residents are allowed to choose a gender-neutral option on their driver's licenses and ID cards, making DC residents the first US citizens with the option to choose a gender other than M/F on driver's licenses and identification cards.

June 28, 1929

Philosopher, author, activist, and pioneering socialist Edward Carpenter (*The Intermediate Sex, Intermediate Types Among Primitive Folk, Civilization: Its Cause and Cure*) – the only English writer before World War I to publicly defend the homosexual's rightful place in society – dies in England at the age of 84 after suffering a stroke.

June 28, 1935

Actor John Inman - best known for his role as Mr. Humphries on the British sitcom *Are You Being Served?* and who was named BBC TV personality of the year in 1975 - is born in Preston, Lancashire, England.

June 28, 1969

In the early morning hours, approximately 3 a.m., rioting begins outside the Stonewall Inn in the Greenwich Village neighborhood of New York City during a routine gay bar raid. The riots become a key turning point the modern gay rights movement.

June 28, 1970

The first Gay Pride marches take place in New York, Chicago, and Los Angeles to commemorate the anniversary of the Stonewall Riots. In New York City it is called the Christopher Street Liberation Day Parade.

June 28, 2003

Screenwriter and crime fiction novelist George Baxt - best known for creating the gay black detective Pharaoh Love in a series of five books (*A Queer Kind of Death, Swing Low Sweet Harriet, A Queer Kind of Love,* etc.) as well as a series of 13 celebrity murder novels (*The Tallulah Bankhead Murder Case, The Dorothy Parker Murder Case*, etc.) - dies at age 80 in New York City.

June 28, 2005

Activist Brenda Howard, known as the Mother of Pride for her work in coordinating the Christopher Street Liberation Day March and rally on the first anniversary of the Stonewall Riots, dies of cancer at age 58 in New York City.

June 28, 2012

Psychiatrist, psychoanalyst and author Richard Isay – a pioneer in changing the way analysts viewed gay people and the author of *Being Homosexual, Commitment and Healing*, and *Becoming Gay* – dies of cancer at age 77 in New York City.

June 29, 1892

Activist Henry Gerber - founder of the Society for Human Rights, the first recognized gay rights organization in the U.S. which also published the first American publication for homosexuals, *Friendship and Freedom* - is born in Bavaria, Germany.

June 29, 1994

Writer, poet, performance artist, dancer, and activist Assotto Saint (*The Road Before Us, Spells of a Voodoo Doll*) - who also founded the Metamorphosis Theater and the art techno band Xotica - dies of an AIDS-related illness.

June 29, 1999

Allan Carr - producer of such films as *Grease, Can't Stop the Music* and *Where the Boys Are '84* and the stage musical *La*

Cage aux Folles (for which he won a Tony Award) - dies of liver cancer at age 62 in Beverly Hills, CA.

June 29, 2017

Leatherman, photographer, entrepreneur, and activist Chuck Renslow (The Gold Coast, Kris Studio, International Mr. Leather, The Leather Archives and Museum) dies of heart failure at age 87 in Chicago, IL.

———————————◯———————————

June 30, 1923

Gad Beck - the last known gay Jewish survivor of the Holocaust and Lambda Literary Award nominee for *An Underground Life: Memoirs of a Gay Jew in Nazi Berlin* - is born in Berlin, Germany.

June 30, 1984

The Unitarian Church votes to approve ceremonies that unite same-sex couples.

June 30, 2005

The new gay-oriented programming cable network, Logo, is launched by MTV.

June 30, 2016

The Secretary of Defense announces that the Pentagon is lifting the ban on open trans people serving in the military.

JULY

July 2015

The issue of *Vanity Fair* magazine featuring trans celebrity Caitlyn Jenner, photographed in her Malibu home by Annie Liebovitz. The issue introduced Jenner with the cover headline, "Call me Caitlyn."

July 1, 1804

Novelist, feminist writer, and bohemian memoirist George Sand, the pen name of Amandine/Amantine Aurore Lucile Dudevant (*Indiana, Consuelo, Mauprat, Marianne, Valentine*) - best known for her rustic novels of love and class - is born in Paris, France.

July 1, 1899

Actor Charles Laughton (*Mutiny on the Bounty, Witness for the Prosecution, Spartacus, The Night of the Hunter*) - who was nominated for three Oscars and won once for *The Private Life of Henry VIII* (1933) - is born in Yorkshire, England.

July 1, 1925

Actor Farley Granger (*Strangers on a Train, Rope, Hans Christian Anderson, One Life to Live*) - who also wrote the 2007 memoir *Include Me Out: My Life from Goldwyn to Broadway* - is born in San Jose, CA.

July 1, 1933

Choreographer, muralist, and prolific erotic artist Dom
Orejudos aka Etienne aka Stephen (*The Tin Soldier*,
Metamorphosis of the Owls, *The Gold Coast* murals and
International Mr. Leather contest posters) - whose ballet *The
Charioteer* inaugurated color broadcast on WTTW in Chicago
- is born in Chicago, IL.

July 1, 1943

Willem Arondeus – artist, writer, and member of the Dutch
Resistance during WWII – is executed at age 48 in Haarlem,
The Netherlands, for blowing up the Nazi's registration
building. He instructs his attorney to declare his homosexuality
after his death so the public would know that gays are not
cowards.

July 1, 1962

Alan L. Hart - the transgender novelist, physician, and medical
researcher who championed the radiological diagnosis of
tuberculosis decades before epidemiological testing becomes
available, saving thousands of lives – dies of heart failure at
age 71.

July 1, 2005

Singer, songwriter, record producer Luther Vandross (*Here and
Now*, *A House is Not a Home*, *Never Too Much*) - who won
eight Grammy Awards and had every one of his 14 albums go
either platinum or multi-platinum - dies at age 54 of a heart
attack in Edison, N.J.

---○---

July 2, 1902

Harlem Renaissance era writer and painter Richard Bruce Nugent – whose short story *Smoke, Lillies and Jade* is regarded by many to be the first publication by an African-American author to openly depict homosexuality – is born in Washington, DC.

July 2, 1920

Lambda Literary Award winning novelist and memoirist Donald Windham (*Lost Friendships*, *The Dog Star*, *The Hero Continues*, *Tanaquil*, *Two People*) - an intimate friend of Tennessee Williams, Lincoln Kirstein, Paul Cadmus, and Truman Capote - is born in Atlanta, GA.

July 2, 1934

The Motion Picture Production Code aka The Hays Code, a list of guidelines adopted by major studios to ensure "decency" in movies (which had been in effect since 1930) is given the power to enforce those guidelines by the MPPDA (Motion Picture Producers and Distributors of America). One of the guidelines strongly discourages any and all depiction of homosexuality.

July 2, 1951

Early transgender activist Sylvia Rivera - who was a member of the Gay Activists Alliance and the Gay Liberation Front but who was outspoken about the place transgender people had in the early gay rights movement and who later helped found S.T.A.R. (Street Transgender Action Revolutionaries) with Marsha P. Johnson - is born in New York City.

July 2, 1966

Billie Jean King wins her first Women's Singles title at Wimbledon. King won her first Doubles trophy there in 1962 and in her career won a total of 20 Wimbledon titles.

July 2, 1987

Innovative musical theater director and choreographer Michael Bennett (*Follies*, *A Chorus Line*, *Dreamgirls*, *Ballroom*) - who received Tony nominations for every musical he was associated with and won a total of eight awards - dies at age 44 from an AIDS-related illness in Tucson, AZ.

July 2, 2012

Journalist, news correspondent, CNN anchor, and media personality Anderson Cooper officially and publicly comes out as gay in a statement which says, "The fact is, I'm gay..." He cites the importance of LGBT visibility as a factor in his choosing to do so.

―――――――――○―――――――――

July 3, 1901

Sculptress and artist Thelma Wood - who enjoyed the bohemian lifestyle in Europe and whose lovers included Berenice Abbott and Djuna Barnes - is born in Kansas.

July 3, 1981

The New York Times first reports that physicians in New York and California have tracked 41 cases of a rare and often rapidly fatal cancer in otherwise healthy gay men – eight of whom passed within two years of diagnosis. The syndrome would soon be referred to as GRID (Gay-Related Immune Disorder).

———————————○———————————

July 4, 1844

Professional sculptor Edmonia Lewis, who became the first woman of African-American and Native American heritage to achieve international fame and recognition in the fine arts world, is born in Greenbush, NY. Her pieces include *The Old Arrow Maker, Forever Free, The Death of Cleopatra*, and *Hiawatha*.

July 4, 1855

Gay poet Walt Whitman publishes *Leaves of Grass* which is destined to become a classic of American literature.

July 4 ,1947

Songwriter and music executive Jacques Morali – a pioneer in the French disco sound and the creator of the group The Village People who wrote many of their hits (*Macho Man, YMCA, In The Navy*) as well as those for The Ritchie Family (*Best Disco in Town*) – is born in France.

July 4, 1965-1969

Early homophile organizations such as the Mattachine Society and Daughters of Bilitis hold annual picket protests in front of Independence Hall on Philadelphia, PA. to remind the American people that gays and lesbians have no basic civil rights protections. Participants include gay and lesbian rights activists Frank Kameny, Barbara Gittings, Craig Rodwell, Kay Tobin Lahusen, Lilli Vincenz, and Jack Nichols. Kameny famously insisted on a dress code for participants – jackets and ties for the men and dresses for the women – to convey the group's respectability.

July 4, 2008

Science fiction author, critic, and poet Thomas M. Disch (*The Dreams Our Stuff is Made Of, 334, The Genocides, On Wings of Song, The Word of God, Camp Concentration*) - who was nominated for several Hugo and Nebula awards for his fantasy/speculative fiction writing and won a Hugo Award for his non-fiction writing - commits suicide at age 68 in New York City. Disch was also the author of the popular children's book *The Brave Little Toaster: A Bedtime Story for Small Appliances*.

July 5, 1889

Multi-talented writer, designer, artist, and filmmaker Jean Cocteau (*Orpheus, Beauty and the Beast, Les Enfants Terribles*) - who won France's film award the Prix Louis Delluc - is born in Maisons-Laffitte, France.

July 5, 1904

Historian, writer, and scholar Harold Acton (*The Villas of Tuscany*, *The Last Medici*, *The Bourbons of Naples*) - and an inspiration for Evelyn Waugh's classic novel *Brideshead Revisited* - is born in Florence, Italy.

July 5, 1942

William B. Kelley, longtime gay activist and lawyer who was an important figure in the early LGBT rights movement, is born near Kennett, MO.

July 5, 2007

Actor Kerwin Mathews (*The 7th Voyage of Sinbad, Maniac, The 3 Worlds of Gulliver, Jack the Giant Killer, The Devil at 4 O'clock*) - popular in several swashbuckling and action films of the 1950s and early 1960s - dies of a heart attack at age 81 in San Francisco, CA. He is survived by his partner of 46 years Tom Nicoll.

July 5, 2011

Artist Cy Twombly (*Leaving Paphos Ringed With Waves, Lepanto, Scent of Madness*) - primarily known for his large, scribbled, and graffiti-like paintings - dies of cancer at age 83 in Rome, Italy.

July 5, 2011

Drag legend and performer extraordinaire, community activist, and icon Vicki Marlane dies of an AIDS related illness at age 76 in San Francisco, CA.

―――――――――――○―――――――――――

July 6, 1907

Iconic self-taught surrealist painter Frida Kahlo (*Self-Portrait With Thorn Necklace, Self-Portrait with Cropped Hair, Frieda and Diego Rivera*) is born in Coyoacan, Mexico.

July 6, 1941

Author Michael Grumley (*After Midnight, Hard Corps: Studies in Leather and Sadomasochism, Life Drawing*) - a founding member of the gay men's writing group the The Violet Quill which included Edmund White, Felice Picano, Andrew Holleran, and Grumley's partner, Robert Ferro - is born in Davenport, IA.

July 6, 1943

Vietnam Air Force Sgt. Leonard Matlovich – the first gay service member to purposely out himself in order to challenge the military's ban on gays serving openly – is born in Savannah, GA. Matlovich, recipient of a Purple Heart and a Bronze Star, was a veteran of three tours in Vietnam.

July 6, 1992

The body of transgender activist Marsha P. Johnson is found floating in the Hudson River in New York City. She was 48. Johnson was a participant in the Stonewall riots, a popular member of New York's gay art scene, and instrumental in founding the organization S.T.A.R. (Street Transvestite Action Revolutionaries).

July 6, 1999

U.S. Army Private Barry Winchell becomes a focal point of the Don't Ask, Don't Tell debate when he is brutally murdered at age 21 by a fellow soldier in Fort Campbell, Kentucky.

July 7, 1899

Film director George Cukor (*The Women*, *My Fair Lady*, *Gaslight*, *The Philadelphia Story*, *A Star is Born*) - who was nominated for five Oscars and won once - is born in New York City.

July 7, 1978

Martina Navratilova wins her first Women's Singles title at Wimbledon, her first of 9 Singles trophies. In her career, she won a total of 20 Wimbledon titles in singles, doubles, and mixed doubles categories.

July 7, 1990

Best selling Brazilian rock singer and composer Cazuza - who gained fame as the lead singer of the group Barao Vermelho and later recorded solo - dies of AIDS-related lung cancer at age 32 in Rio de Janeiro, Brazil.

July 7, 2012

Barry Frank marries long-time partner, James Ready, becoming the first member of Congress to marry someone of the same sex while in office.

───────────────○───────────────

July 8, 1906

Architect Philip Johnson – who would establish the Department of Architecture and Design at the New York Museum of Modern Art in 1930, and who is celebrated for championing both the International and Post-Modern styles of architecture – is born in Cleveland, OH.

July 8, 1933

Peter Orlovsky, actor, poet (*Leper's Cry, Clean Asshole Poems and Smiling Vegetable Songs, Straight Hearts Delight*) – and partner of Allen Ginsberg – is born in New York City.

July 8, 1979

Robert Opel – photographer and owner of Fey-Way Studios art gallery is slain at age 39 in his San Francisco shop. Opel's greatest fame came when he streaked behind presenters David Niven and Elizabeth Taylor at the 46th Annual Academy Awards in 1974.

July 8, 1980

The National Democratic Party's rules committee announces that it will no longer discriminate against homosexuals. The following month it becomes the first major political party in the U.S. to endorse a gay rights plank in the party platform that will be adopted at their National Convention.

July 8, 1994

Actor Dick Sargent *(Operation Petticoat, The Ghost and Mr. Chicken)* - and best known as the second Darrin Stephens on

Bewitched - dies at age 64 of prostate cancer in Los Angeles, CA.

July 8, 2018

Heartthrob, actor, and singer Tab Hunter (*The Girl He Left Behind, Damn Yankees, Polyester, Lust in the Dust*) dies of cardiac arrest at age 86 in Santa Barbara, CA.

———————————————⊖———————————————

July 9, 1893

Journalist and radio personality Dorothy Thompson (*On the Record, I Saw Hitler, Let the Record Speak*) - once the second most influential woman in the U.S. behind First Lady Eleanor Roosevelt - is born in Lancaster, N.Y.

July 9, 1933

Neurologist, naturalist. historian, and author Oliver Sacks (*The Man Who Mistook His Wife for a Hat, Awakenings, Musicophilia, The Mind's Eye, An Anthropologist on Mars*) is born in London.

July 9, 1936

Writer, poet, playwright, and activist June Jordan (*Some of Us Did Not Die, Directed By Desire: The Collected Poems of June Jordan*) author of the *American Poetry Review* column "The Black Poet Speaks of Poetry" and regular columnist for the *Progressive* - is born in New York City.

July 9, 1987

Activist, poet, writer, and journalist Michiyo Fukaya (*Lesbian Lyrics, A Fire is Burning It is in Me: The Life and Writings of Michiyo Fukaya*) - commits suicide. As the representative of the Lesbian and Gay Asian Collective which formed during the First National Third World Lesbian and Gay Conference during the 1979 March on Washington - Fukaya gave the eloquent speech "Living in Asia America: An Asian American Lesbian's Address Before the Washington Monument."

July 10, 138 A.D.

Hadrian – the Roman emperor best known for rebuilding the Pantheon as well as constructing Hadrian's Wall to mark to northern limit of Roman Britain – dies at age 62 in Baiae, Italy.

July 10, 1871

Writer Marcel Proust - whose *Remembrance of Things Past* was published in seven parts between 1913-1927 and is considered a masterpiece of literature - is born in Auteuil, France.

July 10, 1927

Artist Louise Abbema (*Flora*, *The Seasons*, *Sarah Bernhardt*, *A Game of Croquet*) – commonly associated with the Belle Epoque – dies at age 73 in Paris, France.

July 10, 2014

Laverne Cox becomes the first transgender person nominated

for an Emmy Award (Outstanding Guest Actress In a Comedy Series) for her role as Sophia Burset in the Netflix series *Orange is the New Black.*

July 11, 1895

Witty socialite Dorothy "Dolly" Wilde - niece of Oscar Wilde and a lover of Natalie Clifford Barney who also had an affair with Alla Nazimova - is born in London, England.

July 11, 1931

Heartthrob, actor, and singer Tab Hunter (*The Girl He Left Behind, Damn Yankees, Polyester, Lust in the Dust*) is born in Manhattan.

July 11, 1946

Stonewall Award winning activist, author, and film aficionado Vito Russo (*The Celluloid Closet*) is born in New York City. Russo was one of the earliest activists to study the impact of the media and entertainment industry representation of gays and lesbians. He also organized queer cinema screenings for the Gay Activists Alliance and later was a founding member of the Gay and Lesbian Alliance Against Defamation (GLAAD).

July 11, 1973

Bestselling writer Nobuko Yoshiya (*Flower Tales, Two Virgins in the Attic, To the Ends of the Earth*) - an out lesbian in Japan in the 1920s who also began her own magazine *Black Rose* - dies of colon cancer at age 77 in Kamakura, Japan.

July 11, 1987

Dr. Tom Waddell dies of an AIDS-related illness at age 49 in San Francisco, CA. A former Olympic decathlete (1968), Waddell was also the founder of The Gay Olympics (later the Gay Games) in San Francisco in 1982. In 1976, Waddell and then lover Charles Deaton, became the first homosexual couple to appear in the "Couples" section of *People Magazine*.

July 11, 1988

Lambda Literary Award nominee Robert Ferro (*The Family of Max Desir*, *The Blue Star*, *Second Son*) - a member of the gay men's writing group The Violet Quill which included Edmund White, Andrew Holleran, and Felice Picano - dies of an AIDS-related illness at age 46 in Ho-Ho-Kus, N.J.

July 11, 1989

Noted film actor Sir Laurence Olivier (*Rebecca, The Entertainer, Wuthering Heights, Spartacus, Marathon Man, Hamlet, Sleuth*) dies of renal failure at age 82 in West Sussex, England.

July 11, 1991

Writer Gale Wilhelm - whose novels included the early lesbian themed romances *We Too Are Drifting* (1935) and *Torchlight to Valhalla* (1938) - dies of cancer at age 83.

July 11, 2014

Chris Mosier becomes the first openly transgender man inducted into the National Gay and Lesbian Sports Hall of Fame.

―――――――――――○―――――――――――

July 12, 1864

Scientist, botanist, agricultural chemist, and inventor George Washington Carver - who was committed to the improvement of farming and is credited with, among other things, the concept of crop rotation - is born into slavery in Diamond Grove, MO.

July 12, 1934

Pianist Val Cliburn – who won the first quadrennial International Tchaikovsky Piano Competition in Moscow – is born in Shreveport, LA.

July 12, 1945

Painter Russell Cheney (*Kittery Point*, *Portrait of Howard Lathrop*) - a master at capturing New England life and landscapes - dies of a heart attack at age 64 in Kittery, ME.

July 12, 1950

Acclaimed interior decorator (and former actress) Elsie de Wolfe aka Lady Mendl (*Elsie de Wolfe's Recipes for Successful Dining*, *After All*, *The House in Good Taste*) dies at age 84 in Versailles, France.

―――――――――――○―――――――――――

July 13, 1935

Writer and feminist theorist Monique Wittig (*Les Guerilleres*, *The Straight Mind and Other Essays*, *The Lesbian Body*) is born in Dannemarie in Haut-Rhin, France.

July 13, 1945

Stage and silent film actress and producer Alla Nazimova (*Salome*, *Camille*, *Blood and Sand*, *The Red Lantern*) – a central figure in Hollywood's early lesbian scene, whose grand home, The Garden of Allah was a hotspot for Hollywood's elite, and who was also the godmother of former First Lady Nancy Reagan – dies of a coronary thrombosis at age 66 in Los Angeles, CA.

July 13, 1954

Iconic self-taught surrealist painter Frida Kahlo (*Self-Portrait With Thorn Necklace*, *Self-Portrait with Cropped Hair*, *Frieda and Diego Rivera*) dies of a pulmonary embolism at age 47 in Coyoacan, Mexico.

July 13, 1954

Actress and comedian Danitra Vance (*Saturday Night Live*, *Little Man Tate*, *Limit Up*) - recipient of an NAACP Image Award and winner of an Obie Award (for Off-Broadway work) - is born in Chicago, IL.

July 13, 1970

Roger Edens film producer and composer (*Easter Parade*, *Good News*, *Annie Get Your Gun*, *For Me and My Gal*, *Babes in Arms*, *Strike Up the Band*, *On the Town*) - who won three Oscars for his musical film scores - dies of cancer at age 64 in Los Angeles, CA.

July 13, 1987

Poet and writer Robert Francis (*Stand Here With Me*, *The Orb*

Weaver, We Fly Away, The Trouble with Francis) - who was recognized for his work by the Academy of American Poets - dies at age 85 in Southampton, N.Y.

July 14

International Non-Binary People's Day, an annual day celebrating the contributions of non-binary people and focusing on the issues affecting them, is celebrated.

July 14, 1895

19th century progenitor of the modern gay rights movement, Karl Ulrichs (*Research on the Riddle of Man-Manly Love*) – one of the first to proclaim that Uranians (aka lesbians and gay men) are natural and not diseased, criminals, or sinful – dies at age 69 in L'Aquila, Italy.

July 14, 1917

Playwright, stage director, and screenwriter Arthur Laurents (*West Side Story, Gypsy, Rope, The Way We Were*) - winner of two Tony Awards and nominated for two Oscars - is born in Brooklyn, N.Y.

July 14, 1926

Comic, actor, and one of the 20th century's foremost female impersonators, Charles Pierce – who did impressions of screen divas and actresses from Joan Crawford to Bette Davis to Carol Channing – is born in Watertown, N.Y.

July 14, 1954

Playwright Jacinto Benavente (*The Governor's Wife*, *Bonds of Interest*, *The Lady of the House*) - a Nobel Prize winner in literature - dies at age 87 in Madrid, Spain.

July 14, 2014

Singer, songwriter, musician, writer Vange Leonel (*Esse Mundo, Noite Preta, Madame Oraculo*) dies of ovarian cancer at age 51 in Sao Paulo, Brazil.

July 15, 1997

Fashion designer Gianni Versace - who built an $800 million dollar empire in a decade - is murdered at age 50 outside his home in Miami Beach, FL.

July 15, 2003

The TV series *Queer Eye for the Straight Guy* debuts on Bravo to become the network's most popular program and establishing the genre of Gay Reality TV. The series won the Emmy for Outstanding Reality TV series in 2004.

July 16, 1943

Writer Reinaldo Arenas *(Before Night Falls, Old Rosa, Farewell to the Sea)* - who supported and later rebelled against Fidel Castro's Cuban government before fleeing to the U.S. - is born in Oriente, Cuba.

July 16, 1995

Poet, essayist, educator, and novelist Sir Stephen Spender (*World Within World, The Temple, Vienna, Selected Poems*) - whose work centered on social issues and the class struggle and who was the only non-U.S. citizen (to date) to serve as U.S. Poet Laureate - dies of heart failure at age 86 in London, England.

July 16, 1995

Novelist and poet May Sarton (*Mrs. Stevens Hears the Mermaids Singing, As We Are Now, Journal of a Solitude)* - well-known for her published journals - dies of breast cancer at age 83 in York, ME.

July 16, 1997

Seven time Oscar-nominated film editor William H. Reynolds - who won the award for *The Sound of Music* and *The Sting* but also edited such classics as *The Day The Earth Stood Still, Hello, Dolly!, Fanny, The Turning Point, Three Coins in the Fountain, Love is a Many Splendid Thing, The Godfather, The Sand Pebbles*, and *The Great White Hope* - dies of cancer at age 87 in South Pasadena, CA.

July 17, 1898

Photographer Berenice Abbott (*Nightview, New York, Hardware Store on the Bowery, Flatiron Building, Under the El at the Battery, James Joyce)* - who after living in bohemian Paris during the 1920s, became a frequent documenter of the life and landscape of New York City - is born in Springfield, OH.

July 17, 1914

Writer James Purdy (*On Glory's Course, Malcolm, Eustice Chisholm and the Works, Narrow Rooms, Jeremy's Version*) - who was nominated for the National Book Award as well as the Pen/Faulkner Award for Fiction - is born in Hicksville, OH.

July 17, 1945

Ethyl Eichelberger, drag performer. playwright, actor, and outrageous presence in New York's theatrical scene, is born in Pekin, IL. Eichelberger became a popular figure in experimental theater and was best known for his writing, appearing in over 40 plays, and his solo works of impersonations of 'Grand Dames' of history including, Nefertiti, Lucrezia Borgia, Clytemnestra, Medea, Jocasta, etc.

July 17, 2005

Oscar nominated screenwriter, novelist, and biographer Gavin Lambert (*Inside Daisy Clover, Sons and Lovers, Nazimova, On Cukor, Natalie Wood*) - who is best known for chronicling life in Hollywood - dies of pulmonary fibrosis at age 80 in Los Angeles, CA.

July 18, 1899

Author Horatio Alger Jr., best known for his juvenile rags-to-riches novels (*Ragged Dick, The Young Bank Messenger, Paul the Peddler, The Life of Edwin Forrest*) dies at age 67 in Natick, MA.

July 18, 1950

Glenn M. Hughes, "the biker" in the musical group The Village People (*YMCA, In the Navy, Go West*) is born in New York City.

July 18, 1983

Representative Gerry Studds (Democrat from Massachusetts) becomes the first openly gay member of Congress after he comes out on the floor of the House after a former page revealed the two had a homosexual relationship a decade earlier.

July 18, 1996

Student and bisexual activist Stephen Donaldson aka Robert Anthony Martin Jr. (founder of the Student Homophile League in 1965 – now known as the Columbia Queer Alliance) dies of an AIDS-related illness at age 49.

––––––––––––––––⊙––––––––––––––––

July 19, 1875

Activist, journalist, and poet Alice Dunbar Nelson (*Violets and Other Tales, Give Us Each Day*) – a prominent figure in the Harlem Renaissance – is born in New Orleans, LA.

July 19, 1923

Mystery writer Joseph Hansen (*The Man Everybody Was Afraid Of, Skinflick, The Boy Who Was Buried This Morning, A Country of Old Men: The Last Dave Brandstetter Mystery*) is born in Aberdeen, S.D.

July 19, 1943

NFL pro-football player Jerry Smith – star receiver and record-holding tight end for the Washington Redskins 1965-1977 - the first prominent U.S. athlete to announce he was suffering from AIDS – is born in Eugene, OR.

July 20/21 356 BC

Alexander III of Macedonia, better known as Alexander the Great – who, by age 30 had created one of the largest empires in the ancient world and was undefeated in battle – is born in Pella, capital of Macedonia.

July 20, 1948

Poet, fiction writer, and educator Manuel Ramos Otero (*The Story of the Woman and the Sea, La novelabingo*) - considered one of the most important openly gay Puerto Rican authors of the century and who also founded the short lived publishing house El Libro Viaje - is born in San Juan, Puerto Rico.

July 20, 1958

Actor Franklin Pangborn (*Hail the Conquering Hero, Now Voyager, International House*) - whose fussy mannerisms and delivery enlivened over 200 films and television shows - dies following cancer surgery at age 69 in Santa Monica, CA.

---○---

July 21, 1899

Poet Hart Crane (*The Bridge, White Buildings*) is born in Garrettsville, OH.

July 21, 2000

Tony DeBlase - one-time publisher of *Drummer* magazine, designer of the Leather flag, and co-founder of Chicago's Leather Archives and Museum with Chuck Renslow - dies of liver failure at age 57 in Portland, OR.

---○---

July 22, 1889

Unique and highly stylized film director James Whale (*Frankenstein, The Bride of Frankenstein, The Invisible Man, The Old Dark House*) is born in Dudley, England.

July 22, 1980

Activist Marty Mann, author (*Marty Mann's New Primer on Alcoholism, Marty Mann Answers Your Questions About Drinking and Alcoholism*), the first woman to publicly identify herself as a member of Alcoholics Anonymous, and the third woman to ever seek help from Alcoholics Anonymous, dies at age 75 following a stroke in Bridgeport, CT.

July 22, 1990

Author Manuel Puig (*Kiss of the Spider Woman, Betrayed By Rita Hayworth, Heartbreak Tango*) - whose work has been translated into over a dozen languages - dies of a heart attack following gallbladder surgery at age 57 in Cuernavaca, Mexico.

July 22, 1992

Painter, photographer, filmmaker, performance artist, writer and activist David Wojnarowicz (*Close to the Knives*) dies of an AIDS-related illness at age 37 in Manhattan, N.Y.

July 22, 2011

Pakistani-American poet and activist Ifti Nasim (*Myrmecophile, Narman, Selected Poems 1980-2000*) whose poetry was said to be the first direct statement of gay longings and desire to appear in the Urdu language dies of a heart attack in Chicago at age 64.

———————————○———————————

July 23, 1816

Stage actress Charlotte Cushman –acclaimed for playing both male and female roles interchangeably, and at one time acknowledged as the greatest living actress – is born in Boston, MA.

July 23, 1899

Businesswoman and activist Ruth Ellis (*Living With Pride: Ruth C. Ellis @ 100*) – who operated an African American social sanctuary known as The Gay Spot for 27 years out of her Detroit home – is born in Springfield, IL.

July 23, 1909

Writer/academic Samuel Steward (*Dear Sammy: Letters from Gertrude Stein and Alice B. Toklas, Parisian Lives*) aka tattoo artist Phil Sparrow aka erotic novelist Phil Andros (*The Greek Way, When in Rome*) is born in Woodsfield, OH.

July 23, 1966

Actor Montgomery Clift (*From Here to Eternity, A Place in the Sun, The Misfits, Raintree County, Red River, Suddenly, Last Summer*) - who was nominated for four Oscars - dies of a heart attack/coronary occlusion at age 45 in New York City.

July 23, 1924

Oscar nominated screenwriter, novelist, and biographer Gavin Lambert (*Inside Daisy Clover, Sons and Lovers, Nazimova, On Cukor, Natalie Wood*) - who is best known for chronicling life in Hollywood - is born in Sussex, England.

July 23, 1982

Artist and art dealer Betty Parsons, who championed the avant-garde and is known primarily for her work with and promotion of Abstract Expressionism, dies at age 82 from a stroke in New York City.

July 23, 1998

Sex researcher, psychiatrist and author Fritz Klein establishes the American Institute of Bisexuality to promote bisexual research and education.

July 23, 2009

One of the most successful African American authors of all time E. Lynn Harris (*Invisible Life, Just As I Am. And This Too Shall Pass*) – the Lambda Literary Award winning writer who had ten books on *The New York Times* bestseller list and was one of the first to write about men on the "down-low" – dies of a heart ailment at age 54 in Los Angeles, CA.

July 23, 2012

Physicist, educator, and astronaut Sally Ride - a member of NASA's class of 1978 (the first to include women) - who in 1983 became the first woman to enter into low Earth orbit - dies of pancreatic cancer at age 61 in La Jolla, CA. Among her many honors and awards, Ride received the NASA Space Flight Medal twice, was inducted into The Aviation Hall of Fame, The National Women's Hall of Fame, and was posthumously awarded The General James E. Hill Lifetime Space Achievement Award.

July 23, 2015

The Equality Act is introduced in Congress that would make LGBTQ individuals a protected class and grant them basic legal protections in areas of life including education, housing, employment, credit, and more.

―――――――⊖―――――――

July 24, 1989

Photographer and performance artist Mark Morrisoe (*Mark Morrisoe: My Life, Mark Morrisoe*) - who often colored and wrote on his Polaroid snapshots, utilized varied photographic mediums, and experimented with Super 8 film stills in his art as well - dies of an AIDS-related illness at age 30 in Jersey City, NJ.

―――――――⊖―――――――

July 25, 1865

Transgender military surgeon and advocate for improved

hospital conditions, Dr. James Miranda Barry dies from dysentery in London, England.

July 25, 1951

Illustrator J.C. Leyendecker – who popularized The Arrow Collar Man, created the popular imagery of Baby New Year and Mrs. Santa Claus, and did numerous covers for *The Saturday Evening Post* – dies of an acute coronary occlusion at age 77 in New Rochelle, New York.

July 25, 1966

Poet Frank O'Hara (*Lunch Poems*, *Love Poems*, *The Selected Poems of Frank O'Hara*) - who worked at the Museum of Modern Art, was a member of the New York School of poets, and was the posthumous winner of the National Book Award for Poetry - is struck and killed at age 40 on a Fire Island beach by a dune buggy.

July 25, 1983

San Francisco General Hospital opens the first AIDS ward in the U.S. and is fully occupied within days.

July 25, 1985

The publicist of actor Rock Hudson issues a press release announcing that the actor has AIDS. The news marks a watershed moment in AIDS coverage by the general media.

July 25, 1989

TV and film director/producer Arthur Lubin (*Buck Privates, Francis, Hold That Ghost, The Incredible Mr. Limpet*) - and creator of the television sitcom *Mr. Ed* - is born in Los Angeles, CA.

July 25, 2003

Film director John Schlesinger (*Darling, Sunday Bloody Sunday, Yanks, Marathon Man*) - who won an Academy Award for his direction of *Midnight Cowboy* - dies at age 77 in Palm Springs, CA.

———————————————○———————————————

July 26, 1994

W. Dorr Legg – co-founder of both the early homophile organization ONE Inc., and the 1950s interracial homophile social club Knights of the Clock – dies at age 89 of natural causes in Los Angeles, CA.

July 26, 2009

Dancer and contemporary choreographer Merce Cunningham *(Ocean, Biped, Rainforest, Second Hand)* - winner of numerous awards and honors such as being named a "Living Legend" by the Library of Congress - dies at age 90 in New York City.

July 26, 2016

TV personality and pay-per-call psychic Miss Cleo (Youree Dell Harris) dies of colon cancer at age 53 in Palm Beach County, FL.

July 26, 2018

With the opening of *Head Over Heels*, Peppermint becomes the first ever trans person to originate a principle role on Broadway.

―――――――――○―――――――――

July 27, 774 AD

Monk, artist, and scholar Kukai – founder of the Shingon or "True Word" school of Buddhism – is born in Zentsuji, Japan.

July 27, 1919

Activist Martin Block is born in New York City. He was the first chairman of ONE Inc., which he co-founded with William Dale Jennings and Antonio Sanchez (aka Don Slater), and also served as the first editor of *ONE Magazine*.

July 27, 1946

Writer Gertrude Stein (*Tender Buttons*, *The Autobiography of Alice B. Toklas*, *Three Lives*) – a U.S. expatriate in Paris known for her salon as well as her literary and artistic influence – dies of stomach cancer in Paris, France.

July 27, 1946

Student and bisexual activist Stephen Donaldson aka Robert Anthony Martin Jr. (founder of the Student Homophile League in 1965 – now known as the Columbia Queer Alliance) is born in Utica, N.Y.

July 27, 1967

England and Wales decriminalize homosexual acts between consenting adults over the age of 21.

July 27, 1979

Politician, feminist, and activist Marielle Franco (Socialism and Liberty Party/PSOL) is born in Rio de Janeiro, Brazil.

July 27, 1982

The term AIDS (Acquired Immune Deficiency Syndrome) is first officially proposed, eventually replacing the previous terms GRID (Gay Related Immune Deficiency) or simply The Gay Plague.

July 27, 2015

The Boy Scouts of America announces that the national executive board of the organization has ratified a resolution removing the national restriction on openly gay leaders and employees."

―――――――――――――○―――――――――――――

July 28, 1929

Writer Henry Blake Fuller (*With the Procession*, *Bertram Cope's Year*) - a pioneer in the realist style of writing - dies of heart disease at age 72 in Chicago, IL.

July 28, 1941

Director and screenwriter Colin Higgins (*Harold and Maude*,

9 to 5, Foul Play, Silver Streak) is born in Noumea, New Caledonia.

July 28, 1969

Actress, performer, and activist Alexis Arquette (*Pulp Fiction, The Wedding Singer, Bridge of Chucky*) is born in Los Angeles, CA.

July 28, 1985

The first AIDS Walk is held in Los Angeles, CA. The fundraiser is organized by AIDS Project Los Angeles.

July 29, 1905

Dag Hammarskjöld – Nobel Peace Prize winning diplomat and Secretary General of the United Nations (1953-1961) credited with coining the term "planned economy" – is born in Jonkoping, Sweden.

July 29, 1930

Modern dancer and choreographer Paul Taylor (*Three Epitaphs, Esplande and Runes, The Book of Beasts*) is born in Wilkinsburg, PA.

July 29, 1977

Actor David Lochary (*Female Trouble, Mondo Trasho, Pink Flamingos*) - associated with the early films of John Waters - dies of a PCP overdose at age 32 in New York City.

July 30, 1904

Poet, playwright, writer, translator Salvador Novo (*Our Land, Short History of Coyoacan, Mexico City in 1867*) - who was also a chronicler of politics, history, culture and social life in Mexico City - is born in Mexico City.

July 30, 1969

The U.S. film *Midnight Cowboy* by John Schlesinger – which eventually would go on to win Oscars for Best Picture, Director and Adapted Screenplay – is released in theaters to great commercial success in spite of its "Adults Only" X-Rating.

July 30, 1981

The New York Daily News runs an article on top tennis star Martina Navratilova who comes out as a lesbian.

July 31, 1932

Key early gay and lesbian rights activist Barbara Gittings is born in Vienna, Austria. Gittings organized the New York chapter of the Daughters of Bilitis, was editor of the DOB's magazine *The Ladder*, co-founded the National Gay Task Force, and helped form the first gay caucus within an organization (with the American Library Association) which helped promote positive gay and lesbian literature. Gittings was also a major influence in having homosexuality removed from the American Psychiatric Association's list of mental illnesses.

July 31, 2003

Pope John Paul II approves a 12 page set of guidelines issued by the Vatican that warns politicians that it is immoral to support same-sex unions.

July 31, 2012

Novelist, essayist, playwright, and politico Gore Vidal (*The City and the Pillar*, *Myra Breckinridge*, *Burr*, *Palimpsest*, *Lincoln*) - who won a National Book Award, National Book Critics Circle Award, was a candidate for both the U.S. House and Senate, and co-founder of the U.S. Peace Party with Dr. Benjamin Spock - dies from pneumonia complications at age 86 in Hollywood Hills, CA.

AUGUST

August 1966

Three years before Stonewall, transgender patrons at Compton's Cafeteria in the Tenderloin district of San Francisco begin to riot when a policeman's attempt to arrest one of them is met with coffee thrown in his face. The fighting spills into the streets and is followed by picketing the following day. The protests eventually lead to the creation of the National Transsexual Counseling Unit in 1968.

August 1981

The foundation of the Gay Men's Health Crisis (GMHC) - a not-for-profit community based organization - is formed when 80 men meet in Larry Kramer's New York apartment after the Center for Disease Control (CDC) begins reporting the emergence of a rare cancer (Kaposi's sarcoma) among gay men.

───────────────○───────────────

August 1, 1936

Designer Yves Saint Laurent - whose collections revolutionized the world of fashion and who was the first living fashion designer to be given a solo exhibition at the Metropolitan Museum of Art - is born in Oran, Algeria.

August 1, 1949

BAFTA Award winning director/producer Nigel Finch (*Stonewall, Arena: Did You Miss Me?, The Lost Language of Cranes, Kenneth Anger, The Errand*) is born in Tenterden, England.

August 1, 1957

Actor Taylor Negron (*The Last Boy Scout, Angels in the Outfield, Vamps, Fast Times at Ridgemont High*) is born in Glendale, CA.

August 2, 1924

Novelist, essayist, activist, and playwright James Baldwin (*Giovanni's Room, Go Tell it on the Mountain, The Fire Next Time*) – National Book Award nominee and a passionate, literary voice during the turbulent days of the mid-20th century Civil Rights Movement – is born in New York City.

August 2, 1972

Novelist, playwright, poet, therapist, and social critic Paul Goodman (*The Empire City, Growing Up Absurd, Making Do*) dies of a heart attack at age 60 in North Stratford, N.H.

August 2, 1997

Author William S. Burroughs (*Naked Lunch, The Wild Boys, The Soft Machine, Cities of the Red Night, Junkie, Queer*) - one of the key writers of the Beat Generation - dies at age 83 from heart attack complications in Lawrence, KS.

August 3, 1916

Actor and best-selling gay author Gordon Merrick (*The Lord Won't Mind, The Great Urge Downward, One for the Gods*) is born in Bala Cynwyd, PA.

August 3, 1942

Tony DeBlase - one-time publisher of *Drummer* magazine, designer of the Leather flag, and co-founder of Chicago's Leather Archives and Museum with Chuck Renslow - is born in South Bend, IN.

August 3, 1954

Novelist Colette (*The Vagabond, Cheri, Gigi, Claudine in Paris, The Gentle Libertine*) - whose literary forte was passion and love and who did not shy away from the sensual in her work - dies at age 81 in Paris, France. Colette was only the second woman in history to be made a grand officer of the Legion of Honor.

August 3, 1974

The Lesbian Connection - a periodical for and about lesbians which helped to build a social, political, and news network among lesbians begins publication. The magazine/newspaper is founded and run by the lesbian-feminist collective Ambitious Amazons.

---○---

August 4, 1870

Author Hans Christian Andersen (*The Snow Queen, The Red Shoes, The Ugly Duckling, The Little Match Girl, The Emperor's New Clothes, The Little Mermaid, The Princess and the Pea*) dies at age 70 in Copenhagen, Denmark. Though the writer of books, plays, and poems, Anderson is primarily remembered for over 160 fairy tales.

August 4, 1993

Activist Steve Endean - the nation's first professional lobbyist for gays and lesbians who established the Gay Rights National Lobby in 1978 and launched the Human Rights Campaign Fund in 1980 - dies of AIDS-related complications at age 44 in Washington, DC.

---○---

August 5, 1920

Figurative painter George Tooker (*Subway, Waiting Room, Government Bureau*) - awarded the National Medal of Arts and elected to the National Academy of Design - is born in New York City.

August 5, 1943

Baritone William Parker, creator of the *AIDS Quilt Songbook*, is born in Butler, PA.

August 5, 1984

Widely recorded sacred music composer and organist Calvin

Hampton - well known for his weekly Friday midnight concerts at Calvary Church in New York City - dies of an AIDS-related illness at age 45 in Port Charlotte, FL.

August 5, 1988

Director and screenwriter Colin Higgins (*Harold and Maude*, *9 to 5*, *Foul Play*, *Silver Streak*) dies of an AIDS-related illness at age 47 in Beverly Hills, CA.

August 5, 2000

Oscar winning actor Sir Alec Guinness (*The Bridge on the River Kwai*, *Star Wars*, *Dr. Zhivago*, *Kind Hearts and Coronets*) dies of liver cancer in Sussex, England.

August 5, 2007

Educator, feminist, and author Anna Livia (*Bruised Fruit*, *Relatively Norma*, *Bulldozer Rising*) dies in her sleep at age 51 in California. Livia is best known academically for linguistics - co-writing the volume *Queerly Phrased,* which dealt with gender and development of queer linguistics, and delving into the feminist aspects of language with *Pronoun Envy.*

August 5, 2012

Astrologer and member of the Sisters of Perpetual Indulgence, Sister Boom Boom (aka Jack Fertig) dies at age 57 in San Francisco, CA.

August 5-21, 2016

The Human Rights Campaign estimates that there are at least 41 openly lesbian, gay and bisexual Olympians competing in the Olympics.

August 6, 1885

The Parliament in Britain votes to make homosexual acts a criminal offense.

August 6, 1908

Helen Jacobs, winner of nine Grand Slam tennis titles, and the first female tennis player named the *Associated Press* Female Athlete of the Year, is born in Globe, AZ.

August 6, 1928

Artist, filmmaker, underground icon, and self-marketing genius Andy Warhol (*Campbell's Soup Cans, Trash, Chelsea Girls, Eight Elvises*) - a leading figure in the Pop Art movement - is born in Pittsburgh, PA.

August 6, 1929

Racy and frank memoir writer Mary MacLane (*The Story of Mary MacLane, Men Who Have Made Love To Me, Tender Darkness*) - known as "the Wild Woman of Butte" - dies at age 48 in Chicago, IL.

August 6, 1938

Actor and cult film director Paul Bartel (*Eating Raoul, Lust in the Dust, Death Race 2000, Rock 'n' Roll High School*) is born in Brooklyn, N.Y.

August 6, 1948

Activist Steve Endean - the nation's first professional lobbyist for gays and lesbians who established the Gay Rights National Lobby in 1978 and launched the Human Rights Campaign Fund in 1980 - is born in Davenport, IA.

August 6, 1983

New wave countertenor Klaus Nomi (*Encore, Simple Man, Eclipsed: The Best of Klaus Nomi*) dies at age 39 of an AIDS-related illness in New York City.

August 7, 1843

Pioneering gay author Charles Warren Stoddard (*For the Pleasure of His Company, Summer Cruising in the South Seas, In the Footprints of the Padres*) is born in Rochester, N.Y.

August 7, 1911

Oscar nominated film director and screenwriter Nicholas Ray (*Rebel Without a Cause, Johnny Guitar, 55 Days At Peking, The Savage Innocents*) is born in Galesville, WI.

August 7, 2013

Educator, reality TV personality Sean Sasser whose commitment ceremony to Pedro Zamora on the reality series *The Real World: San Francisco* in 1994 was considered a landmark television event, dies of cancer at age 44 in Washington DC.

―――――――――○―――――――――

August 8, 1922

Rudi Gernreich, a fashion designer (the topless monokini) and core Mattachine Society member (along with Harry Hay, Chuck Rowland, Bob Hull, and William Dale Jennings) is born in Vienna, Austria.

August 8, 1951

Award winning author and journalist Randy Shilts (*And The Band Played On*, *Conduct Unbecoming*, *The Mayor of Castro Street*) - who became the first full-time openly gay journalist to cover gay politics for the mainstream U.S. press when he was hired in 1981 by *The San Francisco Chronicle* - is born in Davenport, IA.

August 8, 1984

Popular supporting comic actor Richard Deacon - well known for his regular television sitcom roles which included Mel Cooley on *The Dick Van Dyke Show*, Fred Rutherford on *Leave It to Beaver*, and Roger Buell on *The Mothers-In-Law* - dies at age 63 of heart disease in Los Angeles, CA.

August 8, 1985

Silent film actress who epitomized the flapper image, Louise Brooks (*Pandora's Box*, *Diary of a Lost Girl*, *Beggars of Life*) - author of the memoir *Lulu In Hollywood* - dies of a heart attack at age 78 in Rochester, N.Y.

August 9, 1874

Composer, conductor, and director for the Paris Opera - Reynaldo Hahn (*Ciboulette*, *A Chloris*, *If My Verse Had Wings*) - rumored lover at one time of writer Marcel Proust - is born in Caracas, Venezuela.

August 9, 1878

Furniture and textile designer as well as architect Eileen Gray - a pioneer in the Modern Movement in architecture and designer of stringently functional furniture - is born in Enniscorthy, Ireland.

August 9, 1914

Writer, cartoonist, comic strip author, and illustrator Tove Jansson (*The Moomins*, *Moominland Midwinter*, *The Summer Book*, *Sun City*) is born in Helsinki, Finland.

August 9, 1967

Playwright and author Joe Orton (*Entertaining Mr. Sloane*, *Loot*, *What the Butler Saw*) is murdered at age 34 by his lover Kenneth Halliwell in London, England.

August 9, 1967

Actor Anton Walbrook (*The Life and Death of Colonel Blimp,
The Red Shoes, The Queen of Spades*) dies of a heart attack at
age 67 in Bavaria, Germany.

August 9, 2007

Logo hosts the first U.S. Presidential forum on LGBT issues,
sponsored by the Human Rights Campaign. Six Democratic
candidates participate –including Hillary Clinton and Barack
Obama – all Republican candidates decline.

August 9, 2012

Writer and essayist David Rakoff (*Fraud, Don't Get Too
Comfortable, Half-Empty*) - winner of the Lambda Literary
Award as well as the Thurber Prize for American Humor - dies
of cancer at age 47 in Manhattan, New York.

―――――――――⊖―――――――――

August 10, 1994

The Australian film *The Adventures of Priscilla, Queen of the
Desert* opens in theaters. The film will achieve cult status and
go on to win an Academy Award for Costume Design.

―――――――――⊖―――――――――

August 11, 1890

Cardinal John Henry Newman *(Apologia Pro Vita Sua, Loss
and Gain)* – who was Beatified by the Catholic Church in 2010
– dies of pneumonia at age 89 in Edgbaston, Birmingham,

England. At his insistence, his remains share the grave of his life-companion Fr. Ambrose St. John.

August 11, 1913

Author Sir Angus Wilson (*The Middle Age of Mrs. Eliot*, *The Old Men at the Zoo*, *A Bit Off the Map*) is born in Bexhill, Sussex, England.

August 11, 1949

Actor Ian Charleston (*Gandhi*, *Opera*) - best known for his role as Eric Liddell in the 1981 film *Chariots of Fire* - is born in Edinburgh, Scotland.

August 11, 1953

Novelist, short story writer, and army officer John Horne Burns (*The Gallery, Lucifer With a Book*) dies at age 36 of a cerebral hemorrhage in Italy.

August 12, 1859

America the Beautiful author and the woman who popularized Mrs. Santa Claus - Katharine Lee Bates is born in Falmouth, MA.

August 12, 1866

Playwright Jacinto Benavente (*The Governor's Wife*, *Bonds of Interest*, *The Lady of the House*) - a Nobel Prize winner in literature - is born in Madrid, Spain.

August 12, 1867

Educator, classicist and author Edith Hamilton - whose books on mythology (*Mythology*, *The Greek Way*, *The Roman Way*) have become staples in education - is born in Dresden, Germany.

August 12, 1880

Author Radclyffe Hall – whose seminal lesbian novel *The Well of Loneliness* has never been out of print since its initial publication in 1928 – is born in Bournemouth, England.

August 12, 1901

Poet and writer Robert Francis (*Stand Here With Me*, *The Orb Weaver*, *We Fly Away*, *The Trouble with Francis*) - who was recognized for his work by the Academy of American Poets - is born in Upland, PA.

August 12, 1907

Gladys Bentley (*How Much Can I Stand?*, *Worried Blues*, *Red Beans and Rice*) - iconic gender-bending blues singer of the Harlem Renaissance who typically wore her trademark white tuxedo and top hat and was known for her suggestive lyrics and delivery - is born in Philadelphia, PA.

August 12, 1962

TV personality and pay-per-call psychic Miss Cleo (Youree Dell Harris) is born in Los Angeles, CA.

August 12, 1990

Ethyl Eichelberger, drag performer, playwright, actor, and outrageous presence in New York's theatrical scene, dies at age 45 in New York City. Eichelberger became a popular figure in experimental theater best known for writing, appearing in over 40 plays, and his solo works of impersonations of 'Grand Dames' of history including, Nefertiti, Lucrezia Borgia, Clytemnestra, Medea, Jocasta, etc.

August 12, 1992

Avant-garde composer, musical theorist, and writer John Cage (*4'33"*, *The Seasons*, *Sonatas and Interludes*) dies following a stroke at age 79 in New York City.

August 12, 2009

Harvey Milk is posthumously awarded the Medal of Freedom by President Barack Obama.

August 13, 1895

Painter and feminist Hannah Gluckstein aka Gluck (*Medallion*, *Gluck*, *Sir James Crichton-Brown*, *Rage*, *Rage Against the Dying of the Light*) - who painted primarily portraits, landscapes, and flowers - is born in London, England.

August 13, 1952

Fashion photographer Herb Ritts *(Notorious, Duo, Work, Africa)* - known for his clean composition and his work with celebrity portraits - is born in Los Angeles. Among his many photos was the shot of Cindy Crawford mock shaving k.d. lang on the cover of the August 1993 issue of *Vanity Fair*.

August 13, 1982

Choreographer and director Charles Walters (*Easter Parade, High Society, Please Don't Eat the Daisies*) - who was nominated for an Oscar for Best Director for *Lili* - dies of lung cancer at age 70 in Malibu, CA.

August 14, 1906

Fashion photographer Horst P. Horst (*Horst: 60 Years of Photography*) - who often worked with *Vogue* and *House & Garden* was also known for his shots of celebrities and interiors - is born in Saxony-Anhalt, Germany.

August 14, 1940

Playwright, lyricist, writer and director Tom Eyen (*Dreamgirls, Women Behind Bars, The Neon Woman, Ol' Red Hair is Back*) is born in Cambridge, OH.

August 14, 1991

Author and AIDS educator Allen Barnett - whose collection of stories *The Body and Its Dangers and Other Stories* was the winner of the PEN/Ernest Hemingway Citation and who helped establish the Gay and Lesbian Alliance Against Defamation (GLAAD) - dies at age 36 of an AIDS-related illness in New York City.

August 14, 2012

Actor Ron Palillo - best known for his role as Arnold Horshack on the ABC sitcom *Welcome Back, Kotter* - dies of a heart attack at age 63 in Palm Beach Gardens, FL. He was survived by Joseph Gramm, his partner of 41 years.

August 14, 2018

Christine Hallquist wins the Vermont Democratic primary, becoming the first openly transgender gubernatorial candidate for a major party.

August 15, 1971

The pioneering but short-lived organization, the Homosexual Liberation Front, is formed in Mexico City in response to the firing of a Sears employee for alleged homosexual behavior.

August 15, 2017

Lambda Award winning author and health care analyst Mark Merlis (*American Studies, An Arrow's Flight, JD: A Novel, Man About Town*) dies from pneumonia brought on by Lou Gehrig's disease at age 67 in Philadelphia, PA.

⭘

August 16, 1888

Colonel T.E. Lawrence aka Lawrence of Arabia (*The Seven Pillars of Wisdom*) - best known for his war activities in the Middle East during WWI - is born in Tremadog, Wales.

August 16, 1902

Harlem Renaissance era author, editor, poet and playwright Wallace Thurman - whose novel *The Blacker the Berry* addresses such controversial issues as homosexuality, abortion, and intra-racial prejudice - is born in Salt Lake City, UT.

August 16, 1923

Pierre Seel – the only French person to testify openly about his experience as a homosexual Holocaust survivor of a Nazis concentration camp during WWII – is born in Haguenau, France.

August 16, 1978

Actress Jean Acker (*Never Say Quit, Dream Girl*) - one time lover of Alla Nazimova and whose marriage to Rudolph Valentino lasted less than six hours - dies at age 84 in Los Angeles, CA.

⭘

August 17, 1965

Writer and poet Jack Spicer (*My Vocabulary Did This To Me, After Lorca, The Holy Grail*) - often associated with the San Francisco Renaissance and winner of the National Book Award - dies as a result of alcoholism on San Francisco, CA.

August 17, 2002

The New York Times announces that it will publish same-sex commitment ceremony notices and some types of formal registration of gay and lesbian partnerships in the *Sunday Styles* section under Weddings/Celebrations.

August 17, 2007

The first gay male kiss on a daytime soap happens on *As The World Turns* when Luke Snyder (Vam Hansis) and Noah Meyer (Jake Silberman) kiss.

———————————————○———————————————

August 18, 1990

President George H.W. Bush signs the Ryan White Care Act, a federally funded program for people living with AIDS.

———————————————○———————————————

August 19, 1923

Jim Kepner – founder and curator of the International Gay and Lesbian Archives, and principal associate of ONE, Inc. – is born in Galveston, TX.

August 19, 1929

Ballet impresario Sergei Diaghilev - founder of the Ballet Russes in 1909 which toured worldwide and eventually became the catalyst for the Royal Ballet - dies of diabetes complications at age 57 in Venice, Italy.

August 19, 1936

Spanish poet and dramatist Federico Garcia Lorca (*The House of Bernarda Alba, Blood Wedding, Yerma*) - who was lionized as The Finest Poet of Imperial Spain as well as a member of the avant-garde artists' group the Generation of '27- is shot and killed at age 38 near Alfacar, Granada, Spain.

August 19, 1987

Actor Hayden Rorke (*Pillow Talk, Father's Little Dividend*) – best known for his portrayal of Dr. Bellows on the classic 1960s sitcom *I Dream of Jeannie* – dies of multiple myeloma at age 76 in Toluca Lake, CA.

August 19, 2013

Jose Sarria aka the Widow Norton, who in 1961 became the first openly gay candidate for public office in the United States and who also founded the Imperial Court System, dies of cancer at age 90 in Albuquerque, NM.

August 20, 1948

Perry Watkins - who, in 1990, was one of the first U.S. soldiers to challenge the ban on gays in the U.S. military and have some success with the issue before the Supreme Court - is born in Joplin, MO.

August 20-22, 1976

The first Michigan Womyn's Music Festival takes place near Hart, MI. The international womyn-only cultural event, communal festival, workshops, and celebration of womyn's music was held for decades.

―――――――――○―――――――――

August 21, 1872

Art Nouveau illustrator and author Aubrey Beardsley - the controversial artist known primarily for his unique, decadent, and dramatic black ink drawings - is born in Brighton, England.

August 21, 1923

A key figure in the early gay movement, Don Slater - editor of *ONE Magazine* and co-founder of ONE Inc. and who later chaired the organization the Homosexual Information Center - is born in Pasadena, CA.

August 21, 1928

Educator James Gruber - a gay activist and early member of the Mattachine Society who also founded a motorcycle group called The Satyrs - is born in Des Moines, IA.

August 21, 1944

Actor David Lochary (*Female Trouble*, *Mondo Trasho*, *Pink Flamingos*) - associated with the early films of John Waters - is born in Baltimore, MD.

August 21, 1983

After 15 previews the Broadway musical *La Cage aux Folles,* with music and lyrics by Jerry Herman from a book by Harvey Fierstein, opens at the Palace Theatre on Broadway and will run a total of 1,761 performances and win 6 Tony Awards. The musical also enjoyed award winning Broadway revivals in 2004 and 2010.

August 21, 1994

Actress and comedian Danitra Vance (*Saturday Night Live, Little Man Tate, Limit Up*) - recipient of an NAACP Image Award and winner of an Obie Award (for Off-Broadway work) - dies of breast cancer at age 40 in Markham, IL.

August 21, 2008

The largest greeting card company in the U.S., Hallmark Greeting Cards, introduces a line of cards for same-sex weddings/commitment ceremonies.

August 22, 1764

Architect and interior designer Charles Percier (*The Arc de Triomphe du Carrousel*) - a government architect with partner Pierre Francois Leonard Fontaine under Napoleon Bonaparte - is born in Paris, France.

August 22, 1894

Willem Arondeus – artist, writer, and member of the Dutch Resistance during WWII who blew up the Nazi's registration building and was subsequently executed - is born in Naarden, The Netherlands.

August 22, 1924

Tony Award winning playwright, author, and actor James Kirkwood (*P.S. Your Cat is Dead*, *A Chorus Line*, *Diary of a Mad Playwright: Perilous Adventures on the Road with Mary Martin and Carol Channing*) is born in Los Angeles, CA.

August 23, 1926

Silent screen actor, and film icon Rudolph Valentino (*The Four Horseman of the Apocalypse*, *Camille*, *Cobra*, *The Hooded Falcon*, *The Sheik*, *Son of the Sheik*, *Blood and Sand*) - known as "The Sheik" and "The Latin Lover" and many times considered the first male sex symbol of the movies - dies at age 31 from a perforated ulcer and blood poisoning in New York City.

August 23, 1931

Entertainer and transgender activist Coccinelle (*Dias de Viejo Color*, *Los Viciosos*) - who among other things helped found Devenir Femme (To Become a Woman), an organization providing emotional and practical assistance for those seeking gender confirmation surgery and whose marriage was the first transgender union officially acknowledged by the French government - is born Jacques Charles Dufresnoy in Paris, France.

August 24, 1917

Activist Chuck Rowland (core Mattachine Society member along with Harry Hay, William Dale Jennings, Bob Hull, and Rudi Gernreich, who was also active with ONE, Inc. and the Church of One Brotherhood) is born in Gary, S.D.

August 24, 1987

Civil Rights activist and pioneer Bayard Rustin - a leading proponent of non-violent protest – dies at age 75 of a perforated appendix in New York City. A political advisor and strategist, Rustin was the architect of the 1963 March on Washington for Jobs and Freedom, where Dr. Martin Luther King Jr. delivered his famous *I Have a Dream* speech.

August 24, 1988

Actor Leonard Frey (*The Boys in the Band*, *Fiddler on the Roof*) - who was nominated for a Tony Award as well as an Oscar - dies at age 49 of an AIDS-related illness in New York City.

August 25, 1916

Golden era film actor and top box office star Van Johnson (*The Caine Mutiny, Two Sailors and a Girl, Brigadoon, Thirty Seconds Over Tokyo, The Last Time I Saw Paris*) is born in Newport, R.I.

August 25, 1918

Conductor of the New York Philharmonic for over 1,000 performances and legendary composer Leonard Bernstein (*On The Town, Candide, West Side Story*) - who won three Tony Awards, an Emmy, numerous Grammys, received the Kennedy Center Honor, and was inducted into the Songwriters Hall of Fame - is born in Lawrence, MA.

August 25, 1956

Researcher and sexologist Dr. Alfred Kinsey (*Sexual Behavior in the Human Male, Sexual Behavior in the Human Female*) - founder in 1947 of the Institute for Sex Research at Indiana University - dies of a heart ailment and pneumonia at age 62 in Bloomington, IN.

August 25, 1984

Versatile writer and later celebrity Truman Capote (*In Cold Blood, Breakfast at Tiffany's, The Grass Harp, A Christmas Memory, Other Voices, Other Rooms*) - winner of an Edgar Award for excellence in crime writing and who even appeared in the film *Murder By Death* - dies at age 59 of liver cancer in Los Angeles, CA.

August 26, 1904

Writer Christopher Isherwood (*A Single Man, The Berlin Diaries, Christopher and His Kind*) - whose work inspired *Cabaret* - is born in Cheshire, England.

August 26, 1929

Leatherman, photographer, entrepreneur, and activist Chuck Renslow (The Gold Coast, Kris Studio, International Mr. Leather, The Leather Archives and Museum) is born in Chicago, IL.

August 26, 1952

Primetime Emmy Award winning actor Michael Jeter (*Evening Shade*, *Grand Hotel: The Musical*, *The Green Mile*) is born in Lawrenceburg, TN.

August 26, 2003

Country western singer Wilma Burgess (*Don't Touch Me*, *Fifteen Days*, *Tear Time*, *Baby*, *Misty Blue*) - who had 15 singles from 1965-1975 on the Billboard Country and Western chart - dies at age 64 of a massive heart attack in Nashville, TN.

August 26, 2009

Producer, crime writer, novelist and journalist Dominick Dunne (*The Two Mrs. Grenvilles*, *People Like Us*, *The Way We Lived Then*, *An Inconvenient Woman*) - who also covered the O.J. Simpson murder trial for *Vanity Fair* - dies of bladder cancer at age 83 in Manhattan, New York.

August 27, 1967

Music entrepreneur and manager of such acts as the Beatles, Gerry & The Pacemakers, and Cilia Black - Brian Epstein dies at age 32 of a drug overdose in London, England.

August 27, 1991

Actor, musician, and narrator Gordon Heath (*Animal Farm, The Madwoman of Chaillot, Othello, Mr. Arkadin*) - who also operated the cafe L'Abbaye on Paris' Left Bank - dies at age 72 in Paris, France.

August 27, 1991

The Advocate magazine outs Assistant Secretary of Defense and Pentagon spokesman Pete Williams in a cover story by journalist Michelangelo Signorile. The piece was originally set to be published in *OutWeek* which was shut down due to internal problems.

August 27, 2006

Lambda Literary Award winning visual artist, editor, and poet Tee Corinne (*Cunt Coloring Book, Women Who Loved Women, Intricate Passions, Intimacies, Dreams of the Woman Who Loved Sex*) dies of liver cancer at age 62 in Southern Oregon.

August 27, 2008

Activist and Daughters of Bilitis co-founder Del Martin (*Lesbian/Woman, Lesbian Love and Liberation*) dies from complications from a bone fracture at the age of 87 in San Francisco, CA. In addition to starting the Daughters of Bilitis in 1955, Martin and partner Phyllis Lyon also were one of the first lesbian couples to join the National Organization for Women and worked to form the Council on Religion and the Homosexual to help unite churches and gays.

August 28, 1825

19th century progenitor of the modern gay rights movement, Karl Ulrichs (*Research on the Riddle of Man-Manly Love*) – one of the first to proclaim that Uranians (aka lesbians and gay men) are natural and not diseased, criminals, or sinful – is born in Aurich, then part of the Kingdom of Hanover in modern day Germany.

August 28, 1921

Character actress Nancy Kulp – best known for her portrayal of Miss Jane Hathaway on the classic 1960s sitcom *The Beverly Hillbillies* – is born in Harrisburg, PA.

August 28 - September 2 1982

The first Gay Games are held in San Francisco, CA. Over 1300 gay and lesbian athletes from 28 states and 10 nations compete for medals.

August 28, 1991

The Chicago-based Leather Archives and Museum – founded by Chuck Renslow and Tony DeBlase – is incorporated in the state of Illinois as the National Gay and Lesbian Archives. The name was officially changed to The Leather Archives and Museum on May 28, 1992.

August 29, 1844

Philosopher, author, activist, and pioneering socialist Edward

Carpenter (*The Intermediate Sex, Intermediate Types Among Primitive Folk, Civilization: Its Cause and Cure*) – the only English writer before World War I to publicly defend the homosexual's rightful place in society – is born in Hove, England.

August 29, 1867

Karl Heinrich Ulrichs becomes the first self-proclaimed homosexual to speak out publicly for the rights and welfare of Uranians (aka Urninds/Lesbians and Urnings/Gays) when he pleads at the Congress of German Jurists in Munich for a resolution urging the repeal of anti-homosexual legislation.

August 29, 1929

Lambda Literary Award winning poet Thom Gunn (*The Man with Night Sweats, Boss Cupid*) is born in Gravesend, England.

August 29, 1993

Dorian Corey, drag performer and fashion designer who appeared at Wigstock as well as the documentary *The Queen* (1968) and the documentary, *Paris is Burning* (1990), dies of AIDS at age 56 in Manhattan, NY.

August 29, 2018

Modern dancer and choreographer Paul Taylor (*Three Epitaphs, Esplande and Runes, The Book of Beasts*) dies of renal failure at age 88 in Manhattan.

August 30, 1768

William "Kitty" Courtenay, 9th Earl of Devon - who became infamous in England for his homosexuality and was subsequently exiled - is baptized.

August 30, 1956

Psychologist (and straight ally) Dr. Evelyn Hooker delivers her paper *The Adjustment of the Male Overt Homosexual* at the American Psychiatric Association (APA) Convention in Chicago. Her research findings indicate that heterosexuals and homosexuals do not significantly differ which becomes a milestone in the rapidly shifting clinical perception of homosexuality.

August 30, 1958

Danny Sotomayor – the first nationally syndicated openly gay political cartoonist, and co-founder of ACT-UP/Chicago – is born in Chicago, IL.

August 30, 2015

Neurologist, naturalist, historian, and author Oliver Sacks (*The Man Who Mistook His Wife for a Hat, Awakenings, Musicophilia, The Mind's Eye, An Anthropologist on Mars*) dies of cancer at age 82 in Manhattan.

August 31, 1945

Theater actor Timothy Meyers – who won fame and received a Tony nomination as the original Kenickie in the Broadway production of *Grease*, and was featured in numerous other shows – is born in New Orleans, LA.

August 31, 1963

Award-winning film director, writer and actor Rituparno Ghosh (*Chitrangada, Raincoat, Unishe April, Chokher Bali, The Last Lear*) is born in West Bengal, India.

August 31, 1977

U.S. Army Private Barry Winchell – who will become a focal point of the Don't Ask, Don't Tell debate when he is brutally murdered at age 21 by a fellow soldier – is born in Kansas City, MO.

August 31- September 2, 1979

The Spiritual Conference for Radical Faeries – organized by Harry Hay, Mitch Walker, John Burnside, and Don Kilhefner – convenes in an ashram near Benson, AZ. to explore ideas of gay liberation and spirituality. The retreat/conference gives birth to the organization The Radical Faeries.

August 31, 1995

Lambda Literary Award nominated writer and AIDS activist Steven Corbin (*No Easy Place To Be, Fragments That Remain, One Hundred Years From Now*) dies of an AIDS-related illness at age 41 in New York City.

SEPTEMBER

September 1985

The AIDS Medical Foundation merges with the similar organization National AIDS Research Foundation to become amfAR, the Foundation for AIDS Research with a founding committee of Dr. Mathilde Krim, Dr. Michael S. Gottlieb, and Dame Elizabeth Taylor.

―――――――――○―――――――――

September 1, 1815

Sculptress Emma Stebbins - the lover of actress Charlotte Cushman and whose sculpture *Angel of the Waters* adorns New York City's Central Park - is born in New York City.

September 1, 1868

Adolph de Meyer – photographer of such celebrities as Mary Pickford, John Barrymore, Lillian Gish, and Billie Burke – is born in Paris, France.

September 1, 1967

Poet, writer, and editor Siegfried Sassoon (*The War Poems of Siegfried Sassoon, Memoirs of an Infantry Officer*) - a soldier and leading poet of WWI - dies of stomach cancer at age 80 in Heytesbury, England.

September 1, 1977

Oscar-nominated actress and jazz/blues/gospel vocalist Ethel Waters (*The Member of the Wedding, Pinky, Cabin in the Sky*) - whose autobiography was called *His Eye is on the Sparrow* and whose best remembered recordings include *Stormy Weather, Miss Otis Regrets,* and *Am I Blue?* - dies of heart disease at age 80 in Chatsworth, CA.

September 1, 1977

The first meeting of the national gay and lesbian organization, the Log Cabin Republicans is held. The name of the group is in reference to the first Republican President of the U.S., Abraham Lincoln, who was born in a log cabin.

September 2, 1925

Lambda Literary Award winning queer theologian, psychotherapist, and author John J. McNeill *(The Church and the Homosexual, Taking a Chance on God*) is born in Buffalo, NY.

September 2, 1929

Actor and entertainment personality Victor Spinetti *(The Taming of the Shrew, The Little Prince, Voyage of the Damned)* - whose memorable roles include the Beatles' films *A Hard Day's Night, Magical Mystery Tour,* and *Help* and who won Broadway's Tony Award in 1965 for Best Supporting of Featured Actor in a Musical for *Oh, What a Lovely War* - is born in Gwent, Wales.

September 2, 1943

Artist and poet Marsden Hartley (*Handsome Drinks*, *The Ice Hole*, *Art and the Personal Life*, *German Officer*, *Twenty-five Poems*) - whose work was often influenced by the rugged rural landscape and people of Maine - dies at age 66 in Ellsworth, ME.

September 2, 1946

Grammy Award winning recording artist, songwriter, and musician Billy Preston (*Will It Go Round in Circles*, *Nothing From Nothing*) is born in Houston, TX.

September 2, 2013

At age 63, endurance swimmer and lesbian Diana Nyad becomes the first person to swim from Cuba (Havana) to Florida (Key West) without the aid of a shark cage. Nyad's journey of 110 miles was completed in 53 hours and was her fifth attempt at the feat.

September 3, 1849

Writer Sarah Orne Jewett (*The Country of Pointed Fires*, *A White Heron*, *Strangers and Wayfarers*) - known for her realistic and regional depiction of her Maine world - is born in South Berwick, ME.

September 3, 1959

Actor Merritt Butrick (*Square Pegs*, *Zapped!*, *Fright Night Part II*) - probably best remembered as David, the son of Admiral James T. Kirk in *Star Trek II: The Wrath of Khan* and *Star Trek III: The Search for Spock* - is born in Gainesville, FL.

September 3, 2005

Oscar-winner Ang Lee's *Brokeback Mountain* starring Heath Ledger and Jake Gyllenhaal – as teenage cowboys who embark on a doomed life-long affair in the 1960s – is first released to critical acclaim, moderate financial success, and eventually three Oscars.

––––––––––––––––––––○––––––––––––––––––––

September 4, 1905

Writer Mary Renault (*The Persian Boy*, *The Last of the Wine*, *The Charioteer*) – who is principally responsible for bringing the bisexuality of Alexander the Great into the public realm – is born in Forest Gate, Essex, England.

September 4, 1920

Food journalist and author Craig Claiborne (*The New York Times Cookbook*, *Craig Claiborne's Southern Cooking*, *The Chinese Cookbook*, *The Best of Craig Claiborne*) - food editor and restaurant critic for *The New York Times* - is born in Sunflower, MS.

September 4, 1934

Drag legend and performer extraordinaire, community activist, and icon Vicki Marlane is born Donald Sterger in Crookston, MN.

September 4, 1938

Actor Leonard Frey (*The Boys in the Band, Fiddler on the Roof*) - who was nominated for a Tony Award as well as an Oscar - is born in Brooklyn, N.Y.

September 4, 1957

The Wolfenden Report, a study for laws governing sexual behavior in Great Britain is released. The report was groundbreaking by recommending that the law be concerned only with public acts and refrain from legislating morality. It suggests the decriminalization of homosexual behavior in private between consenting adults over the age of 21.

September 4, 1991

Actor and author Tom Tryon - whose roles included his Golden Globe nominated performance in *The Cardinal* and roles in such films as *In Harm's Way* and *The Story of Ruth* dies of stomach cancer at age 65 in Los Angeles, CA. Tryon's best-selling novels include *The Other, Crowned Heads,* and *Harvest Home.*

September 5, 1838

Architect and interior designer Charles Percier (*The Arc de Triomphe du Carrousel*) - a government architect with partner Pierre Francois Leonard Fontaine under Napoleon Bonaparte - dies at age 74 in Paris, France.

September 5, 1912

Avant-garde composer, musical theorist, and writer John Cage (*4'33"*, *The Seasons*, *Sonatas and Interludes*) is born in Los Angeles, CA.

September 5, 1946

Freddie Mercury, lead singer of the glitter rock band Queen (*Bohemian Rhapsody*, *We Are the Champions*, *Don't Stop Me Now*, *Another One Bites the Dust*, *We Will Rock You*, *You're My Best Friend*) is born in Stone Town, Zanzibar.

September 6, 1860

Hull House founder, social welfare advocate, and Nobel Peace Prize recipient - Jane Addams (*Newer Ideals of Peace*, *Peace and Bread in a Time of War*) is born in Cedarville, IL.

September 6, 1947

Flamboyant, glittery, and oftentimes androgynous singer Sylvester (*You Make Me Feel Mighty Real*, *Dance Disco Heat*, *Do Ya Wanna Funk*) - who had one platinum and five gold records - is born in Los Angeles, CA.

September 6, 1948

Hibiscus – founding member and creative director of the gay liberation theater and performance collective The Cockettes – is born in Bronxville, N.Y.

September 6, 2017

Feminist writer, educator, and activist Kate Millett (*Sexual Politics, Flying, The Loony Bon Trip*), dies of a heart attack at age 82 in Paris.

———————————○———————————

September 7, 1913

Novelist Valerie Taylor (*The Girls in 3-B*, *Journey to Fulfillment*, *Return to Lesbos*) - whose work embodied the golden age of lesbian pulp fiction - is born in Aurora, IL.

September 7, 1957

Singer/songwriter Jermaine Stewart (*We Don't Have to Take Our Clothes Off*, *The Word is Out*, *Say It Again*) is born in Columbus, OH.

September 7, 1971

Oscar nominated actress Spring Byington (*You Can't Take it With You, December Bride, Please Don't Eat the Daisies*) - longtime companion of actress Marjorie Main - dies of cancer at age 84 in Hollywood, CA.

———————————○———————————

September 8, 1504

The Michelangelo masterpiece, the statue of David, is unveiled in Florence, Italy.

September 8, 1873

Primarily known for his theatrical piece *Ubu Roi,* author and playwright Alfred Jarry is born in Laval, France. Jarry was a pioneer of the Theater of the Absurd, and even developed a logic of it called pataphysics.

September 8, 1886

Poet, writer, and editor Siegfried Sassoon (*The War Poems of Siegfried Sassoon, Memoirs of an Infantry Officer*) - a soldier and leading poet of WWI - is born in Matfield, England.

September 8, 1907

Expatriate writer Gertrude Stein first meets Alice B. Toklas in Paris, France. The two would preside over one of the most celebrated salons in Europe and remain together until Stein's death in 1946. Thereafter much of Toklas' time and energy, until her 1967 death, was spent in preserving the memory of her late partner.

September 8, 1934

Composer and conductor Sir Peter Maxwell Davies (*Eight Songs for a Mad King, Kommilitonen, Caroline Mathilde, The Doctor of Myddfai*) is born in Lancashire, England.

September 8, 1975

Sgt. Leonard Matlovich is featured on the cover of *TIME Magazine* above the headline *I Am a Homosexual: The Gay Drive for Acceptance* – thus ushering in the idea of gays serving openly in the military into the national consciousness.

September 8, 1991

Golden Globe winning actor Brad Davis *(Midnight Express, Chariots of Fire, Querelle, Sybil)* dies at age 41 of an AIDS-related illness in Los Angeles, CA.

September 8, 1995

The film *To Wong Foo Thanks for Everything, Julie Newmar* (starring Patrick Swayze, Wesley Snipes, and John Leguizamo as three drag queens travelling cross-country) is released.

September 8, 2003

Popular Emmy Award winning daytime television talk show *Ellen* aka *The Ellen DeGeneres Show*, hosted by out comedienne Ellen DeGeneres, makes its debut.

September 8, 2008

The political news and commentary program, *The Rachel Maddow Show,* debuts on MSNBC.

September 8, 2014

Finland releases stamps celebrating noted homoerotic artist Tom of Finland.

September 8, 2016

The Lady Chablis, the trans star of the book and later the film *Midnight in the Garden of Good and Evil,* is born in Quincy, FL.

September 9, 1911

Novelist, playwright, poet, therapist, and social critic Paul Goodman (*The Empire City, Growing Up Absurd, Making Do*) is born in New York City.

September 9, 1949

Figure skater John Curry (1976 Olympic and World Champion) is born in Birmingham, England.

September 9, 1992

The Lesbian Avengers march in Queens, N.Y. – their first official action – to protest the School Board's refusal to implement the Rainbow Curriculum.

September 10, 1886

Avant-garde poet, novelist, translator, and self-proclaimed "pagan mystic" H.D. aka Hilda Doolittle, (*Hymen, Helen in Egypt, Hermetic Definition, The Gift, HERmoine*) - who helped define what is now called "free verse poetry" - is born in Philadelphia, PA.

September 10, 1889

Novelist (*Reuben Sachs, The Romance of a Shop*), poet, essayist and the first Jewish woman to attend Cambridge University, Amy Levy, commits suicide at age 26 in London.

September 10, 1942

Singer and stage actor Gilbert Price - who received Tony nominations for *Lost in the Stars*, *The Night That Made America Famous*, and *Timbuktu!* - is born in New York City.

September 10, 2008

Poet Reginald Shepherd (*Otherhood*, *Fata Morgana*, *Some Are Drowning*, and *Angel, Interrupted*) - who was nominated for a National Book Critics Circle Award and a Lambda Literary Award - dies of cancer in Pensacola, FL.

―――――――――――○―――――――――――

September 11, 1935
Pioneering female mountaineer Freda Du Faur, who is credited as the first woman to climb New Zealand's tallest mountain, Mount Cook and became a leading amateur climber of her day, commits suicide at age 52 in Dee Why, Australia.

September 11, 1961

KQED, a public television station in San Francisco, airs the 60 minute program *The Rejected,* the first documentary about homosexuality broadcast in the United States. In 2002 GLAAD (The Gay and Lesbian Alliance Against Defamation) presented KQED with the Pioneer Award in recognition of *The Rejected* as the start of LGBT programming. In 1967 CBS will become the first network to air a documentary program about homosexuality with the episode of *CBS Reports*, "The Homosexuals".

September 11, 1993

The HBO film *And the Band Played On* airs. Based on the book by Randy Shilts, the film's all-cast includes Alan Alda, Lily Tomlin, Matthew Modine, Richard Gere, and Anjelica Houston.

September 11, 2001

New York Fire Department Chaplain Father Mychal F. Judge dies in the terrorist attacks on the World Trade Center in New York City after performing the Last Rites on a fallen firefighter. He is subsequently accorded the solemn honor of being named Victim 0001 of 9/11.

September 11, 2001

Public relations executive Mark Bingham – one of four who attempted to take control of ill-fated United Airlines Flight 93 from terrorist hijackers – dies when the airliner crashes near Shanksville, PA. before reaching the U.S. Capitol Building in Washington, DC.

September 11, 2011

Gay rights activist and author Arthur Evans (*Witchcraft and the Gay Counterculture*) - a member of the Gay Liberation Front and later a co-founder of the Gay Activists Alliance - dies at age 68 of a massive heart attack in San Francisco, CA.

September 11, 2016

Actress, performer, and activist Alexis Arquette (*Pulp Fiction, The Wedding Singer, Bridge of Chucky*) dies from complications of HIV at age 47 in Los Angeles, CA.

---⊖---

September 12, 1956

Singer and actor Leslie Cheung (*A Better Tomorrow*, *Farewell My Concubine*) - considered one of the founders of "Cantopop" - is born in Kowloon, Hong Kong.

September 12, 1992

Oscar nominated actor Anthony Perkins (*Fear Strikes Out*, *Friendly Persuasion*, *The Black Hole*) - best known as Norman Bates in *Psycho* and who also won Best Actor at the Cannes Film Festival in 1961- dies at age 60 of an AIDS-related illness in Hollywood, CA.

September 12, 1993

Actor Raymond Burr (*Perry Mason*, *Ironside*, *Rear Window*) - who was nominated for eight primetime Emmy Awards and won twice - dies of cancer at age 76 in Healdsburg, CA.

September 12, 2017

Activist Edith "Edie" Windsor dies at age 88 in Manhattan. Windsor was the primary plaintiff in the Supreme Court case United States vs. Windsor which overturned part of the Defense of Marriage Act and is considered a huge legal victory for the same sex marriage movement in the U.S.

September 13, 1885

Alain Locke – writer (*The Negro in America*), philosopher, educator and "Dean" of the Harlem Renaissance who also edited several collections including *The New Negro: An Interpretation* – is born in Philadelphia, PA.

September 13, 1922

Civil rights leader Dr. Antonia Pantoja – recipient of the Presidential Medal of Freedom and founder of the Puerto Rican Forum and ASPIRA (Spanish for "Aspire", this not-for-profit group emphasizes pride, education, and commitment to community) – is born in San Juan, Puerto Rico.

September 13, 1931

Male to female gender pioneer Lili Elbe - who was eventually classified as "intersex" and the subject of the 1933 biography *Man into Woman* and the novel *The Danish Girl* (2000) - dies in Germany at age 48 after complications from her fifth operation for gender confirmation surgery.

September 13, 1959

Adrian aka Adrian Adolph Greenberg – one of Hollywood's premier costume designers whose film credits include *The Women*, *The Wizard of Oz*, *Camille*, *Dinner at Eight* and *The Great Ziegfeld* – dies of a heart attack at age 56 in Hollywood, CA.

September 13, 1977

The ABC sitcom *Soap* debuts featuring Billy Crystal as gay son Jodie Dallas.

September 13, 1991

Author Peter McGehee (*Boys Like Us, Beyond Happiness, Sweetheart, The IQ Zoo*) dies of AIDS-related toxoplasmosis at age 35.

———————————○———————————

September 14, 1934

Feminist writer, educator, and activist Kate Millett (*Sexual Politics, Flying, The Loony Bon Trip*), is born in St. Paul, MN.

September 14, 1954

Painter, photographer, performance artist, filmmaker, writer and activist David Wojnarowicz (*Close to the Knives*) is born in Red Bank, N.J.

September 14, 2002

Actor and comedian Michael Greer who played the prison drag queen in the stage and film versions *Fortune and Men's Eyes* and whose best known comedy bit was a monologue as *Mona Lisa* while holding a gilded frame - dies of lung cancer at age 59 in Riverside, CA.

———————————○———————————

September 15, 1889

Writer and poet Claude McKay (*Home to Harlem, Banjo, Banana Bottom, Harlem: Negro Metropolis*) a key figure in the Harlem Renaissance, is born in Clarendon, Jamaica.

September 15, 1941

A.J. Laurent – activist, and original publisher and co-founder of *The Advocate* – is born in Magnolia Springs, Alabama.

September 15, 1946

Pakistani-American poet and activist Ifti Nasim (*Myrmecophile, Narman, Selected Poems 1980-2000*) whose poetry was said to be the first direct statement of gay longings and desire to appear in the Urdu language, is born in Faisalabad, Pakistan.

———————————————○———————————————

September 16, 1856

Photographer Wilhelm von Gloeden - known primarily for his 20th century pastoral postcards of the men and boys of Sicily, mostly nudes and/or adorned in classical robes or garlands - is born in Wismar, Germany.

September 16, 1882

Pioneering female mountaineer Freda Du Faur, who is credited as the first woman to climb New Zealand's tallest mountain, Mount Cook and became a leading amateur climber of her day, is born in Croydon, Australia.

September 16, 2016

Tony Award winning playwright Edward Albee (*The Sandbox, Who's Afraid of Virginia Woolf?, The Zoo Story, Three Tall Women; The Goat or Who is Sylvia?*) dies of a heart attack at age 88 in Montauk, NY.

September 17, 1730

Military officer Friedrich von Steuben – who served as Inspector General and Major General of the Continental Army during the American Revolutionary War – is born in Magdeburg, Duchy of Magdeburg, Brandenburg, Prussia.

September 17, 1907

Professional sculptor Edmonia Lewis, who became the first woman of African-American and Native American heritage to achieve international fame and recognition in the fine arts world, dies at age 63 in London. Her pieces include *The Old Arrow Maker, Forever Free, The Death of Cleopatra*, and *Hiawatha.*

September 17, 1928

Prolific actor Roddy McDowell (*Lassie Come Home, Planet of the Apes, The Poseidon Adventure, Fright Night, Cleopatra*) - who won a Tony Award in 1960 for his role in *The Fighting Cock* - is born in London, England.

September 17, 1948

Anthropologist Ruth Benedict (*The Chrysanthemum and the Sword, Patterns of Culture*) – partner of Margaret Mead and president of the American Anthropological Association – dies at age 61 in New York City.

September 17, 1975

The Off-Broadway musical *Boy Meets Boy* opens at the Actor's Playhouse; a campy send-up of 1930s Astaire/ Rogers productions, it becomes the first musical written by gays for gays to attract mainstream attention.

———————————○———————————

September 18, 1848

Benjamin Henry Jesse Francis Shepard aka Francis Grierson, composer, pianist, author and spiritualist (*The Valley of Shadows, Lincoln, the Practical Mystic, Modern Mysticism*) is born in Birkenhead, England.

September 18, 1905

Actress and international film icon Greta Garbo (*Camille, Ninotchka, Grand Hotel, Queen Christina, Anna Karenina*) - who was nominated for four Oscars - is born in Stockholm, Sweden.

September 18, 1935

Activist, journalist, and poet Alice Dunbar Nelson (*Violets and Other Tales, Give Us Each Day*) - a prominent figure in the Harlem Renaissance - dies of a heart ailment at age 60 in Philadelphia, PA.

September 18, 1961

Dag Hammarskjöld – Nobel Peace Prize winning diplomat and Secretary General of the United Nations (1953-1961) and also credited with coining the term "planned economy" - dies in a plane crash in Ndola, Zambia.

September 18, 2000

Transgender biographer Dawn Langley Simmons (*Rosalynn Carter: Her Life Story*, *Jacqueline Kennedy: a Biography*, *Princess Margaret*, *Dawn: A Charleston Legend*) dies of Parkinson's Disease at age 77 in Charleston, S.C.

September 18, 2010

Feminist author, cultural critic, and journalist Jill Johnston (*Lesbian Nation: The Feminist Solution*, *The Village Voice*, *Admission Accomplished: The Lesbian Nation Years 1970-75*) - who championed the lesbian separatist movement of the 1970s - dies of a stroke at age 81 in Hartford, CT.

―――――――――○―――――――――

September 19, 1934

Music entrepreneur and manager of such acts as The Beatles, Gerry & The Pacemakers, and Cilia Black - Brian Epstein is born in Liverpool, England.

September 19, 1936

Transgender FTM author, nurse and adventurer Jack Bee Garland – who went by numerous names including Elvira Virginia Mugarrieta, Babe, Bean, Jack Beam, Jack Maines, and Beebe Beam – dies of peritonitis at age 66 in San Francisco, CA.

September 19, 1964

The first gay picket in the U.S. is led by activist Randy Wicker; a group pickets the Whitehall Street Induction Center in New York City to protest the U.S. military's treatment of gay people after the confidentiality of gay men's draft records are violated.

September 19, 1992

Actor Frederick Combs (*The Boys in the Band*) dies of an AIDS-related illness at age 56 in Los Angeles, CA.

September 19, 2010

The beatification of Cardinal John Henry Newman is officially proclaimed by Pope Benedict XVI during his visit to Birmingham, England. In Roman Catholicism, beatification is the recognition of a holy life and/or martyr's death and subsequent entry into Heaven. It also denotes the beatified's capacity to be venerated and to intercede on behalf of individuals who pray in his or her "blessed" name. Beatification is the third of four steps in the canonization process of the Catholic Church and the making of a saint.

September 20, 1762

Architect and interior designer Pierre Francois Leonard Fontaine (*Arc de Triomphe du Carrousel*) - a government architect with partner Charles Percier under Napoleon Bonaparte - is born in Pontoise, France.

September 20, 1917

Activist and businessman Hal Call is born in Trenton, MO. He was a member of the early homophile group The Mattachine Society, and co-founder of Pan Graphic Press which printed *The Mattachine Review*, *The Ladder*, and other homophile publications. He was also the Founder of the gay and lesbian book clearinghouse Dorian Book Service.

September 20, 1918

Actor, musician, and narrator Gordon Heath (*Animal Farm*, *The Madwoman of Chaillot*, *Othello*, *Mr. Arkadin*) - who also operated the cafe L'Abbaye on Paris' Left Bank - is born in New York City.

September 20, 1980

Activist Clark Polak kills himself at age 43 in Los Angeles, CA. Among his accomplishments are creating, publishing, and editing *DRUM* magazine, being president of the Philadelphia-based homophile organization the Janus Society, and the leader of the Homosexual Law Reform Society.

September 20, 2005

Artist, anthropologist and AIDS activist Tobias Schneebaum (*Keep the River on Your Right: A Modern Cannibal Tale*) - who lived for a time with the cannibals of the Amazon - dies at age 83 from complication of Parkinson's disease in Great Neck, NY.

September 20, 2011

The military policy "Don't Ask, Don't Tell" is formally repealed by President Barack Obama after 18 years in a statement that began, "Today, the discriminatory law known as "Don't Ask, Don't Tell" is finally and formally repealed. As of today, patriotic Americans in uniform will no longer have to lie about who they are in order to serve the country they love. As of today, our armed forces will no longer lose the extraordinary skills and combat experience of so many gay and lesbian service members. And today, as Commander in Chief, I want those who were discharged under this law to know that your country deeply values your service."

September 20, 2015

The television series *Transparent* wins big as at the 67th annual Emmy Awards taking home awards for Outstanding Lead Actor in a Comedy Series, Outstanding Directing of a Comedy Series as well as three additional awards.

———————————————○———————————————

September 21, 19 B.C.

Virgil (*The Aeneid, The Georgics, The Eclogues*) - Roman poet of the Augustan period - dies as the result of a fever at age 50 in Brundisium in the Roman Empire and is buried near Naples, Italy.

September 21, 1327

King Edward II of England aka Edward of Caernarfon - who ruled England from 1307-1327 and whose widely documented relationship with lover Piers Gaveston was one of the earliest examples of Medieval Europe's religion-based same-sex joining ritual known as Wedded Brotherhood – was murdered by members of his inner circle at age 43 at Berkeley Castle in Gloucestershire, England.

September 21, 1902

Poet Luis Cernuda (*Selected Poems, Written in Water*) - member of the avant-garde artists' group the Generation of '27 - is born in Seville, Spain.

September 21, 1955

The Daughters of Bilitis – the first known lesbian civil and political rights organization in the U.S. – is established by partners Del Martin and Phyllis Lyon in San Francisco, CA.

September 21, 1998

Multiple Emmy Award winning TV sitcom *Will and Grace* debuts on NBC. It will run a total of eight seasons and become the first successful U.S. sitcom featuring gay main characters. The series will be resurrected in 2017.

September 21, 2010

Author and columnist Dan Savage, with husband Terry Miller, found the internet based *It Gets Better Project* - which comes in response to the escalating number of LGBT youth suicides and features video messages to these teens, (from LGBT adults) that their lives will improve.

September 21, 2015

Photographer, filmmaker, activist Honey Lee Cottrell, who was also the co-founder of the San Francisco Lesbian and Gay History Project, dies at age 69 in Santa Cruz, CA.

September 22, 1840

Landowner, diarist, and business woman Anne Lister – whose encoded diaries were deciphered to reveal intricate details about lesbian life in 19th century Europe – dies of a fever at age 49 while on holiday with her lover Anne Walker at Kutais/Koutais, now known as Kutaisi, Georgia.

September 22, 2015

Lambda Literary Award winning queer theologian, psychoterapist, and author John J. McNeill *(The Church and the Homosexual, Taking a Chance on God)* dies at age 90 in Fort Lauderdale, FL.

September 22, 2018

West Hollywood is the site of America's first citywide Bi Pride event, held the day before Bisexual Visibility Day. September is also Bisexual Awareness Month.

September 23

Bisexuality Day celebrates bisexual pride. Date is also know as Bi or Bisexual Visibility Day.

September 23, 1984

The Leather and BDSM community of San Francisco organizes the first single-day Folsom Street Fair to coincide with the autumnal equinox which it did through 1992. Thereafter the fair became more closely associated with the last Sunday of September.

September 23, 2009

The ABC sitcom *Modern Family* about three different but interconnected families debuts. The program features the gay dads Cameron and Mitchell (played by Eric Stonestreet and Jesse Tyler Ferguson) and their adopted daughter Lily (Aubrey Anderson-Emmons).

———————————————◦———————————————

September 24, 1923

Actor Louis Edmonds (*All My Children*, Roger Collins in the daytime series *Dark Shadows*) - who came out publicly in his biography *Big Lou* - is born in Baton Rouge, LA.

September 24, 1961

Benjamin Sumner Welles – FDR's Under Secretary of State and the Founder of the North Atlantic Treaty Organization (NATO) – dies at age 68 in Bernardsville, NJ.

September 24, 1981

Actress Patsy Kelly (*Rosemary's Baby*, *Freaky Friday*, *Pigskin Parade*) - who won a Tony Award for Best Featured Actress in a Musical for *No, No, Nanette* - dies of cancer at age 71 in Woodland Hills, CA.

September 24, 1982

The CDC (Center for Disease Control) uses the term AIDS (Acquired Immune Deficiency Syndrome) for the first time.

September 24, 1991

Choreographer, muralist, dancer and erotic artist Dom Orejudos aka Etienne aka Stephen (*The Tin Soldier*, *Metamorphosis of the Owls*, *The Gold Coast* murals and *International Mr. Leather* contest posters) - whose ballet *The Charioteer* inaugurated color broadcast on WTTW in Chicago - dies of an AIDS-related illness at age 58.

―――――――――――――○―――――――――――――

September 25, 1987

Tony Award nominated actor and playwright Emlyn Williams - best known for writing the plays *Night Must Fall* and *The Corn is Green* and who also did a good amount of film work - dies at age 81 of complications from cancer in London, England.

September 25, 1990

The compilation album *Red Hot + Blue* is released on the Chrysalis label to raise money for AIDS research and care. One of the first major benefit projects of the music industry, it features an eclectic collection of contemporary artists performing Cole Porter songs. The successful CD becomes the first of several *Red Hot* benefit collections.

September 25, 1993

President Bill Clinton appoints nurse Kristine Gebbie as the nation's first AIDS czar (federal AIDS coordinator) stating that the epidemic required the country to look for "unprecedented remedies to unprecedented problems."

September 26, 1937

Blues singer Bessie Smith (*Nobody Knows You When You're Down and Out, St. Louis Blues, A Good Man is Hard to Find, I Need a Little Sugar in My Bowl*) - "The Empress of the Blues" - dies at age 43 after being critically injured in an auto accident in Clarksdale, MS.

September 26, 1942

Chicana and feminist writer/theorist Gloria Anzaldua (*Borderlands/La Frontera: The New Mestiza*) - winner of an American Book Award as well as a Lambda Literary Award and who also co-edited *This Bridge Called My Back: Writings By Radical Women of Color* - is born in Rio Grande Valley, TX.

September 26, 1946

Feminist and writer Andrea Dworkin (*Pornography: Men Possessing Women, Intercourse, Life and Death: Unapologetic Writings on the Continuing War on Women*) - best known for her strong stance against pornography and winner of the American Book Award in 2001 - is born in Camden, N.J.

September 26, 1948

Photographer and choreographer Arnie Zane - co-founder and co-artistic director of the postmodernist Bill T. Jones/Arnie Zane Dance Company and whose honors include a New York Dance Performance Award - is born in the Bronx, N.Y.

September 27, 1961

Avant-garde poet, novelist, translator, and self-proclaimed "pagan mystic" H.D. aka Hilda Doolittle, (*Hymen, Helen in Egypt, Hermetic Definition, The Gift, HERmoine*) - who helped define was is now called "free verse poetry" - dies following a stroke at age 75 in Zurich, Switzerland.

September 27, 1992

Stage and film actor Keith Prentice (*The Boys in the Band, Dark Shadows, Cruising*) dies at age 52 of AIDS-related cancer in Kettering, OH.

September 27, 2018

With the opening of *The Nap*, Alexandra Billings becomes the first openly trans woman to be featured in a Broadway play. In the play Billings played trans gangster Waxy Bush.

September 28, 2004

Sierra Leone activist FannyAnn Eddy - who in 2002 founded the Sierra Leone Lesbian and Gay Association, an activist and support organization - is assassinated in Freetown, Sierra Leone.

September 28, 2017

Multiple Emmy-winning TV sitcom *Will and Grace,* returns to NBC television for a 9th season. The revived sitcom originally aired on the network from 1998-2006.

---○---

September 29, 1926

The lesbian drama *The Captive* opens at the Empire Theater on Broadway. In February 1927 it will be one of the New York plays closed under the Wales Padlock Law for "depicting or dealing with the subject of sex degeneracy or sex perversion on the stage."

September 29, 1967

Writer Carson McCullers (*The Heart is a Lonely Hunter, The Member of the Wedding, The Ballad of the Sad Cafe, Reflections in a Golden Eye*) - winner of a New York Drama Critics Circle Award - dies from a brain hemorrhage at age 50 in Nyack, N.Y.

September 29, 1970

Character actor Edward Everett Horton (*Shail We Dance, Arsenic and Old Lace, Ziegfeld Girl, Lost Horizon, Springtime in the Rockies, Here Comes Mr. Jordan, F Troop*) - narrator of the *Fractured Fairy Tales* cartoon on *The Rocky and Bullwinkle Show* - dies of cancer at age 84 in Encino, CA.

September 29, 1973

Poet W.H. Auden (*Collected Poems, Tell Me the Truth About Love*) - who among other honors won the Pulitzer Prize for Poetry, The National Book Award for Poetry, and the Bollingen Prize - dies at age 66 in Vienna, Austria.

September 29, 1992

Singer and songwriter Paul Jabara - who wrote such disco hits as *Last Dance*, *The Main Event*, and *It's Raining Men* - dies at age 44 of an complications due to AIDS in Los Angeles, CA.

September 30, 1918

Civil rights activist Robert Sloane Basker - founder of Mattachine Midwest as well as founder of Chicago's first gay and lesbian hotline - is born in East Harlem, New York City.

September 30, 1924

Versatile writer and later celebrity Truman Capote (*In Cold Blood, Breakfast at Tiffany's, The Grass Harp, A Christmas Memory, Other Voices, Other Rooms*) - winner of an Edgar Award for excellence in crime writing and who even appeared in the film *Murder By Death* - is born in New Orleans, LA.

September 30, 1955

Iconic film actor James Dean (*East of Eden, Giant, Rebel Without a Cause*) - who was nominated for two Oscars and one Hollywood's brightest stars during his brief, meteoric career - dies in an accident driving his Porsche Spyder race car at age 24 near Cholame, CA.

September 30, 1989

Composer and music critic Virgil Thomson dies at age 92 in his Chelsea Hotel suite in Manhattan. Thomson collaborated with Gertrude Stein on two operas - *Four Saints and Three Acts and The Mother of Us All* - the latter about the life of Susan B. Anthony. Later in life he was awarded the Kennedy Center Honor as well as a National Book Critics Circle Award.

September 30, 1990

Novelist, poet, playwright, and essayist Patrick White (*Voss, The Eye of the Storm, The Twyborn Affair, Riders in the Chariot*) - who in 1973 won the Nobel Prize in Literature and was named Australian of the Year - dies at age 78 in Sydney, Australia.

OCTOBER

October

U.S. LGBT History Month celebrates the achievements of great figures and important moments in LGBTQ history.

———————————————⊖———————————————

October 1, 1499

Renaissance philosopher Fr. Marsilio Ficino – who coined the term "platonic love" – dies at age 65 in Careggi, Italy. He is credited with bridging the divide between Antiquity and Christianity, which allowed the Renaissance to flourish.

October 1, 1760

William Beckford, art collector, politician, and writer (*Vathek, Memoirs of Extraordinary Painters*) - who chose self-exile after his affair with William Courtney was revealed - is born in London, England.

October 1, 1979

Filmmaker Dorothy Arzner (*The Wild Party, Craig's Wife, Christopher Strong, The Bride Wore Red*) – who invented the boom microphone, was the first woman to direct a talking film, and the first woman to join the Directors Guild of America – dies at age 82 in La Quinta, CA.

October 1, 1989

Denmark becomes the first country to officially and legally recognize same-sex partnerships.

October 1, 2016

Marie Kuda, writer, archivist, editor, lecturer, journalist, publisher (Womanpress), and historian of LGBT culture in Chicago, dies at age 76 in Cicero, IL. Kuda edited and published essential works in lesbian scholarship including *Two Women: The Poetry of Jeannette Howard and Valerie Taylor* and *Women Loving Women: A Select and Annotated Bibliography of Women Loving Women in Literature.*

October 2, 1889

Dr. Margaret "Mom" Chung is born in Santa Barbara, CA. She is the first known American-born Chinese female to become a physician in the U.S., and is credited with successfully lobbying for the creation of the U.S. Women's Naval Reserves – the WAVES.

October 2, 1957

Writer, poet, performance artist, dancer, and activist Assotto Saint (*The Road Before Us, Spells of a Voodoo Doll*) - who also founded the Metamorphosis Theater and the art techno band Xotica - is born in Haiti.

October 2, 1985

Oscar nominated actor Rock Hudson (*Giant, Pillow Talk,*

McMillan and Wife) a top 10 box office star from 1957-1964, dies at age 59 of an AIDS-related illness in Beverly Hills, CA. Hudson became the first major figure to announce that he had AIDS (July 1985) and subsequently donated a quarter of a million dollars to help the fledgling organization the National AIDS Research Foundation (NARF).

———————————————○———————————————

October 3, 1858

Internationally known stage actress Eleonora Duse (*La Dame aux Camelias*, *Francesca da Rimini*, *La Citta Morta*) - noted for her roles in the works of Henrik Ibsen - is born in Vigevano, Italy.

October 3, 1915

Actor Anthony Forwood (*The Story of Robin Hood and His Merrie Men*, *Knights of the Round Table*) and later manager of his partner Sir Dirk Bogarde - is born in Weymouth, England.

October 3, 1925

Novelist, essayist, playwright, and politico Gore Vidal (*The City and the Pillar*, *Myra Breckinridge*, *Burr*, *Palimpsest*, *Lincoln*) - who won a National Book Award, National Book Critics Circle Award, was a candidate for both the U.S. House and Senate, and co-founder of the U.S. Peace Party with Dr. Benjamin Spock - is born in West Point, N.Y.

October 3, 1929

Stage and early film actress Jeanne Eagles (*The Letter, Jealousy, Man Woman and Sin*), who in 1929 became the first actor to receive a posthumous Oscar nomination, dies of a drug overdose at age 39 in New York City.

October 3, 1952

Actor Steve Tracy – who portrayed Percival Dalton on the TV series *Little House on the Prairie* – is born in Canton, OH.

October 3, 1953

Lambda Literary Award nominated writer and AIDS activist Steven Corbin (*No Easy Place To Be, Fragments That Remain, One Hundred Years From Now*) is born in Jersey City, N.J.

October 3, 1998

Prolific actor Roddy McDowell (*Lassie Come Home, Planet of the Apes, The Poseidon Adventure, Fright Night, Cleopatra*) - who won a Tony Award in 1960 for his role in *The Fighting Cock* - dies of lung cancer at age 70 in Studio City, CA.

October 4, 1890

Dr. Alan L. Hart – physician, radiologist, researcher, writer and novelist – is born Alberta Lucille Hart in Halls Summit, KS. She will champion the radiological diagnosis of tuberculosis decades before epidemiological testing becomes available – saving thousands of lives.

October 4, 1897

Professor, serviceperson and author (*The Narrow Land*) Elizabeth Reynard, who helped to establish the WAVES (Women Accepted for Volunteer Emergency Service) and was the first woman to be appointed lieutenant in the United States Navy Reserve, is born in Massachusetts.

October 4, 1970

Electrifying singer and songwriter Janis Joplin (*Piece of My Heart, Mercedes Benz, Summertime, Me and Bobby McGee*) - a main attraction at both Woodstock and the Monterey Pop Festival - dies of a heroin overdose at age 27 in Hollywood, CA.

October 4, 1989

Comedian, writer, and actor Graham Chapman (*Monty Python's Flying Circus, Monty Python and the Holy Grail, The Life of Brian, Yellowbeard, A Liar's Autobiography*) dies at age 48 of throat and spinal cancer in Maidstone, Kent, England.

––––––––––––––––––––––○––––––––––––––––––––––

October 5, 1726

Diplomat, spy, and soldier Chevalier d'Eon - who lived his first 49 years as a man and her next 33 as a woman - is born in Tonnerre, Burgundy, France.

October 5, 1840

Essayist, poet, translator, biographer, memoirist, and literary critic John Addington Symonds (*Memoirs, The Renaissance in Italy* - 7 volumes, *Walt Whitman, Beast 666, The Life of Michelangelo Buonarroti, A Problem in Modern Ethics, Memoirs*) - best known as a cultural historian of the Italian Renaissance - is born in Bristol, England.

October 5, 1962

Sylvia Beach – expatriate, bookseller, publisher, founder of the Paris bookstore Shakespeare and Company, and the first publisher of James Joyce's groundbreaking novel *Ulysses* – dies at age 75 in Paris, France.

October 25, 1968

Educator, reality TV personality Sean Sasser whose commitment ceremony to Pedro Zamora on the reality series *The Real World: San Francisco* in 1994 was considered a landmark television event, is born in Detroit, MI.

October 5, 1969

The Washington Blade, originally called *The Gay Blade*, publishes its first issue.

October 5, 2000

Businesswoman and activist Ruth Ellis (*Living With Pride: Ruth C. Ellis @ 100*) – who operated an African American social sanctuary known as The Gay Spot for 27 years out of her Detroit home – dies at age 101 in Detroit, MI.

October 6, 1898

Film director and Oscar nominated art director Mitchell Leisen (*Midnight, Hold Back the Dawn, I Wanted Wings, The Mating Season, Remember the Night, To Each His Own*) is born in Menominee, MI.

October 6, 1955

Author Peter McGehee (*Boys Like Us, Beyond Happiness, Sweetheart, The IQ Zoo*) is born in Pine Bluff, AR.

October 6, 1968

The first worship service of the Metropolitan Community Church (MCC) takes place with a gathering of 12 people in Reverend Troy Perry's living room in Huntington Park, CA. Its goal is to serve the spiritual needs of gay and lesbian people.

October 6, 1979

Poet Elizabeth Bishop (*Geography III, A Cold Spring, The Complete Poems, North and South*) - whose awards include the Pulitzer Prize and the National Book Award for Poetry - dies of a cerebral aneurysm at age 68 in Boston, MA.

October 6, 1992

Actor Denholm Elliott (*Indiana Jones, A Room with a View, Trading Place*) - who was nominated for an Oscar and won four BAFTA Awards - dies of AIDS-related tuberculosis at age 70 in Ibiza, Spain.

October 6, 2014

The Supreme Court denies review in 5 different marriage cases, allowing lower court rulings to stand, and therefore allowing same-sex couples to marry in Utah, Oklahoma, Virginia, Indiana and Wisconsin and opening the door for marriage equality in Colorado, Kansas, North Carolina, South Carolina, West Virginia and Wyoming.

———————————○———————————

October 7

The Official (Roman Catholic/Eastern Orthodox) Feast Day of Saints Sergius and Bacchus, whose 4th century record of martyrdom describes them as lovers who were executed for being closet Christians.

October 7, 1903

Photographer Herbert List (*Junge Manner, Italy, Photographs 1930-1970, Portraits*) - known for his magazine work with periodicals such as *Vogue* and *Harper's Bazaar* - is born in Hamburg, Germany.

October 7, 1916

Novelist, short story writer, and army officer John Horne Burns (*The Gallery, Lucifer With a Book*) is born in Andover, MA.

October 7, 1943

Author Radclyffe Hall – whose seminal lesbian novel *The Well of Loneliness* has never been out of print since its initial publication in 1928 – dies of colon cancer at age 63 in London, England.

October 7, 1967

The first issue of *The Advocate* (then called *The Los Angeles Advocate*) is published and sold for 25 cents a copy in various Los Angeles gay bars.

October 7, 1990

Poet, fiction writer, and educator Manuel Ramos Otero (*The Story of the Woman and the Sea, La novelabingo*) - considered one of the most important openly gay Puerto Rican authors of the century and who also founded the short lived publishing house El Libro Viaje - dies of AIDS-related complications at age 42 in San Juan, Puerto Rico.

October 7, 1993

Stage and film actor Kenneth Nelson (*The Boys in the Band, The Aldrich Family, Lovely Ladies, Kind Gentleman*) dies at age 63 of an AIDS-related illness in London, England.

October 8

International Lesbian Day is celebrated, a date honoring and celebrating lesbian visibility and culture.

October 8, 1960

Film actor James Lyons (*Poison, I Shot Andy Warhol* - in which he played Billy Name, *Swoon, Safe*) editor (*Far From Heaven, Velvet Goldmine, The Virgin Suicides*), and also an activist and writer – is born in New York.

October 8, 1974

"The Outrage" - an episode of the ABC-TV series *Marcus Welby M.D.* [Season 6, Episode 5] about a gay science teacher who rapes a male student is aired. The Gay Activist Alliance urges sponsors to withdraw support in what becomes the first national campaign against the networks.

October 8, 2009

Mister Marcus (Hernandez) – longtime social columnist for the *Bay Area Reporter* and also referred to as the "Dean of Leather Columnists" - dies at age 77 of complications from diabetes and arteriosclerosis in Pacifica, CA.

October 9, 1830

Neoclassical sculptress and designer Harriet Hosmer (*Zenobia in Chains*, *The Sleeping Faun*, *Daphne*, *Beatrice Cenci*, *The Mermaid's Cradle*) - the foremost American female sculptor of her time - is born in Watertown, MA.

October 9, 1984

In the face of the growing AIDS epidemic, the Health Department in the City of San Francisco petition the courts to pass regulations that lead to the eventual closure of the city's bathhouses.

October 9, 2006

Entertainer and transgender activist Coccinelle (*Dias de Viejo color*, *Los Viciosos*) - who among other things helped found

Devenir Femme (To Become a Woman) an organization providing emotional and practical assistance for those seeking gender confirmation surgery and whose marriage was the first transgender union officially acknowledged by the French government - dies at age 75 dies in Marseilles, France.

October 10, 1853

Architect and interior designer Pierre Francois Leonard Fontaine (*Arc de Triomphe du Carrousel*) - a government architect with partner Charles Percier under Napoleon Bonaparte - dies at age 91 in Paris, France.

October 10, 1915

Transgender Civil War soldier Albert D. J. Cashier dies at age 71 at Watertown State Hospital in Watertown, Illinois.

October 10, 1957

Transgender writer Christine Daniels (who was a sports columnist for *The Los Angeles Times* prior to her transition) is born Mike Penner in Inglewood, CA.

October 10, 1987

Two thousand gay and lesbian couples are "married" in a mass mock wedding outside the Internal Revenue Service building in Washington, DC as part of the Second National March on Washington for Lesbian and Gay Rights.

October 10, 2009

Stephen Gately – one of the two lead singers of the group Boyzone (*Working My Way Back To You, Love Me for a Reason, Words, Father and Son*) – dies from a pulmonary edema at age 33 in Majorca, Spain.

———————————○———————————

October 11, 1934

Photographer Peter Hujar (*Peter Hujar: a Retrospective, Portraits In Life and Death*) - known for his black and white portraits and also being the friend and one time lover of David Wojnarowicz - born in Trenton, N.J.

October 11, 1935

Actor Frederick Combs (*The Boys in the Band*) is born in Portsmouth, VA.

October 11, 1963

Writer and filmmaker Jean Cocteau (*Orpheus, Beauty and the Beast, Les Enfants Terribles*) - who won France's film award the Prix Louis Delluc - dies of a heart attack at age 74 in Milly-la-Foret, France upon hearing of Edith Piaf's death.

October 11, 1987

The Second National March on Washington for Lesbian and Gay Rights takes place.

October 11, 1987

The inaugural display of the AIDS Memorial Quilt, which at the time consisted of 1,920 panels, takes place on the National Mall in Washington, DC. The NAMES Project AIDS Memorial Quilt was conceived in November 1985 by San Francisco-based activist Cleve Jones as a way of honoring those individuals lost to the AIDS pandemic.

October 11, 1987

The National Latino/a Gay and Lesbian Organization (LLEGO) - a non-profit organization, dedicated to serving the needs and concerns of the Latino/a LGBT community on a local and national level, is formed during the Second March on Washington for Lesbian and Gay Rights. Over 70 people from 13 states and Puerto Rico attend the first meeting.

October 11, 1988

This date is officially observed as National Coming Out Day for the first time.

October 11, 1988

Entertainment personality and puppeteer Wayland Flowers – who appeared with his puppet Madame on numerous TV shows and nightclubs and starred in the series *Madame's Place* – dies at age 48 of AIDS-related cancer in Dawson, GA.

October 11, 1989

Actor Paul Shenar (*Scarface*, *Raw Deal*, *The Big Blue*, *Rage of Angels: The Story Continues*) dies at age 53 from an AIDS-related illness in West Hollywood, CA.

October 11, 1989

Longtime Companion, the first widely distributed U.S. film to deal with the subject of AIDS, is released. Among several honors, Bruce Davison is nominated for a Best Supporting Actor Oscar and wins a Golden Globe award for his performance in the film.

October 11, 2011

Key gay rights activist and pioneer Frank Kameny - who believed "Gay is Good" despite the institutionalized homophobia in place at the time, and resolved to transform the way gay people were treated in society - dies at age 86 in Washington DC. Among his many accomplishments, the tireless Kameny was co-founder of the Washington, DC chapter of the Mattachine Society, championed to remove homosexuality from the American Psychiatric Association's list of mental disorders, and was the first openly gay person to run for Congress.

October 11, 2011

Trans race car driver and WWII fighter pilot Roberta Cowell, who was also the first British trans woman to undergo gender confirmation surgery, dies at age 93 in London.

October 11, 2012

The first official installation of The Legacy Walk – an outdoor museum commemorating the contributions of LGBT people to world history and culture – is dedicated in Chicago, IL.

---⊙---

October 12, 1875

Occultist, magician, poet, and painter Aleister Crowley, who called himself the Beast 666 and whose works include *The Diary of a Drug Fiend* and *The Book of Thoth*, is born in Royal Leamington Spa, U.K.

October 12, 1896

The play *A Florida Enchantment* opens on Broadway featuring two women kissing. Ushers offer ice water at the intermission to patrons who feel faint. It is made into a film in 1913.

October 12, 1903

Actress Josephine Hutchinson (*North By Northwest, Son of Frankenstein, The Story of Louis Pasteur*) is born in Seattle, WA.

October 12, 1942

Gay rights activist and author Arthur Evans *(Witchcraft and the Gay Counterculture)* - a member of the Gay Liberation Front and later a co-founder of the Gay Activists Alliance - is born in York, PA.

October 12-15, 1979

The National March on Washington for Lesbian and Gay Rights takes place. The event draws more than 100,000 people from across the U.S. and worldwide. The political rally, the focus of the event, takes place on October 14 for the purpose of visibility, protective civil rights legislation, and equal rights.

October 12-15, 1979

The First National Third World Lesbian and Gay Conference is held to coincide with the National March on Washington for Gay and Lesbian Rights which also prompts the forming of the first Lesbian and Gay Asian Collective in the U.S.

October 12, 1985

Ricky Wilson - original guitarist for the band The B52s who helped give the group their early signature sound, and brother of band member Cindy Wilson - dies at age 32 of an AIDS-related illness in New York City.

October 12, 1998

Matthew Shepard, a college student, is tortured and murdered at age 21 in Fort Collins, CO. He becomes a symbol of the horror of hate crimes.

October 13, 1917

Philanthropist Reed Erickson - founder of the Erickson Educational Foundation, which donated millions to the early development of the LGBTQ movement from 1964-1984 - is born Rita Alma Erickson in El Paso, TX.

October 13, 1937

Activist Clark Polak is born. Among his accomplishments are creating, publishing, and editing *DRUM* magazine, being president of the Philadelphia-based homophile organization the Janus Society, and the leader of the Homosexual Law Reform Society.

October 13, 1959

Playwright Scott McPherson (*Marvin's Room*) - winner of a Drama Desk Award as well as an Outer Critics Circle Award - is born in Columbus, OH.

October 13, 1966

Actor Clifton Webb (*Laura*, *Cheaper By the Dozen*, *The Razor's Edge*, *Sitting Pretty*) - nominated for three Oscars, winner of a Golden Globe Award, and the man who first introduced Irving Berlin's song *Easter Parade* on Broadway - dies of a heart attack at age 76 in Beverly Hills, CA.

October 13, 1987

The first national gay civil disobedience action takes place outside the Supreme Court; nearly 600 demonstrators are arrested for protesting the Hardwick vs. Bowers decision upholding the constitutionality of sodomy laws.

October 13, 1997

Annie Proulx's short story, *Brokeback Mountain*, the eventual basis for the groundbreaking Ang Lee film of the same name, is published in *The New Yorker*. Proulx's story is one of 11 included in her 1999 short fiction collection *Close Range: Wyoming Stories*.

---○---

October 14, 1888

Modernist short story writer Katherine Mansfield (*The Garden Party: And Other Stories, Bliss: And Other Stories, Prelude*) - who enchanted and influenced writers from Virginia Woolf to D.H. Lawrence - is born in Wellington, New Zealand.

October 14, 1892

Benjamin Sumner Welles – FDR's Under Secretary of State and the Founder of the North Atlantic Treaty Organization (NATO) – is born in New York City.

October 14, 1925

The Father of Modern Bodybuilding and Victorian era strongman, the great Eugen Sandow, dies of an aneurysm at age 58 in London.

October 14, 1990

Conductor of the New York Philharmonic for over 1,000 performances and legendary composer Leonard Bernstein (*On The Town, Candide, West Side Story*) - who won three Tony Awards, an Emmy, numerous Grammys, received the Kennedy Center Honor, and was inducted into the Songwriters Hall of Fame - dies of a heart attack in New York City at age 72, five days after announcing his retirement from conducting.

October 14, 2006

Gerry Studds - the first openly gay member of Congress and Massachusetts Democratic Congressman from 1973-1997 and who was an inspiration for many by winning re-election after coming out as gay - dies in Boston, MA. at age 69, several days after suffering a pulmonary embolism while walking his dog.

———————————○———————————

October 15, 70 BC

Virgil (*The Aeneid, The Georgics, The Eclogues*) - Roman poet of the Augustan period - is born in Andes in the Roman Republic.

October 15, 1904

Activist Marty Mann, author (*Marty Mann's New Primer on Alcoholism, Marty Mann Answers Your Questions About Drinking and Alcoholism*), the first woman to publicly identify herself as a member of Alcoholics Anonymous, and the third woman to ever seek help from Alcoholics Anonymous, is born in Chicago, IL.

October 15, 1926

French philosopher, social theorist, historian of ideas, and literary critic Michel Foucault (*The History of Sexuality, Madness and Civilization, The Order of Things*) is born in Poitiers, France.

October 15, 1928

Author and illustrator Louise Fitzhugh (*Harriet the Spy, The Long Secret, Nobody's Family is Going to Change, Sport*) is born in Memphis, TN.

October 15, 1937 (some sources say 1922)

Transgender biographer Dawn Langley Simmons (*Rosalynn Carter: Her Life Story, Jacqueline Kennedy: a Biography, Princess Margaret, Dawn: A Charleston Legend*) is born Gordon Langley Hall in Kent, England.

October 15, 1964

Composer, songwriter, and Broadway legend Cole Porter *(Love For Sale, Can-Can, Anything Goes, Silk Stockings, I Get a Kick out of You, Night and Day, Begin the Beguine, So in Love)*, in failing health for years, dies of kidney failure at age 75 in Santa Monica, CA. Porter is considered one of the principle contributors of the *Great American Songbook* with over 900 songs attributed to him. He was nominated for four Oscars, won one Grammy, won two Tony Awards *(for Kiss Me Kate)*, and was inducted into the Songwriters Hall of Fame.

October 15, 1973

The formation of the National Gay Task Force (later the National Gay and Lesbian Task Force) is announced with the goal of seeking civil rights for gay people.

October 15, 1986

NFL pro-football player Jerry Smith – star receiver and record-holding tight end for the Washington Redskins 1965-1977 - the first prominent U.S. athlete to announce he was suffering from AIDS – dies at age 43 of an AIDS-related illness in Silver Spring, MD.

October 16, 1854

Dramatist, critic, novelist, and poet Oscar Wilde (*The Picture of Dorian Gray*, *The Importance of Being Earnest*, *An Ideal Husband*, *Salome*) - who at the height of his career was accused of being a sodomite and subsequently tried and sentenced to two years at hard labor - is born in Dublin, Ireland.

October 16, 1881

Painter Russell Cheney (*Kittery Point*, *Portrait of Howard Lathrop*) - a master at capturing New England life and landscapes - is born in South Manchester, CT.

October 16, 1945

Author Paul Monette (*Borrowed Time*, *Last Watch of the Night*) - who won the National Book Award in 1992 for his gay memoir *Becoming a Man: Half a Life Story* and was the winner of two Lambda Literary Awards as well as a Stonewall Book Award - is born in Lawrence, MA.

October 17

International Pronoun Day, which Seeks to make asking, sharing, and respecting personal pronouns commonplace, is celebrated.

October 17, 1886

Oscar nominated actress Spring Byington (*You Can't Take it With You, December Bride, Please Don't Eat the Daisies*) - longtime companion of actress Marjorie Main - is born in Colorado Springs, CO.

October 17, 1920

Actor Montgomery Clift (*From Here to Eternity, A Place in the Sun, The Misfits, Raintree County, Red River, Suddenly, Last Summer*) - who was nominated for four Oscars - is born in Omaha, NE.

October 17, 1933

Jeanne Deckers aka The Singing Nun - who became a recording sensation with her song *Dominique* which led to the highly fictionalized filming of her story, *The Singing Nun* - is born in Brussels, Belgium.

October 17, 1950

Academy Award nominated Actor Howard E. Rollins Jr. (*In the Heat of the Night, Ragtime, A Soldier's Story*) is born in Baltimore, MD.

October 17, 1964

Angie Xtravaganza, trans performer, underground superstar, and founding member of the House of Xtravaganza and star of the 1990 documentary *Paris is Burning*, is born Jorge Pequero in New York City.

October 17, 1984

Blues singer, songwriter, and nurse Alberta Hunter (*Nobody Knows You When You're Down and Out, The Darktown Strutters' Ball*) - a member of the Blues Hall of Fame - dies at age 89 in New York City.

―――――――――○―――――――――

October 18, 1875

Mikhail Kuzmin, author of *Wings* (1906) – the first Russian novel to not only center on homosexuality, but to deal with it openly and sympathetically – is born in Yaroslavl, Russia.

October 18, 1947

Trail blazing singer and songwriter Laura Nyro (*Stoned Soul Picnic, Stoney End, Eli's Coming, Wedding Bell Blues, And When I Die*) - a trained pianist who often blended musical styles in her work - is born in The Bronx, N.Y.

October 18, 1973

Editor, memoirist, and author Margaret C. Anderson - who founded and published the art and literature magazine *The Little Review* from 1914-1929 and promoted such writers as Hemingway, Yeats, Pound, and James Joyce (which resulted in obscenity charges) - dies at age 86 in Le Cannet, France.

October 18, 1973

Lambda Legal, founded by William J. Thom in 1971, has its incorporation papers approved, and becomes a NFP organization.

October 19

Spirit Day is celebrated. On this day people wear purple to signify that they stand with LGBTQ youth and speak out against LGBTQ bullying.

October 19, 1433

Renaissance philosopher Fr. Marsilio Ficino – who coined the term "platonic love" – is born in Figline Valdarno, Italy. He is credited with bridging the divide between Antiquity and Christianity, which allowed the Renaissance to flourish.

October 19, 1921

Golden Globe Award winning actor George Nader (*Robot Monster, Carnival Story, Away All Boats*) - who also wrote the 1978 gay science-fiction novel *Chrome* - is born in Pasadena, CA.

October 19, 1932

Actor Robert Reed (*The Defenders, Mannix*) - best known as Mike Brady on *The Brady Bunch* - is born in Highland Park, IL.

October 19, 1945

Underground and cult film legend Divine aka Harris Glenn Milstead (*Pink Flamingos, Polyester, Lust in the Dust, Female Trouble, Hairspray*) - as well as a popular disco/dance and nightclub entertainer - is born in Baltimore, MD.

October 19, 1950

Poet and playwright Edna St. Vincent Millay (*Collected Sonnets, The Ballad of the Harp Weaver, First Fig and Other Poems*) - cultural idol from the heyday of Greenwich Village, winner of the Pulitzer Prize for Poetry in 1923, and winner of the Robert Frost Medal in 1943 - dies at age 58 from a heart attack and is found dead at the foot of her stairs in Austerlitz, N.Y.

October 19, 1950

Disco and Hi-NRG composer and recording artist Patrick Cowley (*Menergy, Right on Target, Do You Warna Funk*) often credited as a pioneer of electronic dance music, is born in Buffalo, N.Y.

October 20, 1954

Poet Arthur Rimbaud (*Illuminations, Rimbaud Complete*) - young genius of modern poetry whose torrid affair with Paul Verlaine ended in disaster - is born in Charleville-Mezieres, France.

October 20, 1873

National Urban League founder Frances Kellor - a social reformer and activist who specialized in the rights and care of immigrants, domestic workers, and women, who championed adult education, and who was responsible for having women's suffrage on national party platforms - is born in Columbus, OH.

---○---

October 21, 1884

Cabaret singer and entertainer Claire Waldoff (*Fritze Bollmann, Hannelore, Es Gibt Nur Ein Berlin*) - who reached the height of her fame in Berlin during the decadent period between 1910-1920 - is born in Gelsenkirchen, Germany.

October 21, 1917

Writer and activist William Dale Jennings - core Mattachine Society member (along with Harry Hay, Chuck Rowland, Bob Hull, and Rudi Gernreich) - and later a founding member of the early homophile organization ONE, Inc. - is born in Amarillo, TX.

October 21, 1941

Lambda Literary Award nominee Robert Ferro (*The Family of Max Desir, The Blue Star, Second Son*) - a member of the gay men's writing group The Violet Quill which included Edmund White, Andrew Holleran, and Felice Picano - is born in Cranford, NJ.

October 21, 2009

The popular off Broadway smash hit musical, *Avenue Q*, opens.

October 21, 2016

The pro-gay film, *Moonlight*, by director/screenwriter Barry Jenkins is released in the U.S. The motion picture will go on to win three Oscars that year for Best Picture, Best Supporting Actor, and Best Adapted Screenplay.

October 21, 2016

Actor and stand-up comedian Kevin Meaney (*30 Rock, Uncle Buck, Plump Fiction, Big*) dies of a heart attack at age 60 in Forestburgh, NY.

―――――――――○―――――――――

October 22, 1844

Actress Sarah Bernhardt (*Le Passant, Zaire, Hamlet, La Tosca, Phedre, The Lady of the Camellias*) is born in Paris, France. Often called "The Divine Sarah", Bernhardt was considered the greatest stage actress of her time. She named a Paris theater in her honor and dabbled in early films.

October 22, 1870

Lord Alfred Douglas – author, and the lover for whom Oscar Wilde stood trial and went to prison – is born in Worcestershire, England.

October 22, 1925

Influential multi-medium artist Robert Rauschenberg (*White Paintings, Black Paintings, Combine, Monogram, Stoned Moon*) - who liked to incorporate materials typically outside the artist's mode into his work - is born in Port Arthur, TX.

October 22, 1932

Abolitionist, women's rights activist, orator, and the first woman to give a political address before Congress, Anna Elizabeth Dickinson, dies of a stroke at age 89 in Goshen, NY.

October 22, 1997

Novelist Valerie Taylor (*The Girls in 3-B*, *Journey to Fulfillment*, *Return to Lesbos*) - whose work embodied the golden age of lesbian pulp fiction - dies at the age of 84 in Tucson, AZ.

October 23, 1893

Actress Jean Acker (*Never Say Quit*, *Dream Girl*) - one time lover of Alla Nazimova and whose marriage to Rudolph Valentino lasted less than six hours - is born in Trenton, N.J.

October 23, 1896

Actress Lilyan Tashman (*So This is Paris*, *Manhandled*, *Bulldog Drummond*, *Girl About Town*, *Gold Diggers of Broadway*, *No, No, Nanette*) - a silent film actress who successfully made the transition to sound films - is born in Brooklyn, N.Y.

October 23, 1910

Actor Hayden Rorke (*Pillow Talk*, *Father's Little Dividend*) – best known for his portrayal of Dr. Bellows on the classic 1960s sitcom *I Dream of Jeannie* – is born in Brooklyn, N.Y.

October 23, 1939

Robert Opel – photographer and owner of Fey-Way Studios art gallery – is born in N.J. Opel's greatest fame came when he streaked behind presenters David Niven and Elizabeth Taylor at the 46th Annual Academy Awards in 1974.

October 23, 1957

Designer and founder of one of the world's top fashion houses - Christian Dior dies at age 52 of a heart attack in Montecatini Terme, Tuscany, Italy.

October 23, 1986

Singer, pianist, songwriter Esquerita (*Oh Baby, Rockin' The Joint, Hey Miss Lucy*) dies at age 50 of complications from AIDS in Harlem, N.Y.

October 24, 1869

Educator and literary critic (*Shakespeare's Imagery and What It Tells Us*) Caroline Spurgeon, who became the first female university professor in London and the second in England, is born in Punjab, India.

October 24, 1939

Writer and activist Paula Gunn Allen (*The Sacred Hoop, Spider Woman's Granddaughters*) - whose book *Studies in American Indian Literature: Critical Essays and Course Designs* is considered a landmark in Native American literary criticism - is born in Albuquerque, N.M.

October 24, 1942

Educator and literary critic (*Shakespeare's Imagery and What It Tells Us*) Caroline Spurgeon, who became the first female university professor in London and the second in England, dies on her 73rd birthday in Tucson, AZ.

October 24, 1946

Warhol underground superstar, trans actress (*Trash, Women in Revolt*) and author (*A Low Life in High Heels*) Holly Woodlawn is born Haroldo Santiago Franceschi in Juana Diaz, Puerto Rico.

October 24, 1969

TIME Magazine's cover story is "The Homosexual in America."

October 24, 2002

Activist Harry Hay (*Radically Gay*), often called "The Father of the Modern Gay Movement" for being founder of the Mattachine Society and also a founding member of the Radical Faeries - dies of lung cancer at age 90 in San Francisco, CA.

October 25, 1882

Sculptress Emma Stebbins - the lover of actress Charlotte Cushman and whose sculpture *Angel of the Waters* adorns New York City's Central Park - dies at age 67 in New York City.

October 25, 1894

Surreal artist, photographer, political activist, and writer Claude Cahun aka Lucy Schwob *(Self-Portraits, Heroines, Aveux non Avenus)* - whose work often was self-portraits and often explored gender - is born in Nantes, France.

———————⊖———————

October 26

Intersex Awareness Day is celebrated to commemorate the first intersex protest, which took place in Boston, MA.

October 26, 1989

Dancer and activist Mabel Hampton - active during the Harlem Renaissance and who appeared in the documentary *Before Stonewall* - dies at age 87 in New York City.

October 26, 1992

Author Melvin Dixon (*Vanishing Rooms*, *Trouble the Water*) dies at age 42 from an AIDS-related illness in Stamford, CT.

October 26, 2011

A.J. Laurent – activist, and original publisher and co-founder of *The Advocate* – dies of prostate cancer at age 70 in Los Angeles, CA.

———————⊖———————

October 27, 1941

Operatic soprano, actress and author Georgette Leblanc (*The Choice of Life*, *Carmen*, *Mary Magdalene*, *La Navarraise*, *Sappho*) dies at age 66 in Cannes, France.

October 27, 1977

John Beresford Fowler, interior designer and antiques expert who specialized in wallpaper, printing, and upholstery, dies of cancer at age 71.

October 27, 1992

U.S. Navy Radioman Petty Officer, Third Class, Allen R. Schindler Jr. becomes a focal point in the national debate about gays serving in the military when he is brutally murdered by a fellow sailor at age 22 in Sasebo, Nagasaki, Japan.

October 27, 2013

Musician, singer, songwriter Lou Reed (The Velvet Underground, *Transformer, Walk on the Wild Side, Coney Island Baby*) dies from liver disease at age 71 in Amagansett, NY.

October 28, 1903

Author Evelyn Waugh (*Brideshead Revisited, Scoop, A Handful of Dust, Vile Bodies, Decline and Fall*) - is born in London, England.

October 28, 1909

Painter Francis Bacon (*Three Studies for Figures at the Base of a Crucifixion, Head I, Painting, Study for the Head of George Dyer*) - whose work often depicted brutal and gruesome scenes - is born in Dublin, Ireland.

October 28, 1842

Abolitionist, women's rights activist, orator, and the first woman to give a political address before Congress, Anna Elizabeth Dickinson, is born in Philadelphia, PA.

October 28, 1966

The Student Homophile League at Columbia University, the oldest gay campus organization, holds its first program.

October 28, 1972

Film director and Oscar nominated art director Mitchell Leisen (*Midnight, Hold Back the Dawn, I Wanted Wings, The Mating Season, Remember the Night, To Each His Own*) dies of heart disease at age 74 in Los Angeles, CA.

October 28, 2009

The Matthew Shepard Act is signed into law by President Barack Obama, expanding the 1996 Hate Crimes Law to include a victim's actual or perceived gender, sexual orientation, gender identity, or disability.

———————————○———————————

October 29, 1925

Producer, crime writer, novelist, and journalist Dominick Dunne (*The Two Mrs. Grenvilles, People Like Us, The Way We Lived Then, An Inconvenient Woman*) - who also covered the O.J. Simpson murder trial for *Vanity Fair* - is born in Hartford, CT.

October 30, 1853

Artist Louise Abbema (*Flora, The Seasons, Sarah Bernhardt, A Game of Croquet*) – commonly associated with the Belle Epoque – is born in Etampes, Essonne, France.

October 30, 1930

Cinematographer Nestor Almendros (*Sophie's Choice, Kramer vs. Kramer, The Last Metro, Places in the Heart, The Blue Lagoon*) - who won an Oscar for *Days of Heaven* and who also co-directed *Improper Conduct* in 1984 about the persecution of gays in Cuba - is born in Barcelona, Spain.

October 30, 1968

Silent film actor and MGM box office star Ramon Novarro (*Ben-Hur, Mata Hari, The Student Prince at Old Heidelberg*) – one of the greatest stars of the era – is murdered in North Hollywood, CA.

October 30, 1978

The San Francisco Examiner runs the first of a 13 part series called "Gays and the City" - the most comprehensive examination of homosexuality in the mainstream media up to that point.

October 30, 1990

Female impersonator Craig Russell - whose artistry is captured in the films *Outrageous!* and *Too Outrageous!*, and whose list of impersonations included Peggy Lee, Shirley Bassey, Bette Davis, Barbra Streisand, Mae West, Carol Channing, Sophie

Tucker, Bette Midler, and many others - dies at age 42 from an AIDS-related stroke in Toronto, Ontario, Canada.

October 30, 2014

Tim Cook, the CEO of Apple Inc., comes out publicly as gay, becoming the first openly gay CEO on the Fortune 500 list.

October 31, 1876

Writer Natalie Clifford Barney (*A Perilous Advantage, Adventures of the Mind*) – a U.S. expatriate in Paris known for her artist salon on the West Bank – is born in Dayton, OH.

October 31, 1896

Oscar-nominated actress and jazz/blues/gospel vocalist Ethel Waters (*The Member of the Wedding, Pinky, Cabin in the Sky*) - whose autobiography was called *His Eye is on the Sparrow* and whose notable recordings include *Stormy Weather, Miss Otis Regrets,* and *Am I Blue?* - is born in Chester, PA.

October 31, 1940

Activist Craig L. Rodwell (early gay rights activist and founder of the Oscar Wilde Memorial Bookshop – the first bookstore devoted to gay and lesbian authors and literature) is born in Chicago, IL.

October 31, 1976

Furniture and textile designer as well as architect Eileen Gray - a pioneer in the Modern Movement in architecture and designer of stringently functional furniture - dies at age 98 in Paris, France.

NOVEMBER

November 1, 1883

Jane Heap – the publisher who co-founded the art and literary magazine *The Little Review* with Margaret C. Anderson and became a pioneer of literary modernism – is born in Shawnee, KS.

November 1, 1899

Dada artist of the Weimar Period, Hannah Hoch (*Cut With a Dada Knife Through the Last Weimar Beer Belly*, *The Puppet Balsamine*, *Dada Panorama*, *The Staircase*) - known for her photomontages - is born in Gotha, Germany.

November 1, 1907

Primarily known for his theatrical piece *Ubu Roi,* author and playwright Alfred Jarry dies at age 34 of tuberculosis in Paris, France. Jarry was a pioneer of the Theater of the Absurd and even developed a logic of it called pataphysics.

November 1, 1937

Dr. Tom Waddell is born in Patterson, N.J. A former Olympic decathlete (1968), Waddell was also the founder of The Gay Olympics (later the Gay Games) in San Francisco in 1982. In 1976, Waddell and then lover Charles Deaton, became the first homosexual couple to appear in the "Couples" section of *People Magazine.*

November 1, 1971

The Chicago based lesbian/feminist newspaper *Lavender Woman* releases its first issue. Published by the Lavender Woman collective, the paper will continue with a total of 26 issues until it ceases publication in July 1976.

November 1, 1972

ABC airs the TV-Movie *That Certain Summer* starring Martin Sheen, Hal Holbrook, and Scott Jacoby, the first telefilm to depict a gay dad (Sheen).

November 1, 1996

Rapper, singer, songwriter Lil Peep (*Come Over When You're Sober, Pt. 1, Come Over When You're Sober, Pt. 2)* is born in Allentown, PA.

November 1, 1997

Newspaper columnist, essayist, and activist Jon-Henri Damski (*Angels into Dust, Damski-To-Go*) - who at the time of his death was the longest running columnist published in the U.S. gay and lesbian press - dies of malignant melanoma at age 60 in Chicago, IL.

November 2, 1906

Oscar nominated film, theater, and opera director as well as screenwriter Luchino Visconti (*The Leopard, Death in Venice*) is born in Milan, Italy.

November 2, 1946

Lambda Award winning author Michelle Cliff (*Free Enterprise, No Telephone to Heaven, The Land of Look Behind and Claiming, Abeng*) is born in Kingston, Jamaica.

November 2, 1960

Conductor and composer Dimitri Mitropoulos - conductor at both the New York Philharmonic (where he greatly expanded the repertoire) as well as The Metropolitan Opera - dies at age 64 of heart failure in Milan, Italy while rehearsing Gustav Mahler's 3rd Symphony.

November 2, 1975

Controversial film director, poet, and novelist Pier Paolo Pasolini (*Salo, or the 120 Days of Sodom, Il Decameron, The Gospel According to St. Matthew*) - who was expelled from the Italian Community Party because of his homosexuality - is murdered at age 53 in Rome, Italy.

November 2, 1994

Lambda Literary Award and Stonewall Book Award winning author and AIDS activist David B. Feinberg (*Eighty-Sixed, Spontaneous Combustion, Queer and Loathing: Rants and Raves of a Raging AIDS Clone*) dies of an AIDS-related illness at age 37 in New York City.

November 2, 2017

Professor, author, activist, and editor of *the Journal of Homosexuality* from 1975-2009, John Paul De Cecco, dies at age 92 in San Francisco, CA.

November 2, 2018

The critical and commercial hit film, *Bohemian Rhapsody,* a biopic of Queen front man and rock superstar Freddie Mercury is released. Rami Malek stars as the gay superstar.

November 3, 1889

Transgender soldier and colonel in the Mexican Revolution, Amelio Robles Avila - who was awarded a medal as an Honorary Legionnaire of the Mexican Army - is born Amelia Avila Robles in Xochipala, Guerrero, Mexico.

November 3, 1943

Lambda Literary Award winning visual artist, editor, and poet Tee Corinne (*Cunt Coloring Book, Women Who Loved Women, Intricate Passions, Intimacies, Dreams of the Woman Who Loved Sex*) is born in St. Petersburg, FL.

November 3, 1959

Actor Timothy Patrick Murphy (Mickey Trotter on *Dallas*; *Search for Tomorrow*, *Glitter*, *Sam's Son*, *The Love Boat*) is born in Hartford, CT.

November 4, 1896

Writer and literary editor J.R. Ackerley (*My Father and Myself*, *Hindoo Holiday*, *My Dog Tulip*) is born in London, England.

November 4, 1921

Sam Wagstaff - curator, photography collector (whose collection was comprised of thousands of masterworks) and benefactor of Robert Mapplethorpe - is born in New York City.

November 4, 1933

Barbara Grier - writer, publisher, co-founder of Naiad Press in 1973, and former columnist and editor of the Daughter's of Bilitis' periodical *The Ladder* – is born in Cincinnati, OH.

November 4, 1946

Photographer Robert Mapplethorpe (*The Black Book*, *Some Women*, *Mapplethorpe: Portraits*, *Flowers*) - known for his stark elegant style and controversial subject matter - is born in Queens, N.Y.

November 4, 1995

Poet, performance artist, and activist Essex Hemphill (*Ceremonies*, *Brother to Brother*, *Tongues Untied*, *Black Is...Black Ain't*) dies at age 38 of an AIDS-related illness in Philadelphia, PA.

November 4, 2008

California votes in favor of Proposition 8, that changes the state constitution to say that "only marriage between a man and a woman is valid or recognized."

---○---

November 5, 1963

Poet Luis Cernuda (*Selected Poems*, *Written in Water*) - member of the avant-garde artists' group the Generation of '27 - dies of a heart attack at age 61 in Mexico City, Mexico.

---○---

November 6, 1893

Composer and conductor Pyotr Ilyich Tchaikovsky (*The Nutcracker*, *Swan Lake*, *The 1812 Overture*, *Romeo and Juliet*) - creator of some of the most popular of the world's orchestrations; his work includes concertos, symphonies, ballets, and operas - dies at age 53 of cholera after drinking a glass of tap water in St. Petersburg, Russia.

November 6, 1932

Arthur Bell is born. Bell was an activist, journalist, early member of the Gay Liberation Front, a founding member of the Gay Activists Alliance, a columnist for *The Village Voice*, and the author of *Dancing the Gay Lib Blues* and *Kings Don't Mean a Thing*.

November 6, 1949

Golden Globe winning actor Brad Davis *(Midnight Express, Chariots of Fire, Querelle, Sybil)* is born in Tallahassee, FL.

November 6, 1976

Author Patrick Dennis (*Auntie Mame*, *Little Me*) – the first author to have three books on *The New York Times* bestseller list simultaneously – dies of pancreatic cancer at age 55 in Manhattan, N.Y.

November 6, 1985

Actor Joel Crothers - two time Daytime Emmy nominee for his role as Miles Cavanaugh in *The Edge of Night* and well remembered for his role as Joe Haskell/Nathan Forbes on the daytime soap opera *Dark Shadows* - dies of AIDS-related lymphoma at age 44 in Los Angeles, CA.

November 6, 2012

Seven-term Democratic congresswoman Tammy Baldwin from Wisconsin defeats former Governor Tommy Thompson to become the first openly gay politician elected to the Senate.

November 6, 2018

Democratic candidate Jared Polis wins the Colorado governor race, becoming the nation's first openly gay man to be elected governor.

November 7, 1921

Author, editor, and songwriter Lisa Ben (aka Edythe D. Eyde) who created the first known lesbian publication in the world, *Vice Versa* (which published nine issues from June 1947 - February 1948), is born in San Francisco, CA.

November 7, 1961

Jose Sarria - a waiter and drag entertainer at the Black Cat, runs for a San Francisco City Supervisor spot - becoming the first openly gay candidate to run for political office in the U.S. Out of a field of 32 candidates, with six open seats, he receives 5,600+ votes and comes in 9th - an indication of the growing political force of the gay voting block. As an added claim to fame, in 1964 Sarria declares himself "Empress Jose I, the Widow Norton" thereby founding the Imperial Court System.

November 7, 1978

Influential journalist and writer Janet Flanner - Paris correspondent for *The New Yorker* from 1925-1975 and winner of the National Book Award - dies at age 86 in New York City.

November 7, 1978

Proposition 6 aka The Briggs Initiative appears on the California ballot seeking to ban gays and lesbians from working in California public schools. The drive to defeat the measure was led by political newcomer Harvey Milk, whose high-profile challenge to powerful State Senator John Briggs led to Prop 6's defeat by 58% of the voters. This critical victory for gay and lesbian rights was cause for much jubilation – but it would be short-lived. Harvey Milk was assassinated three weeks later.

November 7, 1989

The airing of the controversial "Strangers" episode [Season 3, Episode 6] of ABC drama series *thirtysomething* causes a stir when two men are shown in bed together, after having sex, for the first time on network TV.

November 7, 1990

Stonewall Award winning activist, author, and film aficionado Vito Russo (*The Celluloid Closet*) dies at age 44 from an AIDS-related illness in Manhattan, N.Y. Russo was one of the earliest activists to study the impact of the media and entertainment industry representation of gays and lesbians. He also organized queer cinema screenings for the Gay Activists Alliance and later was a founding member of the Gay and Lesbian Alliance Against Defamation (GLAAD).

November 7, 1991

Prolific artist Touko Laaksonen aka Tom of Finland - known for his stylized and sexually charged homoerotic art which has had a deep and lasting impact on gay iconography - dies of an emphysema-induced stroke at the age of 71 in Helsinki, Finland.

November 7, 1992

Playwright Scott McPherson (*Marvin's Room*) - winner of a Drama Desk Award as well as an Outer Critics Circle Award - dies of an AIDS-related illness at age 32 in Chicago, IL.

November 7, 2017

Virginia elects Danica Roem to the Virginia House of Delegates. Roem becomes the first openly transgender candidate elected to a state legislature in American history.

November 8

Intersex Day of Remembrance (Intersex Solidarity Day) is observed to highlight issues faced by intersex people. The date also marks the birthday of Herculine Barbin.

November 8, 1838

Memoirist, activist, and intersex person Herculine Barbin, is born in Saint-Jean-d'Angely, France. Barbin was determined female at birth, wrote their autobiography after being declared to be male as an adult. The unwanted change of gender is considered to be a contributing factor to their suicide in February 1868.

November 8, 1957

Pioneering artist George Quaintance – known for his idealized and strongly homoerotic work and whose art was used for the first cover of *Physique Pictorial* — dies of a heart attack at age 55.

November 8, 1998

Actor Jean Marais (*Orpheus, Fantomas, Beauty and the Beast*) - longtime lover of Jean Cocteau and recipient of the Legion of Honor - dies of cardiovascular disease at age 84 in Cannes, France.

November 8, 2009

Professor and activist Dr. Hilda Hidalgo - who held a number of positions in her 23 years at Rutgers University, co-founded several organizations which answered the needs of the Latino community in the Newark, N.J. area, and later became involved with gay rights activism in Florida - dies of pancreatic cancer at age 81.

November 9, 1795

Transgender military surgeon and advocate for improved hospital conditions, Dr. James Miranda Barry is born Margaret Ann Bulkley (there is some dispute as to the exact birth-name), in Belfast, Ireland.

November 9, 1905

Roger Edens film producer and composer (*Easter Parade, Good News, Annie Get Your Gun, For Me and My Gal, Babes in Arms, Strike Up the Band, On the Town*) - who won three Oscars for his musical film scores - is born in Hillsboro, TX.

November 9, 2016

Kate Brown is sworn in as governor of Oregon, a day after she was officially elected to the office. Brown becomes the highest-ranking LGBT person elected to office in the United States. Brown took over the governorship without an election after in February 2016 after John Kitzhaber resigned amidst a criminal investigation.

November 10, 1861

Novelist Amy Levy (*Reuben Sachs, The Romance of a Shop*), poet, essayist and the first Jewish woman to attend Cambridge University, is born in London.

November 10, 1891

Poet Arthur Rimbaud (*Illuminations, Rimbaud Complete*) - young genius of modern poetry whose torrid affair with Paul Verlaine ended in disaster - dies of cancer at age 37 in Marseille, France.

November 10, 1913

Poet, filmmaker, Radical Faerie, and member of the Sisters of Perpetual Indulgence, James Broughton (*Packing Up for Paradise: Selected Poems 1946-1996, Coming Unbuttoned, Hymns to Hermes*) is born in Modesto, CA.

November 10, 1973

Lambda Legal Defense and Education Fund officially meets for the first time in New York City.

November 10, 1992

Sandra Bernhard joins the cast of *Roseanne* as Lunchbox waitress and friend Nancy, the first recurring bisexual character on a sitcom.

November 10, 2011

Barbara Grier - writer, publisher, co-founder of Naiad Press in 1973, and former columnist and editor of the Daughter's of Bilitis' periodical *The Ladder* - dies of cancer at age 78 in Tallahassee, FL.

November 11, 1950

The early homophile organization The Mattachine Society (originally called the Society of Fools) – meets for the first time in the living room of Harry Hay in Los Angeles, CA. Drawing its name from medieval French renaissance secret societies and the papier-mâché masks they wore to their conceal identities, the group's core members – Hay, Rudi Gernreich, William Dale Jennings, Bob Hull, and Chuck Rowland – met in secret and remained anonymous during the group's early years.

November 11, 1985

NBC airs the TV-movie *An Early Frost* airs – the first film to cover the topic of AIDS/HIV broadcast in the U.S.

November 11, 1994

The Real World: San Francisco reality star Pedro Zamora dies at age 22 from an AIDS-related illness in Miami, FL.

November 12, 1648

Nun, poet, feminist, and scholar Sor Juana Ines de la Cruz is born in San Miguel Nepantla, near Mexico City. Sor Juana had a reputation as one of the leading lyric poets of her era, but was censured when she confronted the church about keeping women uneducated. She is currently pictured on Mexico's 200-peso note.

November 12, 1982

Disco and Hi-NRG composer and recording artist Patrick Cowley (*Menergy, Right on Target, Do You Wanna Funk*) often credited as a pioneer of electronic dance music, dies of AIDS at age 32 in San Francisco, CA.

November 12, 2017

Gossip columnist Liz Smith, known as the Grand Dame of Dish, who wrote for *The New York Daily News, The Washington Post*, etc., dies at age 94 in Manhattan.

November 13, 1941

Popular television actor Dack Rambo - Jack Ewing on *Dallas*, Jeff Sonnett on *The Guns of Will Sonnett*, Steve Jacobi on *All My Children* - is born in Earlimart, CA.

November 13, 1952

Beloved bisexual children's book author Margaret Wise Brown (*Goodnight Moon, The Runaway Bunny*) dies of an embolism at age 42 in Nice, France.

November 13, 1955

Educator, feminist, and author Anna Livia (*Bruised Fruit*, *Relatively Norma*, *Bulldozer Rising*) is born Julian Brawn in Ireland. Livia is best known academically for linguistics - co-writing the volume *Queerly Phrased,* which dealt with gender and development of queer linguistics, and delving into the feminist aspects of language with *Pronoun Envy.*

November 14, 1906

Silent film actress who epitomized the flapper image, Louise Brooks (*Pandora's Box*, *Diary of a Lost Girl*, *Beggars of Life*) - author of the memoir *Lulu In Hollywood* - is born in Cherryvale, Kansas.

November 14, 1900

Grammy and Oscar winning composer, author, conductor, and educator Aaron Copland (*Appalachian Spring*, *Third Symphony*, *Fanfare for the Common Man*) - winner of the Pulitzer Prize for Music, Kennedy Center honoree, and recipient of a Guggenheim Fellowship - is born in Brooklyn, N.Y.

November 14, 1991

British new wave film director and winner of two Oscars, Tony Richardson (*Tom Jones*, *A Taste of Honey*, *Look Back in Anger*, *The Loneliness of the Long Distance Runner*, *Blue Sky*) - father of Natasha and Joely Richardson with Vanessa Redgrave - dies of an AIDS-related illness at age 63 in Los Angeles, CA.

November 14, 2003

Actor Gene Anthony Ray - best known for his role as Leroy Johnson in the film and television series *Fame* - dies at age 41 of complications from a stroke in New York City.

November 15, 1952

The Articles of Incorporation are signed for the early gay organization ONE, Inc.

November 15, 1978

Cultural anthropologist, lecturer, and writer Margaret Mead (*Coming of Age in Samoa, Sex and Temperament in Three Primitive Societies, Male and Female*) - who is credited with changing the way we study different cultures and expanding the scope of anthropology - dies of pancreatic cancer at age 76 in New York City.

November 15, 1991

Songwriter and music executive Jacques Morali – a pioneer in the French disco sound and the creator of the group The Village People and wrote many of their hits (*Macho Man, YMCA, In The Navy*) as well as those for The Ritchie Family (*Best Disco in Town*) – dies at age 45 of an AIDS-related illness in Paris, France.

November 15, 1997

Jim Kepner – founder and curator of the International Gay and Lesbian Archives, and principal associate of ONE, Inc. – dies at age 74 following surgery for a perforated intestine in Los Angeles, CA.

November 15, 2002

Writer, painter, and activist Mary Meigs (*The Medusa Head, Lily Briscoe: a Self-Portrait*) who became a spokesperson for elderly lesbians; dies at age 85 in Montreal, Canada following a series of strokes.

November 15, 2017

Rapper, singer, songwriter Lil Peep (*Come Over When You're Sober, Pt. 1, Come Over When You're Sober, Pt. 2*) overdoses at age 21 in Tucson, AZ.

———————————⊖———————————

November 16, 1928

Radcliffe Hall's groundbreaking lesbian novel *The Well of Loneliness,* is judged by the British courts to be obscene and is banned. All existing copies of it are ordered to be destroyed.

November 16, 1931

Theatrical producer Joe Cino - who in 1958 opened Caffe Cino in Greenwich Village, cited as the birthplace of Off-Off Broadway and gay theater - is born Buffalo, N.Y.

November 16, 1952

Major League Baseball player Glenn Burke, who was one of the first professional athletes to come out of the closet while still actively playing and who played for the Los Angeles Dodgers and Oakland Athletics from 1976-1979 – is born in Oakland, CA. He is credited with popularizing the High-Five.

November 17, 1901

"Los 41" takes place in Mexico City when police raid a private gay dance, where 19 of the men are dressed as women, and 41 are arrested. It becomes a scandal, causing even the number 41 to become taboo. For this reason in Mexico there is no 41st division in the military, no number 41 on the payroll, no room 41 in many hotels and hospitals, street numbers skip 41, and some men even skip their 41st birthday for fear of being considered gay.

November 17, 1911

Choreographer and director Charles Walters (*Easter Parade*, *High Society*, *Please Don't Eat the Daisies*) - who was nominated for an Oscar for Best Director for *Lili* - is born in Brooklyn, N.Y.

November 17, 1925

Oscar nominated actor Rock Hudson *(Giant, Pillow Talk, McMillan and Wife)* a top 10 box office star from 1957-1964, is born in Winnetka, IL. Hudson became the first major figure to announce that he had AIDS (July 1985) and subsequently donated a quarter of a million dollars to help the fledgling organization the National AIDS Research Foundation (NARF).

November 17, 1992

Poet, essayist, educator, and activist Audre Lorde (*Zami: A New Spelling of My Name*, *From a Land Where Other People Live*, *Sister Outsider*, *The Black Unicorn*, *The Cancer Journals*) - founding influence of Kitchen Table, Women of Color Press - dies of cancer at age 58 in St. Croix, V.I.

November 17, 1996

Author, editor, historian, and lecturer Martin Greif (*The Gay Book of Days*, *The World of Tomorrow*) dies at age 58 of an AIDS-related illness in Cork, Ireland.

November 18, 1906

Writer Klaus Mann (*Mephisto*, *Der Vulkan*, *The Turning Point*) and son of writer Thomas Mann, is born in Munich, Germany.

November 18, 1909

Belle Epoque poet Renee Vivien (*Roses Rising*, *The Touch*, Prolong *the Night*) - who counted Natalie Clifford Barney and Baroness Heléne de Zuylen de Nyevelt among her lovers - dies at age 32 from lung congestion attributed to pneumonia complicated by alcoholism, drug abuse, and anorexia nervosa in Paris, France.

November 18, 1922

Writer Marcel Proust - whose *Remembrance of Things Past* was published in seven parts between 1913-1927 and is considered a masterpiece of literature - dies of pneumonia and a pulmonary abscess at age 51 in Paris, France.

November 18, 1986

Supermodel Gia Marie Carangi - popular during the late 1970s and early 1980s and portrayed by Angelina Jolie in the 1998 HBO movie *Gia* - dies at age 26 from an AIDS-related illness in Philadelphia, PA.

November 18, 1996

Transgender artist, and sculptor Greer Lankton - known primarily for the strange dolls she crafted from non-traditional materials - is found dead at age 38 in her apartment in Chicago, IL. Lankton's final exhibit has become a permanent installation at Andy Warhol's Mattress Factory in Pittsburgh, PA.

November 18, 1999

Composer, translator, and author Paul Bowles (*The Sheltering Sky, The Stories of Paul Bowles*) - the embodiment of individualism - dies of heart failure at age 88 in Tangier, Morocco.

November 18, 1999

Fashion photographer Horst P. Horst (*Horst: 60 Years of Photography*) - who often worked with *Vogue* and *House & Garden* was also known for his shots of celebrities and interiors - dies at age 93 in Palm Beach Gardens, FL.

―――――――――――――○―――――――――――――

November 19, 1889

Actor Clifton Webb (*Laura*, *Cheaper By the Dozen*, *The Razor's Edge*, *Sitting Pretty*) - nominated for three Oscars, winner of a Golden Globe Award, and the man who first introduced Irving Berlin's song *Easter Parade* on Broadway - is born in Indianapolis, IN.

November 19, 1896

Actor Anton Walbrook (*The Life and Death of Colonel Blimp*, *The Red Shoes*, *The Queen of Spades*) is born in Vienna, Austria.

November 19, 1919

Morris Kight – activist, founder/co-founder of several early gay organizations including Gay Liberation Front/Los Angeles, Aid for AIDS, and the Stonewall Democratic Club – is born in Comanche County, TX.

November 19, 1974

Author and illustrator Louise Fitzhugh (*Harriet the Spy*, *The Long Secret*, *Nobody's Family is Going to Change*, *Sport*) dies of a brain aneurysm at age 46 in New Milford, CT.

November 19, 1979

The play *Bent* by Martin Sherman opens on Broadway at the New Apollo Theatre starring Richard Gere and David Dukes.

—————————————○—————————————

November 20, 1858

Author and educator Selma Lagerlof (*The Wonderful Adventures of Nils*, *Gosta Berlings Saga*) - the first female writer to win the Nobel Prize in Literature (1909) - is born in Varmland, Sweden.

November 20, 1934

Lillian Hellman's play *The Children's Hour* – a play about a student who accuses two teachers of a lesbian affair – premieres on Broadway and becomes a huge hit despite the fact that at the time it was illegal to make any reference to homosexuality on stage.

November 20, 1935

Singer, pianist, songwriter Esquerita (*Oh Baby*, *Rockin' The Joint*, *Hey Miss Lucy*) is born in Greenville, S.C.

November 20, 1999

Transgender advocate Gwendolyn Ann Smith commemorates the first Transgender Day of Remembrance to honor the memory of Rita Hester – a transgender woman who was killed in November 1998 – and all people who have suffered violence due to transphobia.

November 20, 2017

Actor, singer, comedian Jim Nabors *(Gomer Pyle, U.S.M.C., The Andy Griffith Show, The Best Little Whorehouse in Texas)* dies at age 87 in Honolulu, HI.

November 21, 1886

Harold Nicholson – diplomat, diarist, and author (*Public Faces*) – whose marriage to Vita Sackville-West was chronicled by their son in *Portrait of a Marriage* – is born in Tehran, Persia.

November 21, 1952

Essayist, chronicler, and novelist Pedro Lemebel (*Poco Hombre, My Tender Matador, La Esquina Es Mi Corazon)*, is born in Santiago, Chile.

November 21, 1999

Flamboyant actor, writer, critic, personality, gay icon, and raconteur Quentin Crisp (*The Naked Civil Servant, Orlando, How to Have a Lifestyle, Resident Alien*) - dies of a heart attack at age 90 in n Manchester, England.

November 22, 1869

Writer Andre Gide (*The Counterfeiters, Corydon, Lafcadio's Adventures, The Immoralist*) - winner of the Nobel Prize in Literature - is born in Paris, France.

November 22, 1913

Composer, conductor, and pianist Benjamin Britten *(Billy Budd, The Young Person's Guide to the Orchestra, A Midsummer Night's Dream, War Requiem)* - multiple Grammy Award winner and a key figure in 20th century classical music - is born in Suffolk, England.

November 22, 1943

Lyricist Lorenz Hart (*Blue Moon, The Lady is a Tramp, My Funny Valentine, It Never Entered My Mind, I Could Write a Book, Bewitched, Bothered and Bewildered*) - the lyricist half of Rogers and Hart, a member of the Songwriters Hall of Fame, and commemorated on a postage stamp - dies of pneumonia at age 48 in New York City.

November 22, 1975

Writer, journalist, and expatriate Solita Solano - whose circle included Djuna Barnes, Romaine Brooks, Natalie Clifford Barney, and Janet Flanner; and who studied with and was the secretary of spiritual leader G.I. Gurdjieff - dies at age 87 in Orgeval, France.

November 23, 1892

Art Deco artist and designer Erte aka Romain de Tirtoff (*Things I Remember: An Autobiography*) is born in St. Petersburg, Russia.

November 23-24, 1973

A group of gay and lesbian teachers, who want to make upper education more gay friendly, establish the Gay Academic Union at a conference held on the campus of the City University of New York.

—————————————○—————————————

November 24, 1886

Editor, memoirist, and author Margaret C. Anderson - who founded and published the art and literature magazine *The Little Review* from 1914-1929 and promoted such writers as Hemingway, Yeats, Pound, and James Joyce (which resulted in obscenity charges) - is born in Indianapolis, IN.

November 24, 1930

Robert Calhoun – Emmy Award winning TV producer of *As the World Turns*, *Another World*, *Guiding Light* and life partner of actor Farley Granger – is born in Brooklyn, N.Y.

November 24, 1944

Warhol drag superstar of the youth-quaking underground film world Candy Darling (*Flesh*, *Women in Revolt*, *Some of My Best Friends Are*) - who is immortalized in rock songs by Lou Reed and the Rolling Stones - is born James Lawrence Slattery in Queens, NY.

November 24, 1967

The Oscar Wilde Memorial Bookshop – the first U.S. bookstore devoted to gay and lesbian authors and literature – opens at 291 Mercer Street in New York City. It will move to Christopher Street in Greenwich Village in 1973, and eventually close on March 29, 2009.

November 24, 1991

Freddie Mercury, lead singer of the glitter rock band Queen (*Bohemian Rhapsody, We Are the Champions, Don't Stop Me Now, Another One Bites the Dust, We Will Rock You, You're My Best Friend*) dies at age 45 of AIDS complications in Kensington, London, England.

November 24, 2004

Mystery writer Joseph Hansen (*The Man Everybody Was Afraid Of, Skinflick, The Boy Who Was Buried This Morning, A Country of Old Men: The Last Dave Brandstetter Mystery*) dies of heart failure at age 81 in Laguna Beach, CA.

―――――――――――○―――――――――――

November 25, 1896

Composer and music critic Virgil Thomson - who collaborated with Gertrude Stein on two operas - *Four Saints and Three Acts and The Mother of Us All* - the latter about the life of Susan B. Anthony - is born in Kansas City, MO. Later in life Thomson was awarded the Kennedy Center Honor as well as a National Book Critics Circle Award.

November 25, 1956

Lambda Literary Award and Stonewall Book Award winning author and AIDS activist David B. Feinberg (*Eighty-Sixed, Spontaneous Combustion, Queer and Loathing: Rants and Raves of a Raging AIDS Clone*) is born in Lynn, MA.

November 25, 1970

Writer Yukio Mishima (*Confessions of a Mask, Way of the Samurai, The Sound of Waves*) – whose conflicted bisexuality belied his hyper-masculine persona – commits seppuku (ritual suicide) at age 45 in Tokyo, Japan.

November 25, 2005

Pierre Seel – the only French person to testify openly about his experience as a homosexual Holocaust survivor of a Nazi concentration camp during WWII – dies of cancer at age 82 in Toulouse, France.

November 26, 1832

Mary Edwards Walker, surgeon, abolitionist, activist, field service doctor during the Civil War, and the first woman, and to this date the only woman, to win the Congressional Medal of Honor, is born in Oswego, NY.

November 26, 1905

Tony Award nominated actor and playwright Emlyn Williams - best known for writing the plays *Night Must Fall* and *The Corn is Green* and who also did a good amount of film work - is born in Mostyn, Flintshire, Wales.

November 26, 1939

Entertainment personality and puppeteer Wayland Flowers –
who appeared with his puppet Madame on numerous TV shows
and nightclubs and starred in the series *Madame's Place* – is
born in Dawson, GA.

November 26, 1957

Anti-apartheid, gay rights, and AIDS activist Simon
Nkoli - who founded the Gay and Lesbian Organization of
Witwatersrand, was one of the first publicly HIV+ African
men, and who started the group Positive African Men in
Johannesburg - is born in Soweto, South Africa.

November 26, 1957

Visual artist Felix Gonzalez-Torres – known for his minimalist
sculptures and installations which were defined by the AIDS
epidemic –– is born in Guaimaro, Cuba.

November 26, 1970

ABC-TV's *The Dick Cavett Show* airs an episode featuring
representatives of the gay community talking about gay issues.

November 26, 1978

ABC-TV airs *A Question of Love,* a critically acclaimed
television movie starring Gena Rowlands and Jane Alexander
as lesbians who become embroiled in a child custody battle.

November 26, 1987

Photographer Peter Hujar (*Peter Hujar: a Retrospective,*

Portraits In Life and Death) - known for his black and white portraits and also the friend and one time lover of David Wojnarowicz - dies of an AIDS-related illness at age 53.

November 26, 2008

The biographical film *Milk* by Gus Van Sant opens. The film will go on to be nominated for eight Oscars and will win two - for Sean Penn as Best Actor and for Dustin Lance Black's original screenplay.

November 27, 8 BC

Roman poet, critic, and satirist Horace (*Odes*, *The Satires*, *Arts Poetica*) - who has had a profound influence cn both poetry and criticism - dies at age 56 in Rome.

November 27, 1964

Writer and essayist David Rakoff (*Fraud*, *Don't Get Too Comfortable*, *Half-Empty*) - winner of the Lambda Literary Award as well as the Thurber Prize for American Humor - is born in Montreal, Quebec, Canada.

November 27, 1978

Iconic politician Harvey Milk – one of the first openly gay people to be elected to public office when he won a seat on the San Francisco Board of Supervisors and who was posthumously awarded the Presidential Medal of Freedom – is assassinated at age 48, along with Mayor George Moscone, at City Hall in San Francisco, CA

November 27, 1986

Actor Steve Tracy – who portrayed Percival Dalton on the TV series *Little House on the Prairie* – dies of AIDS-related complications at age 34 in Tampa, FL.

November 27, 2007

Author and educator Jane Rule (*Desert of the Heart, After the Fire, One Another's Arms*) dies at age 76 from liver cancer complications on Galiano Island, Canada.

November 27, 2009

Transgender writer Christine Daniels (who was a sports columnist for the *Los Angeles Times* named Mike Penner prior to her transition) commits suicide at the age of 52 in Los Angeles, CA.

———————————— ⊖ ————————————

November 28, 1794
Military officer Friedrich von Steuben – who served as Inspector General and Major General of the Continental Army during the American Revolutionary War – dies at age 64 in Utica, N.Y.

November 28, 1949

Cartoonist Jok Church (*Beakman's World, You Can With Beakman and Jax*) is born in Akron, OH.

---○---

November 29, 1915

Jazz composer and pianist Billy Strayhorn (*Lush Life*, *Take the A Train*, *Satin Doll*) – the frequently unheralded collaborator with Duke Ellington – is born in Dayton, OH.

November 29, 1952

The early gay organization ONE, Inc. holds its first meeting at Studio Bookshop in Hollywood, CA. Under the pseudonym Anthony Ryceman, founding members Martin Block, William Dale Jennings, and Antonio Sanchez aka Don Slater draft the Articles of Incorporation.

November 29, 1984

West Hollywood, CA. becomes the first "gay city" in the U.S. when voters in the previously unincorporated portion of Los Angeles vote to become incorporated on November 6 (1984); as a result when the new city council of West Hollywood formally meets, it has a majority of LGBT members. The general population of the new city is estimated at 40% LGBT.

November 29, 1986

Definitive Hollywood leading man, Cary Grant (*North by Northwest*, *The Philadelphia Story, Charade, Arsenic and Old Lace, An Affair to Remember*), dies of a heart attack at age 82 in Davenport, IA.

———————————————○———————————————

November 30, 1900

Dramatist, critic, novelist, and poet Oscar Wilde (*The Picture of Dorian Gray*, *The Importance of Being Earnest, An Ideal Husband, Salome*) - who at the height of his career was accused of being a sodomite and subsequently tried and sentenced to two years at hard labor - dies at age 46 in Paris, France.

November 30, 1979

Photographer Laura Gilpin (*The Pueblos: A Camera Chronicle, The Enduring Navajo, The Rio Grande*) - known for her pictures of Native Americans - dies at age 88 in Santa Fe, N.M.

November 30, 1987

Novelist, essayist, activist, and playwright James Baldwin (*Giovanni's Room, Go Tell it on the Mountain, The Fire Next Time*) – National Book Award nominee and a passionate, literary voice during the turbulent days of the mid-20th century Civil Rights Movement – dies of esophageal cancer at age 63 in Saint-Paul de Vence, France.

November 30, 1997

Experimental postmodern writer and performance artist Kathy Acker *(My Mother Demonology, Blood and Guts in High School, Pussycat Fever, Literal Madness)* dies of breast cancer at age 50 in Tijuana, Mexico.

November 30, 1998

South African anti-apartheid, gay rights, and AIDS activist Simon Nkoli who founded the Gay and Lesbian Organization of Witwatersrand, was one of the first publicly HIV+ African men, and who started the group Positive African Men in Johannesburg - dies at age 41 from an AIDS-related illness in Johannesburg, South Africa.

DECEMBER

December 1, 1947

Occultist, magician, poet, and painter Aleister Crowley, who called himself the Beast 666 and whose works include *The Diary of a Drug Fiend* and *The Book of Thoth*, dies at age 72 in Hastings, U.K.

December 1, 1952

The New York Daily News headline announces *Ex-GI Becomes Blond Beauty* to herald the arrival of Christine Jorgensen in New York, the first publicly known person to undergo sex-reassignment surgery.

December 1, 1976

Matthew Shepard – a college student whose torture and murder in 1998 will make him a symbol of the horror of hate crimes, and lead to the passage of first-ever LGBT-inclusive federal hate-crimes law – is born in Casper, WY.

December 1, 1988

The first World AIDS Day is observed.

December 1, 1989

Choreographer and dance pioneer Alvin Ailey - founder of the Alvin Ailey American Dance Theater in 1958, choreographer of such productions as *Revelations*, and recipient of the Kennedy Center Honors - dies at age 58 of an AIDS-related illness in Manhattan, N.Y.

December 1, 1989

A Day Without Art is first observed as a national day of action and mourning in response to the AIDS crisis.

December 1, 2011

Actor and comic Alan Sues - best remembered for his work as a regular on *Rowan & Martin's Laugh-In* 1968-1972 - dies of a heart attack at age 85 in West Hollywood, CA.

December 2, 1935

M. Carey Thomas, educator suffragist, and second president of Bryn Mawr College - where she demanded the highest standards from both faculty and students – dies of a coronary occlusion at age 78 in Philadelphia, PA.

December 2, 1946

Fashion designer Gianni Versace - who built an $800 million dollar empire in a decade - is born in Reggio Calabria, Italy.

December 2, 1964

At Cooper Union in New York City, four gay men and lesbians picket the lecture "Homosexuality: A Disease" by a psychoanalyst who claims homosexuality is a mental illness.

December 2, 1990

Grammy and Oscar winning composer, author, conductor, and educator Aaron Copland *(Appalachian Spring, Third Symphony, Fanfare for the Common Man)* - winner of the Pulitzer Prize for Music, Kennedy Center honoree, and recipient of a Guggenheim Fellowship - dies of Alzheimer's disease and respiratory failure at age 90 in Sleepy Hollow, N.Y.

December 2, 2005

The independent comedy/drama *Transamerica* is released about a transsexual woman on a road trip with her long lost son. The film will eventually garner several awards, including a Best Actress Oscar nomination for Felicity Huffman.

―――――――――――○―――――――――――

December 3, 1946

Historian, scholar, and activist Allan Berube *(Coming Out Under Fire: The History of Gay Men and Women in WWII)* - who received a MacArthur Fellowship as well as a Lambda Literary Award and who helped start the San Francisco Gay and Lesbian History Project - is born in Springfield, MA.

December 3, 1984

Popular Portuguese singer, songwriter and innovative entertainer Antonio Variacoes (*Anjo de Guarda, Dar & Receber*) is born in Braga, Portugal.

December 3, 1996

Hawaii's Judge Chang rules the state has no legal right to deprive same-sex couples of the right to marry, making Hawaii the first U.S. state to recognize that gay couples are entitled to the same privileges as heterosexual married couples.

December 3, 2000

The Showtime series *Queer as Folk,* about the lives of five gay men in Pittsburgh, PA., makes its debut, becoming the first hour long TV drama series to chronicle the lives of gay men and lesbians.

––––––––––––––––––––○––––––––––––––––––––

December 4, 1976

English composer, conductor, and pianist Benjamin Britten *(Billy Budd, The Young Person's Guide to the Orchestra, A Midsummer Night's Dream, War Requiem)* - multiple Grammy Award winner and a key figure in 20th century classical music - dies of congestive heart failure at age 63 in Aldeburgh, England.

December 4, 1989

Award winning poet May Swenson (*Dear Elizabeth, New and Selected Things Taking Place, Nature: Poems Old and New*)

- whose many awards and honors include a Bollingen Prize, a nomination for The National Book Award, and a fellowship from the MacArthur Foundation - dies at age 76 from complications due to chronic asthma in Bethany Beach, DE.

December 4, 2013

Luxembourg becomes the first country in the world to have an openly gay Prime Minister Xavier Bettel and an openly gay Deputy Prime Minister Etienne Schneider.

December 5, 1889

Singer and actress Marie-Louise Damien aka Damia (*Napoleon, Tu Ne Sais Pas Aimer, C'est Mon Gigolo*) - part of the Paris circle which included Natalie Clifford Barney, Romaine Brooks, Loie Fuller, etc. - is born in Alsace-Lorraine, France.

December 5, 1984

Berkeley, CA. becomes the first city in the U S. to extend spousal benefits to LGBT city employees and their live in lovers/partners. To qualify, an affidavit of domestic partnership is required.

December 5, 1990

Lambda Literary Award nominated playwright, journalist, composer, and educator Robert Chesley (*Jerker*) - and whose play *Night Sweat* was one of the first produced full-length plays to deal with the AIDS epidemic - dies of an AIDS-related illness at age 47 in San Francisco, CA.

December 5, 1998

The Bisexual Pride Flag, designed by Michael Page, featuring a deep pink stripe and a royal blue stripe separated by a lavender stripe – to represent the continuum of bisexual attraction – is unveiled for the first time.

―――――――――――○―――――――――――

December 6, 1892

Novelist, poet, memoirist, and essayist Sir Francis Osbert Sitwell, 5th Baronet (*Open the Door, Those Were the Days, Great Morning!, Laughter in the Next Room, Before the Bombardment*) is born in London, England.

December 6, 1900

Actress Agnes Moorehead (*The Magnificent Ambersons, Pollyanna, Citizen Kane, Journey Into Fear, Hush Hush Sweet Charlotte*) – nominated for four Oscars and best known for her portrayal of Samantha Stevens' mother Endora in the 1960s sitcom *Bewitched* – is born in Clinton, MA.

December 6, 1955

Commercial and figure photographer George Platt Lynes (*George Platt Lynes: The Male Nudes, When We Were Three, George Platt Lynes: Photographs from the Kinsey Institute*) dies at age 48 of lung cancer in New York City.

December 6, 1988

Actor Timothy Patrick Murphy (Mickey Trotter on *Dallas, Search for Tomorrow*; *Glitter, Sam's Son, The Love Boat*) dies from an AIDS-related illness at age 29 in Sherman Oaks, CA.

December 6, 2010

Hugues Cuenod, a tenor in opera, operetta, and traditional musical theater – who made his debut at the Metropolitan Opera at the age of 84 – dies at age 108 in Vevey, Switzerland.

December 6, 2015

Warhol underground superstar, trans actress (*Trash, Women in Revolt*) and author (*A Low Life in High Heels*) Holly Woodlawn dies of cancer at age 69 in Los Angeles, CA.

December 6, 2018

Bisexual punk rock icon, singer, songwriter, guitarist Pete Shelley, front man of the Buzzcocks, dies of a heart attack at age 63 in Talinn, Estonia.

––––––––––––––⦶––––––––––––––

December 7, 1873

Pulitzer Prize winning writer Willa Cather (*My Antonia, O Pioneers!, Death Comes for the Archbishop*) is born in Gore, VA.

December 7, 1946

Actress Laurette Taylor *(The Glass Menagerie, One Night in Rome, Happiness)* - the original Amanda Wingfield in the Broadway production of *The Glass Menagerie* - dies from a coronary thrombosis at age 63 in New York City.

December 7, 1970

Painter Romaine Brooks (*The Cross of France, White Azaleas*) - who specialized in portraiture with a somber and subdued color palette and who was also the one-time lover of Natalie Clifford Barney - dies at age 96 in Nice, France.

December 7, 1975

Playwright and novelist Thornton Wilder (*The Skin of Our Teeth, Our Town, The Eighth Day, The Bridge of San Luis Rey*) - whose many honors and awards include Pulitzer Prizes both for Fiction as well as Drama and a National Book Award - dies in his sleep of an apparent heart attack at age 78 in Hamden, CT.

December 7, 1990

Cuban writer Reinaldo Arenas (*Before Night Falls, Old Rosa, Farewell to the Sea*) - who supported and later rebelled against Fidel Castro's Cuban government before fleeing to the U.S. - commits suicide at age 47 to relieve his suffering from AIDS in New York City.

December 7, 1995

The Food and Drug Administration (FDA) approves the first protease inhibitor drug for the treatment of HIV.

December 8

Pansexual Pride Day is celebrated.

December 8, 65 BC

Roman poet, critic, and satirist Horace (*Odes, The Satires, Arts Poetica*) - who has had a profound influence on both poetry and criticism - is born in Vesuvia in the Roman Empire.

December 4, 1920

Jeanne Manford, community ally and activist who, in 1973, became the co-founder of the support organization PFLAG, Parents and Friends of Lesbians and Gays, is born in Queens.

December 8, 1939

Marie Kuda, writer, archivist, historian, publisher (Womanpress), activist, and historian of LGBT culture in Chicago, is born in Chicago, IL. Kuda edited and published essential works in lesbian scholarship including *Two Women: The Poetry of Jeannette Howard and Valerie Taylor* and *Women Loving Women: A Select and Annotated Bibliography of Women Loving Women in Literature*.

December 8, 1948

Gay liberation pioneer, women's rights activist, community pioneer, restaurateur, and writer (*Sweet Sixteen*) Vernita Gray is born in Chicago.

December 8, 1950

Singer, songwriter, and music producer Dan Hartman (*I Can Dream About You, Instant Reply, Relight My Fire*) is born in Harrisburg, PA.

December 8, 1954

Surreal artist, photographer, political activist, and writer Claude Cahun aka Lucy Schwob *(Self-Portraits, Heroines, Aveux non Avenus)* - whose work often was self-portraits and often explored gender - dies at age 60 in the Channel Island of Jersey.

December 8, 1981

The 150 member New York City Gay Men's Chorus (NYCGMC) performs at Carnegie Hall at 8:00 p.m. The chorus was founded in August 1980 under the direction of conductor Gary Miller.

December 8, 1996

Academy Award nominated actor Howard E. Rollins Jr. (*In the Heat of the Night, Ragtime, A Soldier's Story*) dies of AIDS-related lymphoma at age 46 in New York City.

December 9, 1717

Art historian and archeologist Johann Joachim Winckelmann *(Reflections on the Painting and Sculpture of the Greeks, History of the Art of Antiquity)* - known as "the founder of modern archeology" - is born in Stendal, Germany. He was the first to differentiate Roman, Greek, and Greco-Roman art and the first to apply scientific archeology to art history.

December 9, 1869

Transgender FTM author, nurse, soldier and adventurer Jack

Bee Garland – who went by numerous names including Elvira Virginia Mugarrieta, Babe, Bean, Jack Beam, Jack Maines, and Beebe Beam – is born in San Francisco, CA.

December 9, 1984

Transgender soldier and colonel in the Mexican Revolution, Amelio Robles Avila - who was awarded a medal as an Honorary Legionnaire of the Mexican Army - dies at age 95 in Xochipala, Guerrero, Mexico.

December 9, 1991

Photographer Berenice Abbott (*Nightview, New York, Hardware Store on the Bowery, Flatiron Building, Under the El at the Battery, James Joyce*) - who after living in bohemian Paris during the 1920s, became a frequent documenter of the life and landscape of New York City - dies at age 93 in Monson, ME.

———————————————○———————————————

December 10
Human Rights Day, which commemorates the day in 1948 the United Nations General Assembly adopted the Universal Declaration of Human Rights, is celebrated.

December 10, 1924

The State of Illinois grants the charter for the Society for Human Rights – the earliest documented homosexual organization in the U.S. which also published the first American publication for homosexuals, *Friendship and Freedom.*

December 10, 1941

Pilot Karen Ulane - whose successful suit against Eastern Airlines, in the wake of being dismissed after her 1980 transition, set a legal precedent for transgender status - is born Kenneth Ulane in Chicago, IL.

December 10, 1965

Avant-garde composer, pianist, and musical theorist Henry Cowell *(The Banshee, Exultation, Suite for Violin and Piano)* - who founded and edited the *New Music Quarterly* and who spent four years in San Quentin (1936-1940) for homosexual conduct - dies at age 68 in Shady, N.Y.

December 10, 1970

Sculptress and artist Thelma Wood - who enjoyed the bohemian lifestyle in Europe and whose lovers included Berenice Abbott and Djuna Barnes - dies of cancer at age 69 in Danbury, CT.

December 10, 1983

In the obituary of Tony Award winning actor David Rounds (Best Featured Actor in a Play for 1980's *Morning's at Seven*) *The New York Times* - for the first time - names a surviving same-sex partner in an obituary.

December 10, 1989

In ACT-UP's biggest and most audacious demonstration, activists gather at St. Patrick's Cathedral in New York City and disrupt Sunday mass to protest the Catholic Church's staunch stance against condom use and AIDS education despite the spread of HIV and the escalating epidemic. More than 5,000 turn out for the demonstration that was done in conjunction with WHAM (Women's Health Action and Mobilization). A total of 111 are arrested both inside and outside the cathedral.

December 10, 2006

The Tony Award winning musical *Spring Awakening* opens at the Eugene O'Neill Theatre.

December 10, 2015

The Color Purple, based on the Alice Walker novel and the Stephen Spielberg film, opens on Broadway at the Bernard B. Jacobs Theatre and will go on to win four Tony Awards.

———————————⊖———————————

December 11, 1913

Actor Jean Marais (*Orpheus*, *Fantomas*, *Beauty and the Beast*) - longtime lover of Jean Cocteau and recipient of the Legion of Honor - is born in Cherbourg, France.

December 11, 1945

Author and editor John Preston (*Mr. Benson*, *I Once Had a Master*, *Franny the Queen of Provincetown*, *Hometowns*) - winner of a Lambda Literary Award as well as the American Library Association's Stonewall Book Award - is born in Medfield, MA.

December 11, 2007

Historian, scholar, and activist Allan Berube (*Coming Out Under Fire: The History of Gay Men and Women in WWII*) - who received a MacArthur Fellowship as well as a Lambda Literary Award and who helped start the San Francisco Gay and Lesbian History Project - dies of complications from stomach ulcers at age 61 in Liberty, NY.

───────────────○───────────────

December 12, 1872

Shakespearean stage actor Edwin Forrest (*Hamlet*, *Macbeth*, *Othello*, *Spartacus*) - a top money earning actor of the 1800s - dies at age 66 in Philadelphia, PA.

December 12, 1968

Theater and film actress Tallulah Bankhead (*Lifeboat*, *A Royal Scandal*, *Devil and the Deep*) - a stage sensation in the 1920s, and later became as famous for her outrageous behavior and larger than life personality as for her acting - dies at age 66 from pneumonia complicated by emphysema and malnutrition in New York City with her supposed final words being "Codeine... bourbon."

December 12, 1972

Brandon Teena – whose rape and murder was the subject of the films *The Brandon Teena Story* and the Academy Award-winning *Boys Don't Cry* – is born Teena Renae Brandon in Lincoln, NE.

December 12, 1999

Artist Paul Cadmus (*YMCA Locker Room*, *Greenwich Village Cafeteria*, *Shore Leave*, *The Fleet's In!*) - known for his oftentimes sensuous and idealized drawings of male figures - dies at age 94 in Weston, CT.

December 12, 2008

Golden era film actor and top box office star Van Johnson (*The Caine Mutiny*, *Two Sailors and a Girl,*. *Brigadoon*, *Thirty Seconds Over Tokyo*, *The Last Time I Saw Paris*) dies at age 92 in Nyack, N.Y.

December 12, 2009

Houston, Texas becomes the largest city in the U.S. with a gay mayor when it elects lesbian Annise Parker 53, to the office in a runoff election. Parker assumed the office and began her term on January 2, 2010

December 13, 1922

Jose Sarria aka the Widow Norton, who in 1951 became the first openly gay candidate for public office in the United States and who also founded the Imperial Court System, is born in San Francisco.

December 13, 1934

Psychiatrist, psychoanalyst and author Richard Isay – a pioneer in changing the way analysts viewed gay people and the author of *Being Homosexual*, *Commitment and Healing*, and *Becoming Gay* – is born in Pittsburgh, PA.

December 13, 1969

U.S. Navy Radioman Petty Officer, Third Class, Allen R. Schindler Jr. – who will become a focal point in the national debate about gays serving in the military when he is brutally murdered by a fellow sailor at age 22 in Sasebo, Nagasaki, Japan – is born in Chicago Heights, IL.

December 13, 1969

Physician Ethel Collins Dunham, the first female member of the American Pediatric Society and recipient of the organization's most prestigious award, the John Howland Medal, dies at age 86 in Cambridge, MA.

December 13, 1983

Writer Mary Renault (*The Persian Boy*, *The Last of the Wine*, *The Charioteer*) – who is principally responsible for bringing the bisexuality of Alexander the Great into the public realm – dies at age 78 in Cape Town, South Africa.

December 15, 1904

W. Dorr Legg – co-founder of both the early homophile organization ONE Inc., and the 1950s interracial homophile social club Knights of the Clock – is born in Ann Arbor, MI.

December 15, 1950

A Senate report entitled *Employment of Homosexuals and Other Perverts in Government* is distributed to members of Congress following an undercover federal investigation into the sexual orientation of government employees that concludes that gays, alcoholics, and neurotics are to be considered security risks.

December 15, 1962

Actor Charles Laughton (*The Hunchback of Notre Dame, Mutiny on the Bounty, Witness for the Prosecution, Spartacus, The Night of the Hunter*) - who was nominated for three Oscars and won once for *The Private Life of Henry VIII* (1933) - dies of kidney/gall bladder cancer at age 63 in Hollywood, CA.

December 15, 1973

The American Psychiatric Association (APA) votes to formally remove homosexuality from the *Diagnostic and Statistical Manual of Mental Disorders*.

December 16, 1899

English playwright, composer, director, actor, and singer Noel Coward (*Private Lives, Hay Fever, Easy Virtue, Blithe Spirit, Design for Living, Quadrille*) - whose many honors include a special Tony Award (1970) for his contributions to the theater and induction into the Songwriters Hall of Fame - is born in Teddington, Middlesex, England.

December 16, 1901

Cultural anthropologist, lecturer, and writer Margaret Mead (*Coming of Age in Samoa, Sex and Temperament in Three Primitive Societies, Male and Female*) - who is credited with changing the way we study different cultures and expanding the scope of anthropology - is born in Philadelphia, PA.

December 16, 1917

Science fiction writer and inventor Arthur C. Clarke *(2001: A Space Odyssey, Rendezvous With Rama, The Fountains of Paradise, A Fall of Moondust, 2010: Odyssey Two)* - winner of multiple Huge and Nebula Awards for fantasy/science fiction writing - is born in Minehead, Somerset, England.

December 16, 1923

Author Gerald Glaskin aka Neville Jackson (*A World of Our Own, No End to the Way, The Road to Nowhere*) - who won the Commonwealth Prize for Literature in 1955 - is born in Perth, Australia. He died in the year 2000, but exact date of his passing is unknown.

December 16, 1965

Popular author W. Somerset Maugham (*The Razor's Edge, The Moon and Sixpence, Of Human Bondage, Rain*) dies at age 91 in Nice, France.

December 16, 1988

Flamboyant, glittery, and oftentimes androgynous singer Sylvester (*You Make Me Feel Mighty Real, Dance Disco Heat, Do Ya Wanna Funk*) - who had one platinum and five gold records - dies of complications from HIV in San Francisco, CA.

December 16, 2018

Angela Ponce, Miss Spain, is the first trans contestant to compete in the Miss Universe pageant.

December 17, 1904

Artist Paul Cadmus (*YMCA Locker Room, Greenwich Village Cafeteria, Shore Leave, The Fleet's In!*) - known for his oftentimes sensuous and idealized drawings of male figures - is born in New York City.

December 17, 1937

Author Bertha Harris (*Lover, Catching Saradove, Confessions of Cherubino, Gertrude Stein*) - who also co-authored *The Joy of Lesbian Sex* - is born in Fayetteville, N.C.

December 17, 1959

Journalist, arts critic, interviewer, broadcaster, and author I.F. Stone *(I.F. Stone: a Portrait; A Portrait in Four Movements: The Chicago Symphony under Barenboim, Boulez, Haitink, and Muti)* is born in Chicago, IL.

December 17, 1987

Writer Marguerite Yourcenar (*Memoirs of Hadrian, Oriental Tales*) - who was the first woman to be elected to the Académie Française - dies at age 84 in Northeast Harbor, ME.

December 18, 1626

Queen Christina of Sweden, who ruled as Queen from 1632 until her abdication in 1654, and who was famous portrayed on film in *Queen Christina* by Greta Garbo, is born in Stockholm, Sweden.

December 18, 1969

The musical *Coco* opens on Broadway – starring Katharine Hepburn as Coco Chanel – featuring what is often considered the first openly gay character in a Broadway musical: Designer Sebastian Baye played by Rene Auberjonois, who won a Tony Award for his performance.

December 18, 2000

Activist and businessman Hal Call dies at age 83 in San Francisco, CA. He was a member of the early homophile group The Mattachine Society, and co-founder of Pan Graphic Press which printed *The Mattachine Review*, *The Ladder*, and other homophile publications. He was also the Founder of the gay and lesbian book clearinghouse Dorian Book Service.

December 18, 2010

The U.S. Senate votes 65-31 to repeal the "Don't Ask, Don't Tell" policy, allowing gays and lesbians to serve openly in the U.S. Military. The vote will be followed by several months' analysis of existing operations, surveying of active-duty personnel, testimony by military branch commanders, and final certification by the Secretary of Defense, the Joints Chiefs of Staff, and the President, to determine the best mechanism for implementing the repeal so as to have the least impact on military readiness.

December 19, 1910

Novelist, playwright, and activist Jean Genet *(Querelle, The Thief's Journal, Our Lady of the Flowers, The Balcony, The Blacks, The Maids)* is born in Paris, France.

December 19, 1994

Popular tenor Vadim Kozin (*Nishchaya, Druzhba*) - who in 1944 was jailed for five years in Stalin's Russia as part of the repression campaign against prominent Soviet performers - dies at age 91 in Magadan, Russia.

December 20, 1865

Acclaimed interior decorator (and former actress) Elsie de Wolfe aka Lady Mendl (*Elsie de Wolfe's Recipes for Successful Dining, After All, The House in Good Taste*) is born in Canada.

December 20, 1978

The San Francisco Gay Men's Chorus - founded by Jon Reed Sims and the world's first chorus to openly identify as gay - holds its first formal concert.

December 20, 1999

Film director Irving Rapper (*Now, Voyager, Deception, Marjorie Morningstar, The Corn is Green, The Glass Menagerie, The Christine Jorgensen Story*) - best remembered for the films he did with Bette Davis - dies at age 101 in Woodland Hills, CA.

———————————————○———————————————

December 21, 1964

Writer, journalist, and photographer Carl van Vechten (*Parties, Peter Whiffle, The Tattooed Countess, Sacred and Profane Memories*) - patron and unofficial publicist of the Harlem Renaissance and also known for the vast photographic portraits of his very wide circle of friends - dies at age 64 in New York City.

December 21, 1969

The Gay Activists Alliance (GAA) is formed by dissident members of the Gay Liberation Front. The group sought to remain politically neutral while focusing on securing basic human rights, dignity and freedom for all gay people. The Greek letter lambda (λ) was selected as the GAA symbol.

December 21, 1989

Photographer and activist Rotimi Fani-Kayode *(Communion, Black Male/White Male Photographs, Traces of Ecstasy)* - known for his staged photos which frequently blend eroticism, symbolism, and his Nigerian roots - dies of an AIDS-related illness at age 34 in London, England

December 21, 1993

President Bill Clinton issues Department of Defense Directive 1304.26 – a compromise policy intended to protect gay and lesbian service members from discharge so long as they did not volunteer information about their sexual orientation. Known colloquially as "Don't Ask, Don't Tell" – the policy runs counter to Clinton's campaign promise to lift the military's ban on homosexuals in the armed forces. "Don't Ask, Don't Tell" will remain in effect for 17 years until it was overturned by the U.S. Senate on December 18, 2010, and formally repealed by President Barack Obama on September 20, 2011.

———————————⊖———————————

December 22, 1934

Harlem Renaissance era author, editor, poet and playwright Wallace Thurman - whose novel *The Blacker the Berry* addresses such controversial issues as homosexuality, abortion, and intra-racial prejudice - dies of tuberculosis at age 32 in New York City.

December 22, 1939

Blues singer Ma Rainey (*Ma Rainey's Black Bottom*, *See See Rider Blues*, *Bo-Weavil Blues*) - one of the earliest known professional blues singers - dies of a heart attack at age 53 in Rome, GA.

December 22, 2001

Writer and performer Lance Loud - known primarily for his appearance on the 1973 PBS reality series *An American Family* in which he came out as a gay man - dies at age 50 of liver failure from Hepatitis C, complicated by HIV, in Los Angeles, CA.

December 22, 2015

Author, editor, and songwriter Lisa Ben (aka Edythe D. Eyde), who created the first known lesbian publication in the world, *Vice Versa* (which published nine issues from June 1947-February 1948), dies at age 94 in Burbank, CA.

December 23, 1888

German-Hungarian novelist, playwright and sculptor Christa Winsloe (*Madchen in Uniform/Girls in Uniform, Life Begins, Half the Violin*) - who boldly explored lesbian and gay themes in her writing during the 1930s and was one time lover of American journalist Dorothy Thompson - is born in Darmstadt, Germany.

December 23, 1993

Activist and author Darrell Yates Rist - co-founder of the Gay and Lesbian Alliance Against Defamation and the author of the travelogue of gay life in the U.S., *Heartlands* - dies of an AIDS-related illness at age 45 in New York City.

December 23, 1993

The Academy Award-winning film *Philadelphia* is released. Directed by Jonathan Demme and starring Tom Hanks and Denzel Washington, it is one of Hollywood's first mainstream films to address AIDS and homophobia. Hanks wins an Oscar for his performance.

December 24, 1930

Dancer and choreographer Robert Joffrey, co-founder and artistic director of the Joffrey Ballet - which he began in 1956 and which often brought ballet to people for the first time - is born in Seattle, WA.

December 24, 1946

Bisexual activist Brenda Howard, known as the Mother
of Pride for her work in coordinating a rally and then
the Christopher Street Liberation Day March on the first
anniversary of the Stonewall Riots, is born in the Bronx, N.Y.

December 24, 1959

Director, screenwriter, playwright, and actor Edmund Goulding
(*Grand Hotel*, *Dark Victory*, *White Banners*, *The Razor's Edge*,
The Great Lie, *Nightmare Alley*, *The Old Maid*) dies during
heart surgery at age 68 in Los Angeles, CA.

December 24, 1990

Actress, comedienne, and storyteller Pat Bond (*Gerty Gerty
Gerty Stein is Back Back Back*, *Murder in the WAC*, *Lorena
Hickok and Eleanor Roosevelt: A Love Story*, *Word is Out*,
Designing Women) dies of emphysema at age 65 in Marin
County, CA.

December 24, 1994

Historian John Boswell (*Christianity, Social Tolerance, and
Homosexuality*, *Same Sex Unions in Premodern Europe*, *The
Kindness of Strangers*) - winner of the American Book Award
and Stonewall Book Award as well as Lambda Literary Award
nominee - dies of an AIDS-related illness at age 47 in New
Haven, CT.

---○---

December 25, 1843

Transgender Civil War soldier Albert D. J. Cashier is born Jennie Irene Hodgers in Clogherhead, Ireland.

December 25, 1908

Flamboyant actor, writer, critic, personality, gay icon, and raconteur Quentin Crisp (*The Naked Civil Servant, Orlando, How to Have a Lifestyle, Resident Alien*) - is born in Sutton, England.

December 25, 1936

Film producer Ismail Merchant (*A Room with a View, Maurice, Howard's End*) - who was nominated for four Oscars - is born in Bombay, India.

December 25, 2016

Singer, songwriter, and record producer George Michael whose many hit records included solo work (*Faith, I Want Your Sex, One More Try*) and with the band Wham! (*Wake Me Up Before You Go-Go, Careless Whisper*) dies of natural causes at age 53 at Goring-on-Thames.

---○---

December 26, 1973

Popular silent film and early talkies actor Billy Haines (*Show People, Alias Jimmy Valentine, Brown of Howard*) – who turned his back on Hollywood when he was given an ultimatum about hiding his homosexuality by entering into a lavender marriage – dies of lung cancer at the age of 73 in Santa Monica, CA.

December 26, 2001

Oscar nominated actor Nigel Hawthorne (*Armistad*, *The Madness of King George*, *Demolition Man*) - who won six BAFTA Awards - dies of a heart attack at age 72 in Radwell, England.

December 26, 2002

Fashion photographer Herb Ritts *(Notorious, Duo, Work, Africa)* - known for his clean composition and his work with celebrity portraits – dies at age 50 from complications from pneumonia in Los Angeles, Among his many photos was the shot of Cindy Crawford mock shaving k.d. lang on the cover of the August 1993 issue of *Vanity Fair.*

December 27, 1901

Oscar nominated actress and entertainment legend Marlene Dietrich (*Morocco*, *Destry Rides Again*, *The Blue Angel*, *Blonde Venus*, *Shanghai Express*, *A Foreign Affair*, *A Touch of Evil*, *Judgment at Nuremberg*, *Witness for the Prosecution*) - who won a special Tony Award as well as the U.S. War Department's Medal of Freedom for her WWII work entertaining troops - is born in Schoneberg, Germany.

December 27, 1932

Fred 'Fritz' Klein – activist, sex researcher, inventor of the Klein Sexual Orientation Grid, and author *(The Bisexual Option, Bisexualities: Theory and Research, Bisexual and Gay Husbands)* and founder of the *Journal of Bisexuality* – is born in Vienna, Austria.

December 27, 1988

Activist, editor, columnist, and author Joseph F. Beam - who was motivated to create and edit the anthology *In the Life* (1986) due to the lack of gay literature by men of color and was also the founding editor of the national magazine *Black/Out* - dies at age 33 of an AIDS-related illness.

December 27, 1990

Activist Chuck Rowland - core Mattachine Society member (along with Harry Hay, William Dale Jennings, Bob Hull, and Rudi Gernreich) who was also active with ONE, Inc. and the Church of One Brotherhood) dies at age 73 in Duluth, MN.

December 27, 1993

Activist, actor, singer, and songwriter Michael Callen (*Zero Patience, Surviving AIDS*) - a founding member of the gay male a cappella singing group The Flirtations - dies of AIDS-related complications at age 38 in Los Angeles, CA.

December 27, 1999

Author and screenwriter Michael McDowell (*The Amulet, Blackwater, The Elementals, Tales From the Darkside, Beetlejuice, The Nightmare Before Christmas*) aka gay mystery writer Nathan Aldyne (*Cobalt*, *Vermilion*, *Canary*) dies of an AIDS-related illness at age 49 in Boston, MA.

December 27, 2000

Oscar nominated actor Alan Bates (*Georgy Girl*, *Women in Love*, *King of Hearts*, *Gosford Park*) - who also won two Tony Awards and one BAFTA Award - dies of pancreatic cancer at age 69 in London, England.

December 27, 2015

Painter, sculptor, and printmaker Ellsworth Kelly (*Houston Triptych*, *Black Ripe*, *Sculpture for a Large Wall*, *Red Curves*, *Red Blue Green)* dies at age 92 in Spencertown, NY.

———————————◯———————————

December 28, 1879

Born Charlotte Darkey Parkhurst in 1812 – transgender stage coach driver, early California settler, fighter, farmer, and expert woodsman Charlie Parkhurst – dies at age 67 of cancer of the tongue in Watsonville, CA.

December 28, 1882

Male to female gender pioneer Lili Elbe - who was eventually classified as intersex and who was the subject of the 1933 biography *Man into Woman* and the novel *The Danish Girl* (2000) - is born Einar Mogens Wegener in Denmark.

December 28, 1888

Hugely influential German silent film director F.W. Murnau (*Nosferatu*, *Sunrise*, *Faust*) - whose films have withstood the test of time - is born in Bielefeld, Germany.

December 28, 1916

Trans gospel quartet singer and soloist Willmer "Little Ax" Broadnax is born in Houston, TX.

December 28, 1932

Author Manuel Puig (*Kiss of the Spider Woman*, *Betrayed By Rita Hayworth*, *Heartbreak Tango*) - whose work has been translated into over a dozen languages - is born in General Villegas, Argentina.

December 29, 1914

Transgender jazz musician and bandleader Billy Tipton is born Dorothy Lucille Tipton in Oklahoma City, OK.

December 30, 1901

Abstract Expressionist painter Beauford Delaney – a France-based U.S. expatriate, often associated with the Harlem Renaissance – is born in Knoxville, TN.

December 30, 1910

Composer, translator, and author Paul Bowles (*The Sheltering Sky*, *The Stories of Paul Bowles*) - the embodiment of individualism - is born in New York City.

December 30, 1948

Author and painter Denton Welch (*In Youth is Pleasure*, *Brave and Cruel*, *Maiden Voyage*, *A Voice Through a Cloud*) dies of tuberculosis at age 33 in Kent, England.

December 30, 1954

Activist, editor, columnist, and author Joseph F. Beam - who was motivated to create and edit the anthology *In the Life* (1986) due to the lack of gay literature by men of color and was also the founding editor of the national magazine *Black/Out* - is born in Philadelphia, PA.

December 30, 2018

The death of Hector Xtravaganza, icon of New York's ballroom scene, founding member of the House of Xtravagnza, HIV activist, and consultant on the TV show Pose consultant, is announced on social media by the House

---

December 31, 1897

Fashion designer Orry-Kelly (Orry George Kelly) - winner of three Academy Awards for Best Costumes for *An American in Paris*, *Les Girls*, and *Some Like it Hot* - is born in Kiama, New South Wales, Australia.

December 31, 1924

Writer, performer, beatnik, and eventually underground film actor Taylor Mead (*Lonesome Cowboys*, *Imitation of Christ*, *The Nude Restaurant*) - often associated with Andy Warhol and The Factory - is born in Gross Pointe, MI.

December 31, 1938

Widely recorded sacred music composer and organist Calvin Hampton - well known for his weekly Friday midnight concerts at Calvary Church in New York City - is born in Kittanning, PA.

December 31, 1964

San Francisco's Council on Religion and the Homosexual – an organization committed to encouraging dialog and tolerance between homosexual activists and religious leaders – holds a costume party fundraiser. When the San Francisco Police Department fails to prevent the fully authorized and permitted event from taking place, its officers arrive to photograph guests and record IDs as they enter and leave. Some arrests are made and rioting results. But the most significant unintended consequence was to expose outraged heterosexual Christians to the harassment experienced routinely by homosexuals.

December 31, 1966

The Canadian homophile organization ASK (The Association for Social Knowledge) opens a community center to serve the gay community in Vancouver.

December 31, 1969

The queer performance group The Cockettes perform for the first time at the Palace Theater in San Francisco, CA.

December 31, 1972

Activist Henry Gerber - founder of the Society for Human Rights, the first recognized gay rights organization in the U.S. which also published the first American publication for homosexuals, *Friendship and Freedom* - dies at age 80 in Washington, DC.

December 31, 1993

Writer/academic Samuel Steward (*Dear Sammy: Letters from Gertrude Stein and Alice B. Toklas, Parisian Lives*) aka tattoo artist Phil Sparrow aka erotic novelist Phil Andros (*The Greek Way, When in Rome*) dies at age 84 in Berkeley, CA.

December 31, 1993

Brandon Teena - the subject of the films *The Brandon Teena Story* and the Academy Award-winning *Boys Don't Cry* - is raped and murdered at age 21 in Humboldt, NE.

December 31, 1994

Influential performance artist, fashion designer, and club personality Leigh Bowery dies at age 33 of an AIDS-related illness in London, England.

INDEX

A

Abbema, Louise 7/10, 10/30
Abbott, Berenice 7/17, 12/9
Academy Awards, The 2/22
Acker, Jean 8/16, 10/23
Acker, Kathy 4/18, 11/30
Ackerley, J.R. 6/4, 11/4
ACT-UP 3/10, 8/24, 12/10
Acton, Harold 2/27, 7/5
Addams, Jane 5/21, 9/6
Adrian/Adrian Adolph Greenberg 3/3, 9/13
Adventures of Priscilla, Queen of the Desert, The 8/10
Advice & Consent 6/6
Advocate, The 8/27, 10/7
After Dark May 1968
AIDS 3/19, 4/15, 4/24, 4/29, 7/25, 7/27, August 1981, 8/18, 9/17, 9/25, 9/25, 10/9, 10/11, 12/1, 12/7,
AIDS term used for the first time 9/24
AIDS czar 9/25
AIDS Memorial Quilt 10/11
AIDS Walk 7/28
Ailey, Alvin 1/5, 12/1
Alan Turing Amnesty Law 1/31
Alarcon, Francisco Xavier 1/15, 2/21
Albee, Edward 3/12, 9/16
Aldridge, Sarah 1/11, 1/27
Alexander III of Macedon aka Alexander the Great 6/10-11, 7/20-21
Alger, Horatio Jr. 1/13, 7/18
All in the Family 2/9
All My Children 2/13, 4/23
Allen, Paula Gunn 5/29, 10/24
Allen, Peter 2/10, 6/18
Almendros, Nestor 3/4, 10/30
AmBi 2/14
amfAR - September 1985

American Family, An 1/11
And the Band Played On 9/11
Anderson, Hans Christian 4/2, 8/4
Anderson, Dame Judith 1/3, 2/10
Anderson, Margaret C. 2/14, 10/18, 11/24
Angels in America 3/25, 5/4
Antonio, Juan 5/4, 5/24
Anzaldua, Gloria 5/15, 9/26
APA (American Psychiatric Association) 8/30, 12/15
Arenas, Reinaldo 7/16, 12/7
Ariston Hotel Baths 2/21
Arnzer, Dorothy 1/3, 10/1
Arondeus, Willem 7/1, 8/22
Arquette, Alexis 7/27, 9/11
As The World Turns 8/17
ASK (The Association for Social Knowledge) April 1964, 12/31
Aucoin, Kevin 12/14, 5/7
Auden, W.H. 2/21, 9/29
Austen, Alice 3/17, 6/9
Avenue Q 10/21
Avila, Amelio Robles 11/3, 12/9
AZT 3/19

B

B.D. Woman's Blues 3/7
Bacon, Francis (statesman, philosopher) 1/22, 4/9
Bacon, Francis (artist) 4/28, 10/28
Baker, Gilbert 3/31, 6/2
Baker, Josephine 4/12, 6/3
Baldwin, James 8/2, 11/30
Baldwin, Tammy 11/6
Balenciaga, Cristobel 1/21, 3/23
Bankhead, Tallulah 1/31, 12/12
Barbin, Herculine 11/8
Barnes, Djuna 6/12, 6/18
Barnett, Allen 5/23, 8/14
Barney, Natalie Clifford 2/2, 10/31
Barry, Dr. James Miranda 7/25, 11/9
Bartel, Paul 5/13, 8/6
Basker, Robert Sloane 4/6, 9/30
Bates, Alan 2/17, 12/27

Bates, Katharine Lee 3/28, 8/12
Baxt, George 6/11, 6/28
Bay Area Reporter, The 4/1
Beach, Sylvia 3/14, 10/5
Beam, Joseph F. 12/27, 12/20
Beardsley, Aubrey 3/16, 8/21
Beaton, Cecil 1/4, 1/18
Beck, Gad 6/24, 6/30
Beckford, William 5/2, 10/1
Before Stonewall 6/27
Belinfante, Frieda 4/26, 5/10
Bell, Arthur 6/2, 11/6
Ben, Lisa 11/7, 12/22
Benavente, Jacinto 7/14, 8/12
Benedict, Ruth 6/5, 9/17
Bennett, Michael 4/8, 7/2
Bentley, Gladys 1/18, 8/12
Berkeley, CA. 12/5
Bernhardt, Sarah 3/26, 10/22
Bernstein, Leonard 8/25, 10/14
Berube, Allan 12/3, 12/11
Berzon, Betty 1/18, 1/24
Bi Pride 9/22
Bi Visibility Day 9/23
Bi-Network 3/25
Billings, Alexandra 9/27
Bingham, Mark 5/22, 9/11
Bisexual Flag 12/5
Bisexuality Day 9/23
Bishop, Elizabeth 2/8, 10/6
Black Cat Tavern 1/1, 2/11
Blass, Bill 6/12, 6/22
Block, Martin 3/4, 7/27
Bogarde, Sir Dirk 3/28, 5/8
Bohemian Rhapsody 11/2
Bond, Pat 2/27, 12/24
Bonheur, Rosa 3/16, 5/25
Bono, Chaz 6/11
Book of Mormon, The 3/24
Boom Boom, Sister 2/21, 8/5
Boswell, John 3/20, 12/24
Bowery, Leigh 3/26, 12/31
Bowie, David 1/8, 1/10
Bowles, Paul 11/18, 12/30
Bowman, Nancy Hunt 2/1, 6/21
Boy Meets Boy 9/17
Boy Scouts of America 7/27

Boys in the Band 3/17, 4/14, 5/31
Brainard, Joe 3/11, 5/25
Briggs Initiative/Proposition 6 11/7
Britten, Benjamin 11/22, 12/4
Broadnax, Willmer "Little Ax" 6/1,
    12/28
Brown, Kate 11/9
Brown, Margaret Wise 5/23, 11/13
Bryant, Anita 6/7
Brokeback Mountain 10/13, 9/3
Brooks. Louise 8/8, 11/14
Brooks, Romaine 5/1, 12/7
Broughton, James 5/17, 11/10
Brown, Forman 1/8, 1/10
Buono, Victor 1/1, 2/3
Burgess, Wilma 6/11, 8/26
Burke, Glenn 5/30, 11/16
Burns, John Horne 8/11, 10/7
Burr, Raymond 5/21, 9/12
Burroughs, William S. 2/5, 8/2
Bush, George W. 2/24
Butler, Octavia 2/24, 6/22
Butrick, Merritt 3/17, 9/3
Byington, Spring 9/7, 10/17
Byron, George Gordon (Lord) 1/22,
    4/19
Byron, Robert 2/24, 2/26

C

Cadmus, Paul 12/12, 12/17
Caffe Cino 3/24, 4/2, 4/13, 11/16
Cage, John 8/12, 9/5
Cahun, Claude 10/25, 12/8
Calhoun, Robert 5/24, 11/24
Call, Hal 9/20, 12/18
Callen, Michael 4/11, 12/27
Can't Stop the Music 6/20
Capote, Truman 8/25, 9/30
Captive, The 9/29
Carangi, Gia 1/29, 11/18
Cardenas, Nancy 3/23, 5/29
Carol 1/15
Carpenter, Edward 6/28, 8/29
Carr, Allan 5/27, 6/29
Carson, Rachel 4/14, 5/27

Carter, Lynne 1/11
Carver, George Washington 1/5, 7/12
Cashier, Albert 10/10, 12/25
Cather, Willa 4/24, 12/7
Cavafy, Constantine 4/29, 4/29
Cazuza 4/4, 7/7
CBS Reports: "The Homosexuals" 3/7
CDC 6/5, 9/24
Center on Halsted, The 6/1
Cernuda, Luis 9/21, 11/5
Chablis, The Lady 3/11, 9/8
Chapman, Graham 1/8, 10/4
Charleston, Ian 1/6, 8/11
Chatwin, Bruce 1/18, 5/13
Cheever, John 5/27, 6/18
Cheney, Russell 7/12, 10/16
Chesley, Robert 3/22, 12/5
Cheung, Leslie 4/1, 9/12
Children's Hour, The 11/20
Chinese Psychiatric Association 4/20
Christian, Meg 1/19
Chrysis, International 3/26
Chung, Dr. Margaret 1/5, 10/2
Church, Jok 4/29, 11/28
Cino, Joe 4/2, 11/16
Civil Unions 4/26
Claiborne, Craig 1/22, 9/4
Clarke, Arthur C. 3/19, 12/16
Clarke, Lige 2/10, 2/22
Cleo, Miss 7/26, 8/12
Cliburn, Val 2/27, 7/12
Cliff, Michelle 6/12, 11/2
Clift, Montgomery 7/23, 10/17
Clinton, Bill 1/19
Cockettes, The 12/31
Coccinelle 8/23, 10/9
Coco 12/18
Cocteau, Jean 7/5, 10/11
Cole, Jack 2/17, 4/29
Colette 1/28, 8/3
Collins, Jason 4/29, 5/6
Color Purple The 12/10
Colorado's Amendment 2 struck down
  5/20
Combs, Frederick 11/19, 10/11
Common Threads 3/26
Compton's Cafeteria - August 1966

Cook, Tim 10/30
Cooper, Anderson 7/2
Cooper's Donuts Riot - May 1959
Copland, Aaron 11/14, 12/2
Corbin, Steven 8/3, 10/3
Corey, Dorian 8/29
Corinne, Tee 8/27, 11/3
Cornell, Katharine 2/16, 6/9
Corner Bar, The 6/21
Cottrell, Honey Lee 1/16, 9/21
Council on Religion and the
  Homosexual 12/31
Courtenay, William "Kitty" 5/26, 8/30
Cox, Laverne 7/10
Coward, Noel 3/26, 12/16
Cowell, Henry 3/11, 12/10
Cowell, Roberta 4/8, 10/11
Cowley, Patrick 10/19, 11/12
Crane, Hart 4/27, 7/21
Crisp, Quentin 11/21, 12/25
Crothers, Joel 1/28, 11/6
Crowley, Aleister 10/12, 12/1
Cuenod, Hugues 6/26, 12/6
Cukor, George 1/24, 7/7
Cullen, Countee 1/9, 3/30
Cunningham, Merce 4/16, 7/26
Curry, John 4/15, 9/9
Curtis, Jackie 2/19, 5/15
Cushman, Charlotte 2/18, 7/23

D

da Vinci, Leonardo 4/15, 5/2
Dall, John 1/15, 5/26
Damien, Marie-Louise aka Damien
  1/31, 12/5
Damski, Jon-Henri 3/31, 11/1
Dan White conviction riots 5/21
Daniels, Christine 10/10, 11/27
Darling, Candy 3/21, 11/24
Daughters of Bilitis 9/21
Davies, Sir Peter Maxwell 3/14, 9/8
Davis, Brad 9/8, 11/6
Dawson's Creek 5/24
Day of Silence 4/27
Day Without Art 12/1

de Acosta, Mercedes 3/1, 5/9
De Cecco, John Paul 4/18, 11/2
de la Cruz, Sor Juana Ines 4/17, 11/12
de Lempicka, Tamara 3/18, 5/16
de Meyer, Adolph 1/6, 9/1
De Pisis, Filippo 4/2, 5/11
de Wolfe, Elsie 7/12, 12/20
Deacon, Richard 5/14, 8/8
Dean, James 2/8, 9/30
DeBlase, Tony 5/28, 7/21, 8/3, 8/28
Deckers, Jeanne 3/29, 10/17
DeGeneres, Ellen 2/25, 4/14, 4/30
Delaney, Beauford 3/26, 12/30
Delanoe, Bertrand 3/18
Denmark recognizes same-sex
   partnerships 10/1
Dennis, Patrick 5/18, 11/6
Dennis, Sandy 3/2, 4/27
d'Eon, Chevalier 5/21, 10/4
Der Eigene 4/1
Dewey's restaurant protest 4/25
Diaghilev, Sergei 3/31, 8/19
Dick Cavett Show, The 11/26
Dickinson, Anna Elizabeth 10/22, 10/28
Die Freundin 5/14
Dietrich, Marlene 5/6, 12/27
Different From the Others 5/28
Dillon, Dr. Michael 5/1, 5/15
Dior, Christian 1/21, 10/23
Disch, Thomas M. 2/2, 7/4
Disney World "Gay Day" 6/1
Divine 3/7, 10/19
Dixon, Melvin 5/29, 10/26
Dollittle, Hilda aka H.D. 9/10, 9/27
Donaldson, Stephen 7/18, 7/27
Don't Ask, Don't Tell 9/20, 12/18, 12/21
Dooley, Dr. Thomas III 1/17, 1/18
Dorval, Marie 1/6, 5/20
Douglas, Alfred Lord 3/20, 10/22
Down Low, The 4/16
Drummer 6/20
Du Faur, Freda 9/11, 9/16
Dunham, Ethel Collins 3/12, 12/13
Dunne, Dominick 8/26, 10/29
Durer, Albrecht 4/6, 5/21
Duse, Eleonora 4/21, 10/3
Dworkin, Andrea 4/9, 9/26

E

Eagles, Jeanne 6/26, 10/3
Early Frost, An 11/11
East Lansing City Council 3/7
Edens, Roger 7/13, 11/9
Eddy, Fannyann 9/28
Edmonds, Louis 3/3, 9/24
Edward II 4/25, 9/21
Eichelberger, Ethyl 7/17, 8/12
Elagabalus 3/11, 3/20
Elbe, Lili 9/13, 12/28
Ellen - sitcom 4/30
Ellen - talk show 9/8
Elliott, Denholm 5/31, 10/6
Ellis, Perry 3/3, 5/30
Ellis, Ruth 7/23, 10/5
Eltinge, Julian 3/7, 5/14
Employment of Homosexuals and Other
   Perverts in Government 12/15
Endean, Steve 8/4, 8/6
England - criminalization of
   homosexuality 8/6
England - decriminalization of
   homosexuality 7/27
Episcopal Church 3/7
Epstein, Brian 8/27, 9/19
Equality, Act, The 7/23
Equality House 3/19
Erickson, Reed 1/3, 10/13
Erte 4/21, 11/23
Esquerita 10/23, 11/20
Evans, Arthur 9/11, 10/12
Evans, Maurice 3/12, 6/3
Executive Order 10450 4/27
Eyen, Tom 5/26, 8/14

F

Falsettos 4/29
Falwell, Reverend Jerry 2/9
Fani-Kayode, Rotimi 12/21
Fanning, Eric 5/17
Fashanu, Justin 2/19, 5/2
Fassbinder, Rainer Maria 5/31, 6/10
Feinberg, David B. 11/2, 11/25

Ferro, Robert 7/11, 10/21
Ficino, Masilio 10/1, 10/19
Finch, Nigel 2/14, 8/1
Firbank, Ronald 1/17, 5/21
First National Third World Lesbian and
    Gay Conference 10/12-10/15
Fitzhugh, Louise 10/15, 11/19
Flanner, Janet 3/13, 11/7
Florida Enchantment, A 10/12
Flowers, Wayland 10/11, 11/26
Folsom Street Fair 9/23
Fontaine, Pierre Francois Leonard 9/20,
    10/10
Forbes, Malcolm 3/11
Ford, Robert 2/2
Forrest, Edwin 3/9, 12/12
Forster, E.M. 1/1, 6/7
Forwood, Anthony 5/18, 10/3
Foucault, Michel 6/25, 10/15
Fowler, John Beresford 6/20, 10/27
Frameline Film Festival 2/9
Francis, Robert 7/13, 8/12
Franco, Marielle 3/14, 7/27
    Frank, Barney 7/7
Frey, Leonard 8/24, 9/4
Friends 1/18
Front Runners 1/6
Fukaya, Michiyo 4/25, 7/9
Fuller, Henry Blake 1/9, 7/28
Fuller, Loie 1/1, 1/15
Fun Home 4/19

G

Garbo, Greta 4/15, 4/19, 9/18, 12/18
Garland, Jack Bee 9/19, 12/9
Garnett, David 2/17, 3/9
Gately, Stephen 3/17, 10/10
Gay Academic Union 11/23-24
Gay Activist's Alliance 12/21
Gay Community Services Center 1/4
Gay Games 8/28
Gay Marriage 6/26, 12/3
Gay Men's Health Crisis - August 1981
Gay Pride Flag/Rainbow Flag 3/19,
    3/31, 6/2, 6/15, 6/25

Gay Pride March 6/28
Geer, Will 3/9, 4/22
Genet, Jean 4/15, 12/19
Gerber, Henry 6/29, 12/31
Gernreich, Rudi 4/21, 8/8
Ghosh, Rituparno 5/30, 8/31
Gide, Andre 2/19, 11/22
Gielgud, Sir John 4/14, 5/21
Gilbert, Peggy 1/17, 2/12
Gilpin, Laura 4/22, 11/30
Ginsberg, Allen 4/5, 6/3
Ginsburg, Steve 4/1
Gittings, Barbara 2/18, 7/4, 7/31
Glaskin, Gerald 12/16
Glee 5/19
Glines, John 6/5
Gluckstein, Hannah 1/10, 8/13
God of Vengeance, The 2/19
Gogol, Nikolai 3/4, 3/31
Gonzalez-Torres, Felix 1/9, 11/26
Goodman, Paul 8/2, 9/9
Gordon-Woodhouse, Violet 1/8, 4/23
Gore, Lesley 2/16, 5/2
Goulding, Edmund 3/20, 12/24
Granger, Farley 3/27, 7/1
Grant, Cary 1/18, 11/29
Grant, Duncan 1/21, 5/8
Gray, Eileen 8/9, 10/31
Gray, Vernita 3/18, 12/8
Greer, Michael 4/20, 9/14
Greif, Martin 2/4, 11/17
Grier, Barbara 11/4, 11/10
Grimke, Angelina Weld 2/27, 6/10
Gruber, James 2/27, 8/21
Grumley, Michael 4/28, 7/6
Guenin, Pierre 2/19, 3/1
Guerin, Daniel 4/14, 5/19
Gunn, Thom 4/25, 8/29
Guinness, Alec 4/2. 8/5

H

Hadrian 1/24, 7/10
Hahn, Reynaldo 1/28, 8/9
Haines, Billy 1/2, 12/26
Hall, Radclyffe 8/12, 10/7, 11/16

Hallmark Greeting Cards 8/21
Hallquist, Christine 8/14
Halston 3/26, 4/23
Hamilton, Edith 5/31, 8/12
Hammarskjold, Dag 7/29, 9/18
Hampton, Calvin 8/5, 12/31
Hampton, Mabel 5/2, 10/26
Hanaford, Phebe 5/6, 6/2
Hanover, Renee 1/5, 4/18
Hansberry, Lorraine 1/12, 5/19
Hansen, Joseph 7/19, 11/24
Haring, Keith 2/16, 5/4
Harris, Bertha 5/22, 12/17
Harris, E. Lynn 6/20, 7/23
Harris, Neil Patrick 2/22
Harrison, Lou 2/2, 5/14
Hart, Alan L. 7/1, 10/4
Hart, Lorenz 5/2, 11/22
Hart, Pearl 3/22, 4/7
Hartley, Marsden 1/4, 9/2
Hartman, Dan 3/22, 12/8
Hartnell, Norman Bishop 6/8, 6/12
Hawthorne, Nigel 4/5, 12/26
Hay, Harry 4/7, 8/31-/9/2, 10/24, 11/11
Hays Code 7/2
Heap, Jane 2/14, 6/18, 11/1
Heath, Gordon 8/27, 9/20
Hemphill, Essex 4/16, 11/4
Hernandez, Mister Marcus 3/22, 10/8
Hibiscus 5/6, 9/6
Hickok, Lorena 3/7, 5/1
Hidalgo, Dr. Hilda 11/8
Higgins, Colin 7/28, 8/5
Highsmith, Patricia 1/19, 2/4
Hirschfeld, Magnus 5/14, 5/14
Hitler, Adolf 2/23
Hoch, Hannah 5/31, 11/1
Hoffman, William M. 4/12, 4/29
Homosexual Law Reform Society 5/12
Homosexual Liberation Front, The 8/15
*The Homosexual Next Door: A
  Sober Appraisal of a New Social
  Phenomenon* 2/22
Horace 11/27, 12/8
Horne, Ken 4/24
Horst, Horst P. 8/14, 11/18
Horton, Edward Everett 3/18, 9/29

Hosmer, Harriet 2/21, 10/9
Hot L Baltimore 1/24
Housman, A.E. 3/26, 4/30
Howard, Brenda 6/28, 12/24
Howard, Brian 1/15, 3/15
Hudson, John Paul 2/20, 4/28
Hudson, Rock 7/25, 10/2, 11/17
Hughes, Glenn M. 3/4, 7/18
Hughes, Langston 2/1, 5/22
Hujar, Peter 10/11, 11/26
Hull, Bob 5/1, 5/31
Human Rights Day 12/10
Hunger, The 4/29
Hunter, Alberta 4/1, 10/17
Hunter, Ross 3/10, 5/6
Hunter, Tab 7/8, 7/11
Hurston, Zora Neale 1/7, 1/28
Hurt, William 3/24
Huston, Bo 5/27, 6/10
Hutchinson, Josephine 6/4, 10/12

I

Illinois Sodomy Laws 1/1, 1/28
Independence Hall picketing 7/4
Inman, John 3/8, 6/28
International Day Against Homophobia,
  Transphobia, and Biphobia 5/17
International Mr. Leather 5/20
International Lesbian Day 10/8
International Non-Binary People's Day
  7/14
International Pronoun Day 10/17
International Transgender Day of
  Visibility 3/31
Intersex Awareness Day 10/26
Intersex Day of Remembrance 11/8
Irons, Evelyn 4/3, 6/17
Isay, Richard 6/28, 12/13
Isherwood, Christopher 1/4, 8/26
It Gets Better Project 9/21

J

Jabara, Paul 1/31, 9/29

Jacobs, Helen 6/2, 8/6
Jackson, Tony 4/20, 6/5
Jansson, Tove 6/27, 8/9
Jarman, Derek 1/31, 2/19
Jarry, Alfred 9/8, 11/1
Jenner, Caitlyn 4/24, July 2015
Jennings, William Dale 5/11, 10/21
Jeter, Michael 3/30, 8/26
Jewett, Sarah Orne 6/24, 9/3
Joffrey, Robert 3/25, 12/24
Johnson, Marsha P. 7/6
Johnson, Philip 1/25, 7/8
Johnson, Van 8/25, 12/12
Johnson, William R. 6/25
Johnston, Jill 3/30, 5/17, 9/18
Joplin, Janis 1/19, 10/4
Jordan, Barbara 1/17, 2/21, 4/24
Jordan, June 6/14, 7/9
Jorgensen, Christine 5/3, 5/30, 12/1
Judge, Father Mychal 5/11, 9/11

K

Kahlo, Frieda 7/6, 7/13
Kameny, Frank 2/22, 5/21, 7/4, 10/11
Kato, David 1/26, 2/13
Kaye, Gorden 1/23, 4/7
Kelley, William B. 5/17, 7/5
Kellor, Frances 1/4, 10/20
Kelly, Ellsworth 5/31, 12/27
Kelly, George Orry 2/27, 12/31
Kelly, Patsy 1/12, 9/24
Kepner, Jim 8/19, 11/15
Keynes, John Maynard 4/21, 6/5
Kight, Morris 1/19, 11/19
King, Billie Jean 7/2
Kinky Boots 4/4
Kinsey, Alfred Dr. 1/3, 6/23, 8/25
Kinsey Report 1/3
Kirkwood, James 4/21, 8/22
Kirstein, Lincoln 1/5, 5/4
Klein, Fred 'Fritz' 5/24, 7/23, 12/27
Knuckles, Frankie 1/18, 3/31
Kondoleon, Harry 2/26, 3/16
Kozachenko, Kathy 4/1
Kozin, Vadim 3/21, 12/19

Kramer, Larry, 3/10, 4/21, 4/27, August 1981
Kuda, Marie 10/1, 12/8
Kukai 4/22, 7/27
Kulp, Nancy 2/3, 8/28
Kuromiya, Kiyoshi 5/9, 5/10
Kuzmin, Mikhail 3/1, 10/18

L

L Word, The 1/18
L.A. Law 2/7
La Cage aux Folles 8/21
La Tourneaux, Robert 6/3
Laaksonen, Touko aka Tom of Finland 5/8, 11/7
Lagerlof, Selma 3/16, 11/20
Lahusen, Kay 7/4
Lambda Legal Defense and Education Fund 10/18, 11/10
Lambda Literary Awards 6/2
Lambert, Gavin 7/17, 7/23
Lankton, Greer 11/18
Larson, Jonathan 1/25, 2/4
Laughton, Charles 7/1, 12/15
Laurent, A.J. 9/15, 10/26
Laurent, Yves Saint 6/1, 8/1
Laurents, Arthur 5/5, 7/14
Lavender Menace, The 5/1
Lavender Woman 11/1
Lawrence v. Texas 6/26
Lawrence, T.E. 5/19, 8/16
Le Gallienne, Eva 1/11, 6/3
Leather Archives and Museum 8/28
Leather Pride Flag 5/28
Leaves of Grass 7/4
Leblanc, Georgette 2/8, 10/27
Legacy Walk, The 10/11
Legg, W. Dorr 7/26, 12/15
Leisen, Mitchell 10/6, 10/28
Leitsch, Dick 5/11, 6/22
Lemebel, Pedro 1/23, 11/21
Leonel, Vange 5/4, 7/14
Lesbian and Gay Asian Collective 10/12-10/15
Lesbian Avengers 5/31, 9/9

Lesbian Cemetery 4/5
Lesbian Connection, The 8/3
Lesbian Herstory Archives, The 3/31
Lesbian kiss on network TV 2/7
Lesbian Nation 3/30
Lesbian Visibility Day 4/26
Levy, Amy 9/10, 11/10
Lewis, Edmonia 4/4, 9/17
Leyendecker, J.C 3/23, 7/25
Liberace 2/4, 4/15, 5/16
LIFE Magazine - Homosexuality in
   America 6/26
Lil Peep 11/1, 11/15
List, Herbert 4/4, 10/7
Lister, Anne 4/3, 9/22
Livia, Anna 8/5, 11/13
Lochary, David 7/29, 8/21
Locke, Alain 6/9, 9/13
Log Cabin Republicans 9/1
Logo 6/30
Longtime Companion 10/11
Lorca, Federico Garcia 6/5, 8/19
Lorde, Audre 2/18, 11/17
Los 41 11/17
Loud, Lance 1/11, 6/26, 12/22
Lowell, Amy 2/9, 5/12
Lubin, Arthur 5/12, 7/25
Ludlam, Charles 4/12, 5/28
Lynde, Paul 1/10, 6/13
Lynes, George Platt 4/15, 12/6
Lyon, Mary 2/28, 3/3
Lyon, Phyllis 6/16, 9/21
Lyons, James 4/12, 10/8

M

Mabley, Jackie "Moms" 3/19, 5/23
MacLane, Mary 5/1, 8/6
Mahoney, John 2/4, 6/20
Main, Marjorie 2/24, 4/10
Mains, Geoff 5/29, 6/21
Making Love 2/12
Manford, Jeanne 1/8, 12/4
Mann, Klaus 5/21, 11/18
Mann, Marty 7/22, 10/15
Mansfield, Katherine 1/9, 10/14

MANual Enterprises v. Day 6/25
Mapes, Jacques 5/4, 6/14
Mapplethorpe, Robert 3/9, 11/4
Marais, Jean 11/8, 12/11
March for Lesbian, Gay, and Bi Equal
   Rights 4/25
Marcus Welby M.D. 10/8
Marlane, Vicki 6/27, 7/5, 9/4
Marlowe, Christopher 2/26, 5/30
Martin, Del 5/5, 6/16, 8/27, 9/21
Mary Tyler Moore Show, The 1/23
Massachusetts legalizes gay marriage
   5/17
Mathews, Kerwin 1/8, 7/5
Matlovich, Leonard 6/22, 7/6, 9/8
Mattachine Society 4/21, 11/11
Matthew Shepard Act 10/28
Matthiessen, F.O. 2/19, 4/1
Maugham, Robin 3/13, 5/17
Maugham, W. Somerset 1/24, 12/16
Maupin, Armistead 1/10-1/12, 5/24
McAlmon, Robert 2/2, 3/9
McBean, Angus 6/8, 6/9
McCowen, Alec 2/6, 5/26
McCullers, Carson 2/19, 9/29
McDowell, Michael 6/1, 12/27
McDowell, Roddy 9/17, 10/3
McGehee, Peter 9/13, 10/6
McKay, Claude 5/22, 9/15
McNeill, John J. 9/2, 9/22
McQueen, Alexander 2/11, 3/17
McPherson, Scott 10/13, 11/7
Mead, Margaret 11/15, 12/16
Mead, Taylor 5/8, 12/31
Meaney, Kevin 4/23, 10/21
Meigs, Mary 4/27, 11/15
Melchior, Lauritz 3/19, 3/20
Mercer, Mabel 2/3, 4/20
Merchant, Ismail 5/25, 12/25
Mercury, Freddy 9/5, 11/24
Merlis, Mark 3/9, 8/15
Merrick, Gordon 3/27, 8/3
Merrill, James 2/6, 3/3
Metropolitan Community Church 10/6
Meyers, Timothy 3/14, 8/31
Michael, George 6/25, 12/25

Michelangelo aka Michelangelo
   Buonarroti 2/18, 3/6, 9/8
Michigan Womyn's Music Festival
   8/20-22
Middleton, George 4/6
Midnight Cowboy 7/30
Milk 11/26
Milk, Harvey 1/8, 5/21, 5/22, 8/12, 11/7,
   11/27
Millay, Edna St. Vincent 2/22, 10/19
Millett, Kate 9/6, 9/14
Milligan, Andy 2/12, 6/3
Mineo, Sal 1/10, 2/12
Mishima, Yukio 1/14, 11/25
Miss Universe 12/16
Mistral, Gabriela 1/10, 4/7
Mitropoulos, Dimitri 3/1, 11/2
Mizer, Bob 3/27, 5/12
Modern Family 9/23
Molina, Miguel de 3/4, 4/10
Monette, Paul 2/10, 10/16
Moorehead, Agnes 4/30, 12/6
Morali, Jacques 7/4, 11/15
Morgan, Julia 1/20, 2/2
Morley, Angela 1/14, 3/10
Morrisoe, Mark 1/10, 7/24
Mosier, Chris 7/11
Murnau, F.W. 3/11, 12/28
Murphy, Timothy Patrick 11/3, 12/6
Musser, Tharon 1/8, 4/19

N

Nabors, Jim 6/1, 11/20
Nader, George 2/4, 10/19
Nasim, Ifti 7/22, 9/15
National Coming Out Day 10/11
National Gay Conference 3/28
National Gay Task Force 10/15
National Latino/a Gay and Lesbian
   Organization (LLEGO) 10/11
National March on Washington for
   Lesbian and Gay Rights 10/12-10/15
Navratilova, Martina 7/7, 7/30
Nazi Party 2/23
Nazimova, Alla 6/3, 7/13

Negron, Taylor 1/10, 8/1
Nelson, Alice Dunbar 7/19, 9/18
Nelson, Kenneth 3/24, 10/7
New Republic, The - March 1972
New York City Gay Men's Chorus 12/8
New York Times, The 7/3, 8/18, 12/10
Newman, John Henry 2/21, 8/11, 9/19
Nichols, Jack 3/16, 5/2, 7/4
Nicholson, Harold 5/1, 11/21
Nijinski, Vaslav 3/12, 4/8
Nin, Anais 1/14, 2/21
Nkoli, Simon 11/26, 11/30
Nomi, Klaus 1/24, 8/6
Nopcsa, Franz 4/25, 5/3
Normal Heart, The 4/21, 4/27
Novarro, Ramon 2/6, 10/30
Novello, Ivor 1/15, 3/6
Novo, Salvador 1/13, 7/30
Nugent, Richard Bruce 5/27, 7/2
Nureyev, Rudolf 1/6, 3/17, 6/16
Nyad, Diana 9/2
Nyro, Laura 4/8, 10/18

O

O'Donnell, Rosie 2/25
O'Hara, Frank 3/27, 7/25
off our backs 2/27
Olivia Records 1/19
Olivier, Sir Laurence 5/22, 7/11
Olympics, The - transsexuals 5/17
ONE Inc. 1/13, 11/15, 11/29,
ONE Inc. v. Olesen
Opel, Robert 7/8, 10/23
Oprah 4/16
Orange is the New Black 7/10
Orejudos, Dom aka Etienne aka Stephen
   7/1, 9/24
Orlovsky, Peter 5/30, 7/8
Orton, Joe 1/1, 8/9
Oscar Wilde Memorial Bookshop 11/24
Osborne, Robert 3/6, 5/3
Otero, Manuel Ramos 7/20, 10/7
Outing 1/29
OutWeek 1/29, 3/11, 6/26
OutWrite - February 1990

P

Packard, Sophia B. 1/3, 6/21
Page, Tommy 3/3, 5/24
Palillo, Ron 4/2, 8/14
Pangborn, Franklin 1/23, 7/20
Pantoja, Dr. Antonia 5/24, 9/13
Pansexual and Panromantic Awareness
  and Visibility Day 5/24
Pansexual Pride Day 12/8
Parker, Annise 12/12
Parker, Pat 1/20, 6/19
Parker, William 3/29, 8/5
Parkhurst, Charlie 12/28
Parsons, Betty 1/31, 7/23
Pasolini, Pier Paolo 3/5, 11/2
Patner, Andrew 2/3, 12/17
Pears, Peter 4/3, 6/22
Peppermint 7/26
Percier, Charles 8/22, 9/5
Perkins, Anthony 4/4, 9/12
Perkins, Frances 4/10, 5/1
Personal Best 2/5
PFLAG 1/8, 3/26, 12/4
Philadelphia 12/23
Phillips, Katherine 1/1, 6/22
Pierce, Charles 5/31, 7/14
Pink Flamingoes 3/17
Polak, Clark 4/25, 10/13, 9/20
Polis, Jared 11/6
Ponce, Angela 12/16
Pontormo, Jacopo aka Pontormo 1/2,
  5/24
Porter, Cole 6/9, 10/15
Pose 6/3, 12/30
Prentice, Keith 2/21, 9/27
Preston, Billy 6/6, 9/2
Preston, John 4/28, 12/11
Price, Gilbert 1/2, 9/10
Princess Diana 4/8
Proposition 6 11/7
Proposition 8 2/7, 11/4
Protease inhibitor 12/7
Proust, Marcel 7/10, 11/18
Puig, Manuel 7/22, 12/28
Pulse nightclub 6/12

Purdy, James 3/13, 7/17

Q

Quaintance, George 6/3, 11/8
Queen Christina of Sweden 4/19, 12/18
Queer as Folk - U.S. 12/3
Queer as Folk - British - 2/23
Queer Eye for the Straight Guy 7/15
Queer Nation 3/20
Question of Love, A 11/26

R

Rachel Maddow Show, The 9/8
Radical Faeries 8/31-9/2
Rainey, Ma 4/26, 12/22
Rainbow Flag/Gay Pride Flag 3/19,
  3/31. 6/2, 6/15, 6/25
Rakoff, David 8/9, 11/27
Rambo, Dack 3/21, 11/13
Rambova, Natacha 1/19, 6/5
Rapper, Irving 1/16. 12/20
Raucourt, Francoise 1/15, 3/3
Rauschenberg, Robert 5/12, 10/22
Ray, Gene Anthony 5/24, 11/14
Ray, Johnny 1/10, 2/24
Ray, Nicholas 6/16, 8/7
Reagan, Ronald 9/17
Red Hot + Blue 9/25
Red Ribbon 6/2
Redl, Alfred 5/25
Reed, Lou 3/2, 10/27
Reed, Paul 1/28, 5/28
Reed, Robert 5/12, 10/19
Reilly, Charles Nelson 1/13, 5/25
Rejected, The 9/11
Relativity 1/11
Renault, Mary 9/4, 12/13
Rene, Norman 5/24
Renslow, Chuck 6/29, 8/26, 8/28
Rent 4/29
Reynard, Elizabeth 1/9, 10/4
Reynolds, William H. 6/14, 7/16

Rich, Adrienne 3/27, 5/16
Richardson, Tony 6/5, 11/14
Ride, Sally 5/26, 6/18, 7/23
Riggs, Marlon 2/3, 4/5
Rimbaud, Arthur 10/20, 11/10
Rippon, Adam 2/11
Rist, Darrell Yates 12/23
Ritts, Herb 8/31, 12/26
Rivera, Sylvia 2/19, 7/2
Robinson, Gene 3/7
Robinson, Fay Jackson 2/15
Rodwell, Craig L. 6/18, 7/4, 10/31
Roem, Danica 11/7
Rogers, Terri 5/4, 5/30
Rollins, Howard E. Jr. 10/17, 12/8
Romero, Cesar 1/1, 12/15
Rorke, Hayden 8/19, 10/23
Roseanne 3/1, 11/10
Rounds, David 12/10
Rowland, Chuck 8/24, 12/27
Rule, Jane 3/28, 11/27
RuPaul's Drag Race 2/2
Russo, Vito 7/11, 11/7
Rustin, Bayard 3/17, 8/24
Ryan White Care Act 8/18

S

Sacks, Oliver 7/9, 8/30
Sackville-West, Vita 3/9, 6/2
Saint, Assotto 6/29, 10/2
San Francisco Chronicle, The "Tales of
  the City 5/24
San Francisco Examiner, The "Gays and
  the City" 10/30
San Francisco Gay Men's Chorus 12/20
Sand, George 6/8, 7/1
Sandow, Eugen 4/2, 10/14
Sarduy, Severo 2/25, 6/8
Sargent, Dick 4/19, 7/8
Sarria, Jose 8/19, 11/7, 12/13
Sarton, May 5/3, 7/16
Sasser, Sean 8/7, 10/25
Sassoon, Siegfried 9/1, 9/8
Savage, Dan 9/21
Scavullo, Francesco 1/6, 1/16

Schindler, Allen R. Jr. 10/27, 12/13
Schlesinger, John 2/16, 7/25
Schneebaum, Tobias 3/25, 9/20
Schneider, Maria 2/3, 3/27
Scott, Randolph 1/23, 3/2
Second National March on Washington
  for Lesbian and Gay Rights 10/11
Seel, Pierre 8/16, 11/25
Sendak, Maurice 5/8, 6/10
*Serving in Silence: The Magarethe
  Cammermeyer Story* 2/6
Sexual Behavior in the Human Male 1/3
Shelley, Pete 4/17, 12/6
Shenar, Paul 2/12, 10/11
Shepard, Benjamin Henry Jesse Francis
  5/29, 9/18
Shepard, Matthew 10/12, 12/1
Shepherd, Reginald 4/10, 9/10
Shilts, Randy 2/17, 8/8
Signorile, Michelangelo 1/29, 8/27
Simmons, Dawn Langley 9/18, 10/15
Simpson, Ruth 3/15, 5/8
Sip-In 4/21, 5/11, 6/22
Sisters of Perpetual Indulgence 2/21,
  4/15, 8/5
Sitwell, Sir Francis Osbert 5/4, 12/6
Slater, Don 2/14, 8/21
Smith, Bessie 4/15, 9/26
Smith, Jerry 7/19, 10/15
Smith, Liz 2/2, 11/12
Smith, Willi 2/29, 4/17
Smyth, Dame Ethel Mary 4/23, 5/8
Soap 9/13
Society for Human Rights 12/10
Solano, Solita 11/22
Sotomayor, Danny 2/5, 8/30
Spender, Stephen 2/28, 7/16
Spicer, Jack 1/30, 8/17
Spinetti, Victor 6/18, 9/2
Spirit Day 10/19
Spring Awakening 12/10
Springfield, Dusty 3/2, 4/16
Spurgeon, Caroline 10/24
St. Sergius and St. Bacchus feast day
  10/7
Stebbins, Emma 9/1, 10/25
Stein, Getrude 2/3, 7/27, 9/8

Steward, Samuel 7/23, 12/31
Stewart, Jermaine 3/17, 9/7
Stoddard, Charles Warren 4/23, 8/7
Stoddard, Thomas 2/12
Sontewall National Monument 6/24
Stonewall Riots 6/28
Strayhorn, Billy 5/31, 11/29
Studds, Gerry 5/12, 7/18, 10/14
Student Homophile League 4/19, 10/28
Studio 54 2/4 4/26
Sues, Alan 3/7, 12/1
Sullivan, Louis 3/2, 6/16
Swenson, May 5/28, 12/4
Sylvester 9/6, 12/16
Symonds, John Addington 4/19, 10/5

T

Tales of the City 1/10-1/12, 5/24
Tashman, Lilyan 3/21, 10/23
Taylor, Laurette 4/1, 12/7
Taylor, Paul 7/29, 8/29
Taylor, Valerie 9/7, 10/22
Tchaikovsky, Pyotr Ilyich 5/7, 11/6
Teena, Brandon *12/12, 12/31*
Teletubbies 2/9
That Certain Summer 11/1
That's What Friends Are For 1/18
Thesiger, Ernest 1/14, 1/15
thirtysomething 11/7
*This Bridge Called My Back: Writings
By Radical Women of Color* 6/1
Thomas, M. Carey 1/2, 12/2
Thompson, Dorothy 1/30, 7/9
Thomson, Virgil 9/30, 11/25
Thurman, Wallace 8/26, 12/22
Tilden, Bill 2/10, 6/5
TIME Magazine 1/29, 4/14, 9/8, 10/24
The Times of Harvey Milk 3/25
Tipton, Billy 1/21, 12/29
*To Wong Foo Thanks for Everything,
Julie Newmar* 9/8
Toklas, Alice B. 3/7, 4/30, 9/8
Tom of Finland 9/8
Tooker, George 3/27, 8/5
Torch Song Trilogy 6/5, 6/10

Tracy, Steve 10/3, 11/27
Transamerica 12/2
Transparent 2/6, 9/20
Transgender Day of Remembrance
11/20
Transgender Pride Flag 4/16
Tryon, Tom 1/14, 9/4
Turing, Alan 6/7, 6/23
Twombly, Cy 4/25, 7/5

U

Ulane, Karen 5/22, 12/10
Ulrichs, Karl Heinrich 8/29
Unitarian Church 6/30
Upstairs Lounge 6/24
U.S. LGBT History Month - October
U.S. State Department 2/7

V

Valentino, Rudolph 5/6, 8/23
van Vechten, Carl 6/17, 12/21
Vance, Danitra 7/13, 8/21
Vandross, Luther 4/20, 7/1
Variacoes, Antonio 6/13, 12/3
Vanity Fair July 2015
Vatican, The 7/31
Vega, Daniela 3/4
Verlaine, Paul 1/8, 3/30
Versace, Gianni 7/15, 12/2
Vice Versa 6/1, 11/7, 12/22
Vidal, Gore 7/31, 10/3
Vincenz, Lilli 7/4
Vining, Donald 1/24, 6/20
Virgil 9/21, 10/15
Visconti, Luchino 3/17, 11/2
Vivien, Renee 6/11, 11/18
Voeller, Bruce 2/13, 5/12
von Gloeden, Wilhelm 2/16, 9/16
von Steuben, Friedrich 9/17, 12/28

W

Waddell, Dr. Tom 7/11, 11/1

Wagstaff, Sam 1/14, 11/4
Walbrook, Anton 8/9, 11/19
Waldoff, Claire 1/22, 10/21
Walker, Mary Edwards 2/21, 11/26
Wall Street 8/24
Wall Street Journal, The 1/11
Walpole, Sir Hugh 3/13, 6/1
Walters, Charles 8/13, 11/17
Warhol, Andy 2/22, 8/6
Warren, Patricia Nell 2/9, 6/15
Washington Blade, The 10/5
Waters, Ethel 9/1, 10/31
Watkins, Perry 3/17, 8/20
Waugh, Evelyn 4/10, 10/28
Webb, Clifton 10/13, 11/19
Weinberg, George 3/20, 5/17
Welch, Denton 3/29, 12/30
Welles, Benjamin Sumner 9/24, 10/14
West Hollywood 11/29
Whale, James 5/29, 7/22
White, Patrick 5/28, 9/30
White House Picket 4/17
White Night Riots
Whitman, Walt 3/26, 5/31, 7/4
Whitmore, George 4/19
Whyte, John Burlingame 3/22, 5/22
Wicker, Randy 9/19
Wilde, Dorothy "Dolly" 4/10, 7/11
Wilde, Oscar 5/19, 5/25, 10/16, 11/30
Wilder, Thornton 4/17, 12/7
Wilhelm, Gale 4/6, 7/11
Will and Grace 5/18, 9/21, 9/28
Williams, Emlyn 9/25, 11/26
Williams, Jonathan 3/8, 3/16
Williams, Pete 8/27
Williams, Tennessee 2/25, 3/26
Williamson, Cris 1/19
Wilson, Sir Angus 5/31, 8/11
Wilson, Doric 2/25, 5/7
Wilson, Lanford 3/24, 4/13
Wilson, Ricky 3/19, 10/12
Winchell, Barry 7/6, 8/31
Winckelmann, Johann Joachim 6/8, 12/9
Windham, Donald 5/31, 7/2
Windsor, Edith "Edie" 6/20, 9/12
Winfield, Paul 3/7, 5/22
Winsloe, Christa 6/10, 12/23

Wisconsin bans discrimination by
 orientation 3/2
Wittgenstein, Ludwig 4/26, 4/29
Wittig, Monique 1/3, 7/13
Wittman, Carl 1/22, 2/23
Wojnarowicz, David 7/22, 9/14
Wolfenden Report, The 5/12, 9/4
Wong, Anna May 1/3, 2/3
Wood, Grant 2/12, 2/13
Wood, Thelma 7/3, 12/10
Woodlawn, Holly 10/24, 12/6
Woods, Donald W. 6/25
Woolf, Virginia 1/25, 3/28
World AIDS Day 12/1

X

Xtravaganza, Angie 3/31, 10/17
Xtravaganza, Hector 12/30

Y

Yasmine 3/3, 6/25
Yoshiya, Nobuko 1/12, 7/11
Yourcenar, Marguerite 6/8, 12/17

Z

Zamora, Pedro 2/29, 11/11
Zane, Arnie 3/30, 9/26
Zero Discrimination Day 3/1

Owen Keehnen

Writer and grassroots historian Owen Keehnen is the author of several books of fiction including the gay novels The Sand Bar, Love Underground, and Young Digby Swank; the horror novel Doorway Unto Darkness; and the Lambda Literary Award nominated collection Night Visitors. He recently wrote the folklore-bio Dugan's Bistro and the Legend of the Bearded Lady about Chicago's gay downtown glitter scene of the 70s. His fiction, essays, and interviews have appeared in dozens of periodicals nationwide. Keehnen authored the book Tell Us About It with Sukie de la Croix and over 100 of his interviews with various LGBTQ authors and activists were collected in the book We're Here, We're Queer. Keehnen and Tracy Baim have coauthored three historical biographies; Leatherman: The Legend of Chuck Renslow, Jim Flint: The Boy from Peoria, and Vernita Gray: From Woodstock to The White House. Keehnen is the cofounder and senior biographer of the LGBT organization, The Legacy Project that seeks to bring proper recognition to LGBT people and their contributions throughout history. He coedited Nothing Personal: Chronicles of Chicago's LGBTQ Community 1977-1997 and wrote ten of the biographical essays in the LGBT history book Out and Proud in Chicago. He is the author of the Starz collections, a four volume series of interviews with gay porn stars. He's had monologues adapted for the stage, edited the Windy City Times Pride Literary Supplement, and cofounded the horror film website racksandrazors.com. He lives in Chicago with his husband Carl and their dogs. He authored the previous version of the LGBT Book of Days in 2013. He was inducted into the Chicago LGBT Hall of Fame in 2011. For more info www.owenkeehnen.com

Victor Salvo

Victor Salvo was inspired to create the Legacy Project in 1987 while coordinating the Chicago and Illinois contingents to the National March on Washington for Gay and Lesbian Civil Rights. Upon his return to Chicago, he dove into work as a political and AIDS activist over the next twenty years. Victor helped establish several political advocacy groups, worked on numerous electoral campaigns, and co-founded two professional associations, before finally, in 2008, setting in motion his plans to create "The Legacy Walk" – the world's only outdoor museum walk committed to celebrating the contributions LGBT people have made to world history and culture. The Legacy Walk was dedicated in Chicago, Illinois on October 11, 2012, and its companion Legacy Project Education Initiative (LPEI) was established in April 2013. In addition to managing the Legacy Project's administration as its Executive Director, Victor – an avid amateur historian – oversees the process of biographical research and editing that propels the Legacy Walk's evolution through ongoing annual selections and inductions. He also oversees LPEI's expansion into a nationwide LGBT youth advocacy and professional development resource for students, teachers and counsellors. He was inducted into the Chicago Gay and Lesbian Hall of Fame in 1998.

Also by Owen Keehnen

Tell Me About It - with St Sukie de la Croix

Dugan's Bistro and the Legend of the Bearded Lady

Night Visitors

Love Underground

The Matinee Idol

Young Digby Swank

Vernita Gray: From Woodstock to the White House - with
Tracy Baim

The LGBT Book of Days

Gay Press, Gay Power – contributor

The Sand Bar

We're Here, We're Queer

Jim Flint: The Boy From Peoria - with Tracy Baim

Leatherman: The Legend of Chuck Renslow - with Tracy Baim

Doorway Unto Darkness

Nothing Personal: Chronicles of Chicago's LGBTQ
Community 1977-1997 – co-editor

Rising Starz

Ultimate Starz

Out and Proud in Chicago – contributor

More Starz

Starz

www.ingramcontent.com/pod-product-compliance
Lightning Source LLC
Chambersburg PA
CBHW060304030426
42336CB00011B/933